342.083 R661 2010

Román, Ediberto.
Citizenship and its exclusions : a classical,
constitutional, and critical race critique /
34284003680998

DAVENPORT UNIVERSITY
MIDLAND CAMPUS LIBRARY
3555 EAST PATRICK ROAD
MIDLAND, MI 48642-5837

Citizenship and Its Exclusions

CRITICAL AMERICA

General Editors: Richard Delgado and Jean Stefancic

For a complete list of titles in the series,
please visit the New York University Press website at www.nyupress.org.

Citizenship and Its Exclusions

A Classical, Constitutional, and Critical Race Critique

Ediberto Román

NEW YORK UNIVERSITY PRESS
New York and London

NEW YORK UNIVERSITY PRESS
New York and London
www.nyupress.org

© 2010 by New York University
All rights reserved

Library of Congress Cataloging-in-Publication Data
Román, Ediberto.
Citizenship and its exclusions : a classical, constitutional, and critical race critique /
Ediberto Román.
p. cm.
Includes bibliographical references and index.
ISBN-13: 978–0–8147–7607–0 (cl : alk. paper)
ISBN-10: 0–8147–7607–8 (cl : alk. paper)
ISBN-13: 978–0–8147–7653–7 (ebook)
ISBN-10: 0–8147–7653–1 (ebook)
1. Citizenship. 2. Constitutional law. I. Title.
K3224.R66   2010
342.08'3—dc22   2009053607

New York University Press books are printed on acid-free paper,
and their binding materials are chosen for strength and durability.
We strive to use environmentally responsible suppliers and materials
to the greatest extent possible in publishing our books.

Manufactured in the United States of America
10 9 8 7 6 5 4 3 2 1

For Katerina, Christian, Nicholas, and Andres

You are my Brilliant and Beautiful Blessings

Contents

Preface and Acknowledgments   ix

1   Introduction: The Citizenship Construct   1

2   The Creation of the Concept: The Classical Period   15

3   The City-States of the Dark Ages   29

4   The Movement toward Nascent Nation-States   49

5   The Philosophical Influence of the Enlightenment   55

6   The *De Jure* Subordinates   83

7   The *De Facto* Subordinates?   119

8   A New Vision of Citizenship?   147

Notes   159

Index   201

About the Author   209

Preface and Acknowledgments

I have long waited to undertake this project, and in fact it took more than a decade to complete. This apparently exceedingly long time frame was due in part to the fact that I needed such time to fully understand the scope and depth of this undertaking. It is a project that in various forms I have touched upon throughout most of my tenure as a legal academic, in a series of law review articles, book chapters, and a prior book entitled *The Other American Colonies: An International and Constitutional Examination of the United States' Overseas Conquests*. In many respects, this project began well before I first entered law school. It was inspired by a freshman English teacher at Hofstra University. Though I unfortunately have not been able to recall or uncover her name, like millions of unnamed educators around the world, she is an unnamed hero and was instrumental in encouraging me to have faith in my intellect. This confidence allowed me to question dominant and popular narratives. As I developed, I took inspiration from writings that questioned the ethos of American democracy as it applied to ethnic and racial minorities. I first was motivated to write about my own people. Specifically, I had always been troubled by the fact that my relatives who resided in an island that was part of the United States—Puerto Rico—did not enjoy the same rights I enjoyed living in New York City. While both they and I considered ourselves Puerto Rican, we were also American, but we enjoyed different rights associated with being American. Indeed, my family in Puerto Rico seemed less American because they could not vote to elect the leader of our land—the president of the United States—and they were without any representation in the legislative body of our land—the United States Congress. They also seemed in some respects to be part of a foreign land with their own Olympic team and national anthem.

After some preliminary research during college and then in law school, I came to learn that there were special rules—or, more accurately, laws—that applied for certain U.S. citizens. For some, the U.S. Constitution did not apply in the same way as it did for other Americans, like me, who happened to live in a state instead of a U.S. territory. This discovery, though informative, was troubling in that I had always understood that a basic tenet of democracy was that all citizens were supposed to be treated equally. Yet my relatives were less than equal, simply because they lived off-shore from the mainland United States. My research uncovered the folly of my idealistic vision of citizenship.

Over the years, I wrote several articles examining the anomalous status of the Puerto Rican people. These works touched upon other groups of outsiders within the American landscape, such as the inhabitants of the other U.S. overseas territories and even the first people of this land—the indigenous people of the continental United States, Hawaii, and Alaska. As I tried to reconcile the democratic ethos of equality and representative government with a repeated practice of exclusion, I uncovered more and more examples of groups that should have qualified as full citizens of this society but instead were denied such a privileged status. This, I learned, was a not-so-uncommon practice in other Western nation-states, and in fact it was a practice that was as old as the concept of citizenship itself.

After exploring these injustices in several shorter writings, I decided to write a book about the history of American citizenship in order to critically examine whether the democratic ethos of equality actually applied to disfavored groups within U.S. democracy. What those studies, along with more recent examinations, unearthed was a history of a concept that seemed to extol the virtues of equality for all members within a given society but actually legitimated a millennia-long practice of forbidding many members of those societies from enjoying that equality. This work seeks to examine that history and in many respects the history of democracy within Western thought. This is done with the ultimate goal of developing a model of membership in a society—a polity—that is truly inclusive. If for one reason or another this effort fails to meet its lofty goals, my aim is to nonetheless provoke debate over whether such inclusiveness in diverse societies can actually be achieved.

Like other descendents of dependent nations or territories, my family in Puerto Rico exists in what could be described as an alien-citizen paradox, feeling both American and culturally Puerto Rican, and at the same time often being reminded of their otherness. In other words, they are reminded of their status as something other than that of a "real" American. I seek to explore that paradox and similar markers of otherness that have historically followed disfavored groups, such as racial and ethnic minorities. This exploration involves examining Western thought on citizenship over thousands of years, as well as the very construct of democracy itself. This in turn exposes an inordinately and unfortunately long pattern of subordination and discrimination of disfavored groups—including women and racial and ethnic minorities. This pattern has occurred despite the notion that equality is a core precept to the concept of citizenship and despite the fact that those who have essentially always been denied the full rights associated with citizenship have met the stated prerequisites required to achieve the status of full and equal members of society.

I trust this work and others I have written, as well as the works of an increasing number of scholars in the area, will one day have the effect of changing the inferior status of so many Americans who are labeled as different than the "typical" American by virtue of having non-Anglo-sounding names and, primarily, by virtue of speaking languages other than English. I am also hopeful that this examination will spark further debates on the value of citizenship in diverse societies and on whether other concepts or frameworks are needed. The inequality inherent in the citizenship construct and related social justice issues relating to the subordination of disempowered groups are among the reasons why I entered the legal academy and became one of the first mainland legal scholars to address the plight of what I refer to as "American Alien-Citizens."

Because it examines the genesis and evolution of the concept of citizenship in Western democracies, this study is broader than an examination of the subordinate status of one group in the twenty-first century. Indeed, the following analysis will examine the subordinate levels of membership throughout world history. Because it examines a construct as broad and fundamental as citizenship, this study could arguably be described as a study of history itself. In entering into such a study, one of my primary tasks is to continue to question the inferior status of my brothers and sisters not only from Puerto Rico but also in every society (and/or other conceptual legal locale) where labels such as "dependent territory," "dependent state," or "colony" continue to contain the inhabitants of those lands in an inferior status, at least when compared to other inhabitants of those very same societies.

In other words, my effort here is not only to raise the issue that millions of U.S. citizens live in subordination but also to change the landscape of citizenship discourse itself. While I may not be the first to make this attempt, I trust that my historical and legal account of citizenship's beginnings and evolution will cause many readers to reexamine the romanticized notions of equality that emanate from the concept. While I have great admiration for the historians who have fairly recently attempted to address the exclusionary nature of membership, the concepts of citizenship and equality have for too long—indeed, from their very beginning—been theoretical siblings that have been extolled and praised in democratic discourse. Yet throughout history, often because of gender, racial, or ethnic bias, those whom one might think could and should be eligible for full membership in a society and therefore entitled to the label of "citizen" were denied the status and the rights associated with it.

While citizenship has always been associated with a certain idealistic basis, this work seeks to illustrate how the noble notion of equality has always been elusive for disfavored groups. On a basic level, this work seeks to document the evolution of the concept of citizenship in an effort to question whether citizenship was developed as an exclusive concept and whether it continues to be applied as such. This work also seeks to bring perspective and provide a historical basis for volatile contemporary debates concerning membership, including debates about the rights of undocumented workers and about marital rights of various groups.

During the classical or ancient period, when the first Western writings on citizenship developed, the concept, which seemed to suggest inclusivity, was nonetheless unavailable to various groups, such as women, those born outside of the city-state, and the poor. Throughout history, women continued to suffer from this marker of inferior membership. In the United States, it was only in the early part of the twentieth century that the basic rights associated with citizenship, such as suffrage, became available to women. Women's struggle for full membership rights, which will be discussed later in the book, provides but one vivid example of the fact that denials of access to citizenship are not novel, and, perhaps more importantly, have impacted disfavored groups for thousands of years.

Throughout this country's history, as well as the histories of other Western democracies, the labeling of inferior membership has also regrettably turned on constructions of race and ethnicity. The issue pertaining to the full and equal membership of racial and ethnic minorities continues to this day. Though the election of Barack Obama, the first African American United States president, casts doubt among some people as to whether there are in fact labels of inferiority for African Americans as well as other racial and ethnic minorities, the views of many people of color suggest that the election of one well-qualified, brilliant, and charismatic political leader does not instantly change the everyday lives of millions of other minorities. His election is nonetheless a moment to relish, to take pride in, and to generate hope that it marks a beginning of dramatic change in perceptions and acceptance.

I am indebted to numerous traditional and critical scholars who have inspired me to enter the academy and to eventually become a scholar. Three of these scholars are particularly important. The first is Professor Michael Olivas, a champion of civil rights and Latino social justice. He has always been my role model and, where appropriate, my harshest critic. Through his efforts, such as his creation of the "Dirty Dozen List" that sought to shame American law schools into increasing Latino and Latina diversity, he singlehandedly changed the landscape of the legal academy. Scores of Latino and Latina professors, including me, owe our careers to his courage. He is a man with incredible intellect, credentials, and wisdom; but for what I believe are subtle but powerful assumptions about identity, he would have been one of the first Latino law deans in this country. For me, though, and I am sure for dozens of other Latino and Latina professors, he will always be my dean. Indeed, I can recall my proudest day in the academy, when Professor Angela Onuwachi-Willig, another scholar I greatly admire, suggested at the 2006 Southeastern Regional People of Color Conference that I was the next generation of Michael Olivas. While I suspect I could never fill those shoes, I will always seek to follow in his courageous, caring, selfless, and honorable footsteps.

The second scholar is an iconic figure whom I recall meeting during my first year of teaching law. As I was sitting in the back of a conference room at the first Annual LatCrit Scholarship Conference listening to a theoretical panel discussion that I must admit I did not fully comprehend, I noticed someone I was certain was either a runner who had just finished a workout and walked into the wrong room or a nonacademic who happened to decide to attend this particular lecture. In an effort to assist him, I introduced myself, ready to inform him of the nature of the meeting. When he introduced himself as Richard Delgado, whom I knew to be the most prolific scholar in the legal academy, I felt silly but did not want to let on that I had just mistaken him for a lost soul.

Over the years, I tried to keep up with his writings in the hopes of making a better second impression, but it seemed that he and his prolific coauthor on many works, Professor Jean Stefancic, wrote faster than I could read. Nonetheless, I sought to follow their model and tried to be fairly productive in my own right. My efforts were evidently fruitful because he soon became familiar with my work, and I was thrilled when he offered to provide comments on some of my works-in-progress. Eventually this dialogue led to the opportunity to write this book, which will be part of his and Professor Stefancic's Critical America series. I am so proud to be one of the many outstanding scholars who have published in this series. I sincerely thank Professor Delgado for being my scholarly role model and for being the most prolific American legal scholar who happens to be Latino. I will always admire the way he has unabashedly and courageously continued to write amazing works on social justice and racial equality.

The third important scholar and academic leader I want to thank is Dean Kevin Johnson. In many ways, he is one of the leading brilliant voices of the Latina and Latino, and immigrant, communities. Even after my first public lecture, when I challenged him on a position he took in an earlier presentation, he generously offered to review one of my works-in-progress. He eventually proved to be a friend, an invaluable mentor, and someone on whose achievements I try to model my own. No matter how busy his schedule, he has always had time to advise me on my writings and on my career.

I also want to thank Dean Alfredo Garcia for being a friend, advisor, and good soul. Gratitude is also due to Deborah Gershenowitz of New York University Press for being a tough editor and brilliant reader who has pushed me to write this book. I look forward to a long and prosperous working relationship with such a talented professional.

I am also indebted to my colleague and friend Hannibal Travis for his invaluable and challenging comments on an earlier draft of this book. Though formally he is my mentee and I his mentor at our home institution, Florida International University College of Law, I often feel the labels should be reversed. I suspect his brilliance and work ethic will soon have him achieving great heights. A very special thank you is in order for my research assistant, Jarred Reiling, who with severe time constraints undertook incredible research efforts and was an utterly amazing editor of an earlier draft of this book. Finally, I want to thank the thousands of law students I have had the great honor to teach over the last dozen years at Florida International University College of Law, St. Thomas University School of Law, and American University Washington College of Law. Their intellect, energy, and wonderfully diverse and beautiful faces have kept me young on the inside; it's my children, and perhaps a dean or two, who have caused some of my grey hairs.

On a related personal side, I want to thank my beautiful wife, Christina Román, for being my best friend and for having the strength, the wisdom, and, when necessary, though often not requested, the ability to provide me with sorely needed criticism. It is simply an amazing gift to get a chance to see the most beautiful woman in the world by my side every day. My blessings also overflow with my beautiful children. They inspire me and never cease to put proud smiles to my face. Katerina is my beautiful, proud Latina who as each day passes confirms that she is an amazing young woman: noble, accomplished, and kind. Christian is so like his father that it is scary. He has his father's spirit but is brighter, more beautiful, and more loving than his dad could ever aspire to be. He will certainly always make dad proud. Nicholas is a terribly handsome, sneaky, and impressive young man. He will inevitably be both popular and rich—two attributes he must have acquired from his mom. Andres Joaquin, aka AJ, is a ball of energy who will always surprise everyone with his stamina, charm, tenacity, ability, and beauty.

Finally, I want to thank my incredible parents for instilling in their son the pride and belief that he could achieve anything he wanted in this amazing land. Though economics and other obstacles may have limited their chances, they never allowed me to believe I was less than anyone. They instilled a deep pride in my culture, and that pride ensured that I would one day fulfill my dreams. Their teachings also armed me with the much-needed strength to overcome fear and insecurity when such emotions could have slowed or curbed my efforts as a scholar to challenge dominant narratives in this society.

I hope this work and other efforts I have undertaken provide an avenue for some to further engage in debates about membership, race, and ethnicity. In many respects this project was written during a time in my professional life when the value of productivity and academic engagement came into serious question. In other words, this book was written during a time when serious question arose as to whether merit really mattered or whether other reasons were the true basis for advancement. Fortunately, such debates only motivated me to work that much harder on this and other projects in an effort to remain optimistic about the value an academic may have in his or her field. Irrespective of whether my idealism is a function of good judgment or simply naïveté , I am hopeful that scholars and students of many different backgrounds and disciplines will find this project thoughtful, provocative, and useful. For my own purposes, I trust this effort will inspire me to continue to excel as a student of the law and as a scholar. In doing so, I pray that, for as long as I can take a breath, I can assist, and perhaps even inspire, as many as I can along the way.

Introduction

The Citizenship Construct

A Tale of Three Terrorists

Imagine that you reside in a country not unlike the United States, with a similar cultural, economic, racial, and ethnic mix. As in many other countries, the events of September 11, 2001, dramatically changed the lives of the inhabitants of your land. Your country passed a series of special laws specifically designed to enhance national security, and has joined the United States in its military efforts in Afghanistan and Iraq. Your country's law enforcement and military officials, in several high-profile arrests that captured the attention of the populace, took three suspects into custody who allegedly were involved in terrorist-related activities. While these arrests occurred at slightly different times and in different places, their commonality is that the alleged wrongdoers were citizens of your country. However, the commonality ends there. As events have unfolded, your country's treatment of these individuals has varied greatly. Now, for the moment, put yourself in the place of each of these individuals.

In the first arrest, you are a young Caucasian man who grew up in a fairly affluent area of your country. You were captured fighting for the Taliban regime in Afghanistan. As a teenager, you had discovered Islam and allegedly had come to adopt Taliban and al-Qaeda beliefs. You traveled to Egypt and Yemen to learn Arabic, trained for *jihad* in several training camps, and were said to have interacted with Osama bin Laden. After your arrest, you were not subject to the limited-rights regime pursuant to the special laws' "enemy combatant" label. This label would have severely limited your constitutional rights and would have insured that you would have faced military and not civilian laws. You would have probably been detained in your country's offshore military base that held all "enemy combatants" for an indefinite amount of time. You instead proceeded through your country's traditional criminal system. The official spokesperson for your president declared that "the great strength of this country is you will now have your day in court." Almost immediately after your arrest you had access to legal representation. You were able to meet with your family and had them with you throughout the criminal process. After engaging in fairly traditional judicial processes, such as a bail hearing and normal legal discovery procedures, you were allowed to decide whether you would enter into a plea agreement or fight the charges in a civilian criminal trial. After conferring with counsel and family members, you eventually entered a plea agreement, and you have begun to serve a twenty-year prison sentence. This treatment and the arrangement you eventually entered into was far more favorable than the potential of indefinite confinement as an "enemy combatant" or execution for treason.

Now consider for the moment that you are the second individual arrested. You, like the first individual, were born in this country but are of Saudi Arabian descent (though you have never lived in the land of your parents and are largely unfamiliar with it). You were captured in Afghanistan allegedly fighting with Taliban forces. Unlike the first individual, you were immediately treated as an "enemy combatant" and were quickly sent to a military jail. Your government argued that because you are an enemy combatant, it could detain you indefinitely without formal charges or proceedings. Your government decided that you would only be allowed the due process and access to counsel it deemed necessary. After a lengthy confinement in a military jail without any hearing or even charges leveled against you, the Supreme Court of your land ordered that you were entitled to a meaningful hearing and demanded that your government either produce evidence of your crimes or release you.

Your government never used your citizenship status as the basis for subjecting you to the traditional criminal laws and procedures of your land, as it did with the first individual. Instead, your government treated you as one of the scores of foreigners captured in Afghanistan. After weighing its options, ultimately your government declared that you no longer posed a threat to your country and offered you a plea agreement whereby, without ever being convicted of any crime, you would have your citizenship revoked, and you would agree to be deported to your parents' native land. You would also be required to pledge never to return to the land of your birth. Left with few reasonable alternatives, you begrudgingly agreed and left your family and your homeland for a country that was largely foreign to you.

Now put yourself in the place of the third individual. You are an ethnic minority of one of your country's overseas territories. You were arrested in your land because you were suspected of preparing a terrorist attack. Despite being a citizen of your land by virtue of being born there, you were immediately held in indefinite detention as a material witness and later as an "enemy combatant." You were jailed in a military prison for several years without trial. You faced indefinite confinement and only recently have been given the chance to meet with counsel. Even after one of your country's federal judges ordered that you either be charged with a crime or released, your government and its attorney general continued to argue that it had the authority to continue to detain you indefinitely, without trial, for the duration of hostilities in the war on terror. Eventually, after years of detention and, essentially, isolation, a federal judge ordered that you be afforded the right to a civilian criminal trial to determine your guilt or innocence.

Arguably, in each of these three instances you allegedly waged war against your land, yet in each instance you faced dramatically different treatment. Though in each instance you were a citizen of your land, you were different by virtue of your racial or ethnic background. Perhaps by coincidence, in each instance you were treated differently. In the first scenario, you were Caucasian, were afforded your country's traditional criminal process, and almost immediately had your day in court, with right to counsel and other fundamental rights. You were also characterized by your land's media as "a confused young man." In the second scenario, you were of Arab descent, were subject to potentially indefinite confinement, ultimately were convicted of no crime, and were effectively forced to give up the citizenship of the land of your birth and shipped off to a land foreign to you. In the third scenario you were an ethnic minority, were immediately treated as an enemy combatant, a category typically reserved for foreign nationals captured in foreign lands, were imprisoned in an overseas military jail for several years with little or no access to counsel, and only recently faced traditional criminal prosecution.

As is evident to any newspaper reader, the above depiction is not based on fictional portrayals but on the actual events related to the arrests of John Walker Lindh,[1] Yaser Esam Hamdi,[2] and Jose Padilla.[3] While their cases are more complex than the above summaries suggest, the U.S. government's disparate treatment of these three similarly situated individuals has raised serious questions among critics of the judicial system concerning the reasons behind their disparate treatment and what exactly motivated it.[4] Though many believe that this disparity was largely due to racial and class biases,[5] few, if any, scholars have fully explored the subject.[6] Those scholars who have addressed these events typically have limited their analysis to the appropriate application of criminal laws relating to declared enemy combatants like Jose Padilla and Yaser Esam Hamdi.[7] Nonetheless, public criticisms of their treatment tend not to stem from distinctions in legal status established for different groups. Instead, public criticism, to the extent that there has been any, has focused on applying criminal constructs to ethnically diverse groups.[8] Little of the debate has focused on the membership status of those individuals. Ironically, all three alleged wrongdoers had the status of full members of our political community. In other words, they were all U.S. citizens.

Yet as the parable illustrates, they were treated in dramatically different ways. Lindh, a Caucasian, was not treated as a terrorist and was characterized as merely a misguided young man. Hamdi, an Arab American, was effectively forced to renounce his American citizenship and was expatriated to the land of his parents, even though he was born and raised in the United States. Padilla, of Puerto Rican descent, was immediately treated as an enemy combatant and terrorist, with the limited rights associated with such labels. The stark differences in their treatment illustrate the dichotomous and confounding nature of citizenship, particularly when applied to favored versus disfavored groups.

The Citizenship Construct and Its Complexity

The dominant narrative concerning U.S. citizenship does not, even in passing, suggest that some citizens are favored over others. On the contrary, citizenship is generally viewed as the most desired or preferred legal status a member of society can attain. It is a status that invokes the belief that one holding such a position can exercise and be protected by all of the provisions of the Constitution. It is a status that conveys a sense of full membership and inclusion. Yet this membership has historically been exclusive as well as illusory for those who did not fit within unwritten requirements established by those with the title.

Thus, the paradoxical nature and dialectic of citizenship embody both a norm of universal inclusion and one of exclusionary particularism. Perhaps because of the dichotomous nature of the topic as well as its significance in so many areas of study and debate, the subject of citizenship has enjoyed revitalization in academic circles. Accordingly, it has garnered considerable interest over the last few decades, particularly by scholars in legal studies, political theory, social theory, and cultural studies. The historical development of this concept, its importance to Western liberal theory, and its confounding paradoxical nature is the focus of this project.

Ostensibly, citizenship is the guarantee of certain rights and duties, including the right of suffrage and other important constitutional rights.[9] In terms of the citizenship ideal, its importance does not begin and end with the delineated rights identified by the courts and legislatures.[10] Citizenship is considered to define the relationship between the individual and the state.[11] And it is by virtue of an individual's citizenship status that he or she is a member of the political community and is supposed to have equal rights.[12]

The significance of citizenship, however, is not limited to a certain set of rights. Indeed, as Derek Heater explains, "very early in its history the term already contained a cluster of meanings related to a defined legal or social status, a means of political identity, a focus of loyalty, a requirement of duties, an expectation of rights and a yardstick of good social behavior."[13] The status of citizen recognizes that such a person is ordinarily one who possesses legal, social, and political power.[14] Consistent with liberal theory's precepts of liberty and equality, citizenship is thus linked to the notions of freedom and full participation in government.[15] Scholars have long argued that because equality and belonging are inseparably linked, to acknowledge citizenship is to confer "belonging" to the United States.[16]

There is also a long history of judicial pronouncements concerning the importance of citizenship and the centrality of equality to that concept. For instance, Justice Brandeis declared that the loss of citizenship was equivalent to the loss of everything that makes life worth living.[17] Chief Justice Rehnquist more recently observed, "in constitutionally defining who is a citizen of the United States, Congress obviously thought it was doing something, and something important. Citizenship meant something, a status in and relationship with a society which is continuing and more basic than mere presence or residence."[18] Chief Justice Warren described citizenship as "that status, which alone, assures [one] the full enjoyment of the precious rights conferred by our Constitution."[19] Justice Harlan, following the classic Aristotelian construction, observed, "[the] citizenry is the country and the country is its citizenry."[20] Chief Justice Waite declared that citizenship "conveys the idea of membership of a nation."[21]

Citizenship is considered to be the most basic of all rights. As Hannah Arendt once explained, it is "the right to have rights."[22] Accordingly, citizenship is a broadly conceived concept that is typically deemed to be a central component of Western civilization. It has been described as the adhesive that bonds the Constitution[23]—that which binds the people to the republic. Citizenship embodies the strongest link between the individual and the government.[24]

In other words, citizenship is a broad concept that not only signifies the rights afforded in the Constitution but also guarantees an individual's membership in a political community. This guarantee yields an allegiance and protection that binds the citizen and the state, which includes "the sense of permanent inclusion in the American political community in a non-subordinate condition."[25] Thus, citizenship signifies an individual's full membership in a political community where the ideal of equal membership, theoretically, is to prevail.[26] Citizenship refers not only to delineated rights but also to a broad concept of full membership or incorporation into the body politic.[27] A correlative of this concept is a sense of belonging and participation in a community that is the nation.[28]

At least in this country's formal legal pronouncements, there is little doubt about the importance of citizenship, and how central equality is to the concept. Yet the question is often raised whether outsider groups, such as the alleged terrorists/enemy combatants mentioned above, are to be treated similarly if some happen to be Caucasian, like John Walker Lindh, and others happen to be U.S. citizens of families from other countries, like Yasser Hamdi. Thus, the post–September 11 events relating to the abovementioned parable were posed not to raise questions concerning the application of criminal laws.[29] Rather, they were presented to question whether citizenship—the fundamental legal and social label that is arguably the most important identity marker in both its legal construction and its application—includes formal gradations of membership.[30] The question this book seeks to answer is whether different as well as differentiated legal treatment of those within a society—who are supposedly equal in their legal, social, and political status—actually exists.

The book's conclusion, which may be surprising to some, explains that not only is the gradation of membership an old phenomenon but also the creation of subordinate levels of membership is also consistent with citizenship's dark little secret.[31] That secret is the largely unexplored fact that the citizenship construct, although widely accepted as requiring equality among those with the status, also contains a lesser-known aspect that accepts and, arguably fosters differences in the treatment of individuals living in a society. Among citizens, these differences have probably never been a function of the desire or interest of the minority or less-favored groups. To the contrary, to the extent that levels of membership exist, with the less powerful groups possessing less favored status, those subordinate forms of membership derive directly from the desire of favored or majority groups' wishes to maintain their preferred status within their society. As one scholar recently proclaimed, the image of being political, or in other words being a citizen, is "bequeathed to us from the victors: those who were able to constitute themselves as a group, confer rights on and impose obligations on each other, institute rituals of belonging and rites of passage, and, above all, differentiate themselves from others, constructing an identity and an alterity simultaneously."[32]

In many respects, the above observation is the starting point for this entire project. Until relatively recently, few legal scholars have explored the idea that there may have been ancient constructions of citizenship that endorsed creating gradations or levels of membership, and even fewer scholars have extensively explored this phenomenon. Those who have engaged in thoughtful examinations of the full scope of the ancient writings have not examined the impact of levels of membership on the historical development of Western constructions of democracy. That task is exactly what this project seeks to accomplish: tracing the classic construction of citizenship and its tension between members and outsiders, exploring whether the phenomenon of membership gradations was followed by nascent nation-states of Europe, and, finally, investigating how this phenomenon had its impact on the creation and evolution of citizenship in the United States.

In particular, this project seeks to explore how a construct that is universally associated with equality among those within a society simultaneously has a seldom-explored exclusionary practice that not only was accepted but was always seen as necessary by those who are the members of society. Though the concept of citizenship is millennia old, the latter part of the twentieth century witnessed considerable interest in further defining and developing frameworks to explain the components and aspects of citizenship. One scholar recently identified three major recent attempts to discern patterns of citizenship.[33]

The most famous of these influences is that of T. H. Marshall, who, in his lectures titled "Citizenship and Social Class," identified three components or aspects of citizenship: the political (the right of suffrage), the civil (the premise of equality before the law), and the social (the notion of the welfare state). He argued that the concept developed historically in that sequence. Though the subject of some debate, Marshall's rights-based framework is consistent with laudable aspects of the classical construction of citizenship, and his framework is the starting point for most critiques of the concept. Marshall's notion of social citizenship has generated particular interest among citizenship scholars.[34]

Another leading modern theorist is J. G. A. Pocock, who points out a dual development of citizenship. Looking back to its ancient roots, Pocock notes that for the Greeks in general and Aristotle in particular being a citizen was part of a man's natural state, whereas for the Romans, citizenship entailed a legal relationship between a man and the state. Pocock observes that jurisprudence

> brought about some equation of the "citizen" with the "subject," for in defining him as the member of a community of law, it emphasized that he was, in more senses than one, the subject of those laws that defined his community and of the rulers and magistrates empowered to enforce them.[35]

The third leading theorist is Peter Riesenberg, who both expands on and differs from Marshall and Pocock in his book *Citizenship in the Western Tradition: Plato to Rousseau.* Like Pocock, Riesenberg recognizes the gradations of citizenship that developed in the ancient world. However, he also suggests that there are two phases in the history of citizenship. According to Riesenberg, the first period was an

> intimate world and the forces that held it together . . . when most historically and morally conscious people lived in such communities and had remarkably similar ideas about what a good person's conduct should be and how to develop it, generation after generation.[36]

Reisenberg argued that the second period developed after a series of revolutions during the late eighteenth century. This period ushered in the modern era of citizenship. During this period, the notion of the importance of the individual citizen was replaced by a more inclusive, democratic vision of the concept.[37]

A fourth and more recent citizenship theorist is Linda Bosniak. In a series of articles and a book titled *The Citizen and the Alien,* Bosniak adds another dimension to examining the patterns of citizenship. She adds the issue of alienage to the discussion and does not assume the merit of using national boundaries to fix the contours of citizenship.[38] In a wonderfully written and powerful theoretical piece, Bosniak raises two provocative points.

The first, which is consistent with this book's basic premise, uses alienage as the focus of Bosniak's examination, in which she observes that the enforcement of exclusionary citizenship norms against territorially present aliens both directly and indirectly undermines the inclusionary and egalitarian values of Western citizenship theory.[39] The aliens present within the fixed boundaries of a country are the subjects of and form the basis for the vantage point from which Bosniak explores the contours of citizenship; Bosniak's group of aliens fits squarely and neatly within the disfavored group categories addressed in this project. Bosniak's second and more controversial position argues that border norms trump territorial personhood, which results in decisions and positions that are antithetical to liberal democratic values. Her solution is to look at citizenship from a normative, nationalist perspective that would allow us to establish citizenship norms on the basis of a global perspective.[40]

In some respects, this work agrees with all of these theorists, particularly with their recognition that ancient times developed and practiced levels of membership. However, the above writers all make only passing reference to this phenomenon, and this work seeks to demonstrate that marginalizing the phenomenon is an error, since gradation of membership was not only a central component of the construct but was also a central basis for the assurance that the construct would stand the test of time. The notion of gradations of membership and its consequences will be examined from ancient times to the present. In terms of examining citizenship through a global lens, as Bosniak proposes, such an approach is inviting and does bring coherence to an incoherent and dichotomous construct, yet its practicality gives this author pause, at least for the moment. Perhaps upon further reflection and with the aid of global events (which may suggest that the idyllic notion of global citizenship can be achieved), this author will subscribe to this approach.[41]

While Marshall's civic component of citizenship, with its emphasis on equality, is widely accepted in contemporary scholarship and jurisprudence, the application of the construct raises serious questions as to whether the equality component is a merely aspirational ideal limited to preferred members of society. For outsider groups within a society, the equality ideal is indeed aspirational at best and has historically been illusory in too many instances.

This book directly contests the second part of Riesenberg's characterization of the period of citizenship as a more inclusive and democratic vision of citizenship. Riesenberg was correct in observing an increased emphasis on inclusiveness in the literature of citizenship in more recent times. Related to this point, Riesenberg is also correct when he suggests that citizenship is not a static concept but rather has evolved to allow many historically disfavored groups de jure membership. The Western practice, however, especially with respect to ethnic and racial minorities, demonstrates something less than an overriding goal of inclusiveness. In other words, central to this thesis is that the exclusionary aspect of the construct, though far less explored in the literature, is a central component of the construct. To put it bluntly, defining the insiders invariably defines the outsiders. However, the practice of citizenship has not been so coherent. The typical point of demarcation or basis for distinction—national borders—was not the basis for and does not adequately explain the subordination of some groups within those national boundaries, as in the instance of women.

This project is far more critical of the evolution of the practice of granting citizenship than are theorists like Riesenberg or Marshall. However, this work does recognize a slow shift in at least the literature on the subject of citizenship to a more inclusive model. Nonetheless, when history bore witness to the requests for or challenges to inclusion, citizenship in one form or another came at considerable cost when such inclusion did occur. This cost all too often included wars and major unrest, and ultimately typically served the interests of the favored group.

The vivid differences in membership explored here capture greater attention during times of crises.[42] For instance, during the recent debates revolving around the appropriate level of civil rights protections available to accused terrorists and others believed to be terrorists after September 11, some writers have questioned the propriety of the treatment of Arab Americans and Muslim Americans, while others have championed differences in citizenship, effectively arguing that "some Americans are more equal than others."[43] In discussing the post–September 11 civil rights debate, one author observed that "[t]he pertinent question is not one of balancing, but one of determining which segments of American society deserve less constitutional protection than others in national crises."[44] Thus, the concept of citizenship implies a dialectic[45] (a process of intellectual evolution and self-definition by means of the negation and transcendence of opposing ideas) between inclusion within a membership group and exclusion of nonmembers of the group, and as a result exclusion also defines the contours and meaning of the group itself.[46]

The tension in the application of the citizenship construct is not limited to times of crises,[47] but, at least in the domestic sense, it has also repeatedly arisen when disfavored groups sought full membership.[48] Not only are the recent criticisms of this government's treatment of Arab and Muslim citizens after September 11 reminiscent of the World War II Japanese internment cases, which are widely discussed in legal literature,[49] but this treatment is also reminiscent of the exclusion of disfavored groups from the definition of social and political citizenship prevalent throughout several thousand years of recorded history.[50] Specifically, this book intends to document the numerous examples of exclusionary practice associated with citizenship requests in order demonstrate how the concept in Western democracies has resulted in effects that are wholly inconsistent with the purportedly liberal inclusive ethos associated with citizenship.

The last two decades have witnessed what several writers have described as "an explosion of interest in the concept of citizenship."[51] The renewed theoretical focus was sparked by recent worldwide political events and trends, including, but not limited to, increasing voter apathy and long-term welfare dependency in the United States, quickly followed by significant minority participation during the election of the first African American president, the resurgence of nationalist movements in Eastern Europe, and the stresses created by increasingly multicultural and multiracial populations in Western Europe.[52] Recent events suggest that scholarly interest will probably continue to focus on the subject of citizenship: the September 11 terrorist attacks on the United States; the United States' ensuing domestic and global war on terrorism, with its consequences to Arabs and Muslims both at home and abroad; the U.S. government's ineffective efforts at rescuing the largely poor and African American victims of the Louisiana coast after Hurricane Katrina, along with the widespread characterization of those citizens as refugees; the resulting phenomenon of the election of President Barack Obama; and the recent and ongoing ethnic uprisings by African, Muslim, and Arab residents in France and Germany. While these events have led to a significant amount of public and media attention, they have thus far not been the basis for scholarly debate concerning the disparity in citizenship or whether there are in fact gradations of members within Western democracies.

Despite these events and their global impact (or lack thereof) on citizenship discourse, world events have repeatedly warranted the need for a comparison of the inclusive versus the exclusive aspects of the concept. Indeed, this duality appears in the first writings on the subject made over two thousand years ago, when philosophers and politicians focused on equality for members of society and advocated, in the same breath, the exclusion of many who were both desirous of the status and, arguably, otherwise eligible to obtain it.[53] Thus, from its genesis, the construct of citizenship exhibited a confounding paradox of exclusionary as well as inclusive foundations. Yet, the vast majority of the literature on the subject, with the possible exception of recent efforts, focuses on the more appealing, inclusive component of the construct.

The membership facet of citizenship exhibits a subjective psychological or "imagined quality."[54] The formal recognition of rights, as well as the imagined attributes of the status, demonstrates the importance in the construction of self for those within and outside the status classification. These citizen attributes are supposed to define who the people are in "We the People"[55] Michael Walzer observed that "[w]e who are already members do the choosing in accordance to our understanding of what membership means in our community and of what sort of a community we want to have"[56] Accordingly, it is a goal of this work to illustrate how a subject that purportedly stands for inclusion and equality was influenced by consequential human beings, men for the most part, who had their own view of which inhabitants of society were appropriate to be deemed full members capable of being ruled and ruling. With these demarcations crept in individual sentiments, including values and biases. As a result, a basic tenet of democracy—equality of membership—was affected by the human condition, which includes a natural fear of the unknown and with that a fear of the different. In terms of citizenship, this translates into a fear of all who could labeled as outsiders (for example, women, foreigners, the poor, and so on). This work chronicles the evolution of the citizenship concept and with it the ways in which societies have included and excluded members of their communities.

This book's central thesis is essentially straightforward: Western societies have uniformly accepted the aspects of citizenship discourse that have championed equality and inclusion; but at the same time, these same societies have repeatedly denied disfavored groups full social, civil, and political citizenship rights[57] This book compares citizenship's egalitarian aspects with its lesser-known particularized aspects, and their consequences. It is the particularized aspects of the concept that have largely escaped scholarly scrutiny until fairly recently, but it is that history of particularization that has resulted in the exclusion of millions upon millions throughout the annals of time.[58]

In this chapter, I have addressed the notion of the dual nature of citizenship. In chapter 2, "The Creation of the Concept: The Classical Period," I explore the various components of ancient citizenship theory. In chapter 3, "The City-States of the Dark Ages," I examine the role citizenship has played, if any, from the ancient world through the Dark Ages. Chapter 4, "The Movement towards Nascent Nation-States," discusses the revitalization of the concept during the modern period. In chapter 5, "The Philosophical Influence of the Enlightenment," I describe the impact of Enlightenment theorists on the construct and how they influenced the United States' construction and application of the term.

In chapter 6, "The *De Jure* Subordinates," I discuss the domestic development of the concept. I argue that the American experience of citizenship fits squarely within the classical practice associated with the concept as well the application of the construct during the periods following the classical pronouncements and applications. These examinations will demonstrate that American constitutional jurisprudence has followed the historical duality and dialectic of the citizenship construct. Thus, this country's sanctioning the creation and maintenance of formal, or *de jure*, subordinate citizens (including this country's indigenous peoples and inhabitants of its territorial island dependencies) is far from novel.

In chapter 7, "The *De Facto* Subordinates," I question whether American constitutional jurisprudence has also established *de facto* subordinate citizens.[59] Specifically, this section posits that certain groups, such as African Americans, were and perhaps still are less than full citizens despite attaining such status after the passage of the Fourteenth and Fifteenth Amendments to the U.S. Constitution. Unquestionably, the 1954 decision in *Brown v. Board of Education* effectively confirmed the existence of the "separate but equal" paradox from *Plessy v. Ferguson* that created *de facto* subordinates until the 1950s; the *Brown* decision also rejected the subordinate membership that the *Plessy* decision created. Nevertheless, when examining phenomena such as driving while Black, infant mortality, and incarceration rates, questions may still remain whether all members of a society are truly equal.

Finally, in chapter 8, "A New Vision of Citizenship," I seek to establish an inclusive model for citizenship, which should be based on rights as well as status. Building off both Marshall's aspirational vision of a rights-based model for all members of society and Bosniak's caution against placing too much value in national boundaries, this part will seek to make two important points in an effort to change the way we think about citizenship. The first, which is consistent with a large part of the entire project, is to emphasize and seek global recognition of the fact that citizenship has always been a vehicle that extolled inclusion but was used to exclude less favored members of a society. The second is to argue that for the concept of citizenship to maintain a semblance of coherence in light of historical incoherence or hypocrisy, the noble declarations of full membership rights for all those who meet the criteria of members must be applied evenly and without prejudice. This section will look to international pronouncements as well as international court decisions as a basis to provide a floor or baseline for citizenship rights that should be available to all within a society. This new vision will look to Marshall's rights-based framework to provide a standard for all within a society who meet the criteria for membership. Constructions of race, ethnicity, or other illegitimate labels highlighting difference will be cast aside and will thus be irrelevant in this new vision of membership.

The Creation of the Concept

The Classical Period

Originating in the minds of Athenian philosophers like Plato and Aristotle and political leaders like Solon and Lycurgus, the concept of citizenship served a pivotal role in the development of the Western world and of democratic order itself. Indeed, ever since the times of the ancient Greeks, citizenship was expressed as the right to be a formal member of the political community known as the city-state; the citizen's key power was the right to participate and perhaps even to use that right to rule. As one scholar recently put it, "Citizenship has expressed a right to being political, a right to constitute oneself as an agent to govern and to be governed, deliberate with others, and join in determining the fate of the polity to which one belongs."[1] Over twenty-five hundred years old, the concept to this day remains indispensable for the conceptual construction and understanding of basic elements of political and legal order.[2] Though using slightly refined terms, the modern concept of citizenship varies little from the classical concept of the term. The citizen was a member of two forms of human association and organization first established in the ancient world, i.e., the Athenian *polités* and the Roman *cives*.[3]

The Greeks

The Greek city-state created lasting institutions of citizenship. These small political communities were places of commerce, protection, and political and cultural development.[4] The inhabitants of those communities were essential not only for the growth of the communities through commerce, association, and cooperation but also for its literal survival in times of military threat. The *polis* was thus a community of citizens (adult males), citizens without rights (women and children), and noncitizens (resident foreigners and slaves) who lived in a defined area with defined laws and was independent of outside authority.[5] Essentially, the *polis* was an association of male citizens who were joined together in making and carrying out decisions that affected the community.[6]

At least one source concludes that this association was a natural evolution from the military sphere and the right of warriors to approve or reject the decisions of their leaders.[7] Even before the term existed, it was the citizenry, as opposed to others within the city-states, who principally provided the essential task of protecting the community. The role of the individuals who provided the defense for these small political communities had to be recognized by some sort of special status that provided them with certain rights in addition to their primary duty of defending the city-state.[8] This status eventually became known as citizenship. Its importance in the Greek world continually increased as Greek society developed, particularly when resources and powers were significant enough to be challenged.[9] The status of citizenship in ancient Greece became a vehicle for apportionment of land and other privileges as the society continued to develop. However, during these early periods of community living, what the notion of citizenship really was, in addition to what should be the appropriate form of governmental rule, was far from clear.

If not the first, then certainly one of the earliest philosophers of the classical era to examine political life and the construct of citizenship was Plato. Plato's works focused on the development of the ideal developing and stable political community. His view of the ideal *polity* entailed a society where stability and harmony could be achieved. In other words, Plato sought to achieve the perfect state.[10] He even attempted to set forth what should be the precise population of such an ideal community. In his vision, however, not all who resided within the *polity* were equal, nor did everyone enjoy equal rights. During his era, from 428 B.C. to 347 B.C., Plato proposed that the citizens of the *polity* should be divided into four classes of individuals based upon their wealth.[11]

Plato believed that other individuals who resided within the *polity* did not merit the label citizen. He believed that the citizens of the city-state should be divided into categories: the guardians, who were charged with governing; the soldiers, who defended the state; and the producers, who provided the economic engine for the state.[12] According to Plato in his work *The Republic*, citizens of the *polis* were not equal.[13] Though Plato did address citizenship in his work, his remarks about citizenship were a function of his theorizing a stable and harmonious state.[14] In fact, his primary interest was in theorizing about and creating a blueprint for the ideal state.[15] The focus of this interest was to develop a plan for a stable and harmonious polity.[16] Plato's writings came early in the development of the citizenship construct, and as a result, his works were far from exhaustive on this matter. Nevertheless, Plato was not only a philosopher. He was also a teacher, and his most distinguished pupil was the other leading philosopher of this era—Aristotle.[17]

Aristotle was primarily interested in analyzing actual constitutions and examining the principles behind them.[18] However, as a result of such examination and his support of a democratic state, Aristotle spent considerable time exploring the preferred governmental structure. And as part of this analysis, he necessarily spent considerable time writing about the concept of citizenship. In book 3 of *Politics*, Aristotle set forth what is often considered the foundational statement concerning the citizenship concept when he asserted that "a state is composite, like any other whole made up of many parts; these are the citizens, who compose it."[19] In terms of defining those who hold the status of citizen, Aristotle declared,

> Citizens, in the common sense of that term, are all who share in the civic life of ruling and being ruled in turn. In the particular sense of the term, they vary from constitution to constitution; and under an ideal constitution they must be those who are able and willing to rule with a view to attaining a way of life according to goodness.[20]

In a related observation, Aristotle also explained that "he who enjoys the right of sharing in deliberative and judicial office . . . attains thereby the status of a citizen of his state."[21]

Yet even in this early day, the concept appeared to be malleable and elusive to define. In Aristotle's words, "The nature of citizenship, like that of the state, is a question which is often disputed: there is no general agreement on a single definition."[22] For Aristotle, the citizen was a male of known genealogy, a patriarch, a warrior, and the master of the labor of others (typically slaves).[23] Nonetheless, who should be eligible for the status was, as it still is today, a point of some controversy.

Early on, Aristotle questioned whether the status of citizen should be available to everyone within a society. Specifically, he questioned whether women, children, slaves, foreigners, the elderly, and "mechanics" could be citizens.[24] Though inconsistent with an elitist perspective,[25] Aristotle acknowledged, yet bemoaned, the fact that Greek democracies like Athens admitted freeborn adult males to citizenship regardless of property qualifications or occupation.[26] As a result, farmers, artisans, traders, and skilled craftsmen were eligible for citizenship. Despite this reality, Aristotle and Plato insisted that citizenship was incompatible with physical labor.[27] In Aristotle's notion of a well-ordered regime, the status of citizen would only be accorded to those whose *arête* (virtue) would qualify them to participate fully in holding office and other functions associated with ruling.[28]

Aristotle declared that his conceptualization was not merely to engage in the descriptive enterprise of determining citizenship in a relative sense.[29] He was instead interested in defining citizenship in the strictest sense and focused on those individuals who were competent to exercise the civic rights associated with judicial and other governmental tasks.[30] According to one scholar examining Aristotle's elitist vision of citizenship, the lower classes and unskilled workers lacked the excellence associated with just judgment and wise rule, and therefore, they could not be citizens.[31] There indeed appears to be support for the view that Aristotle believed that a man who earns his living has no place in political affairs, and such a person should be classified with resident aliens or slaves, or at least as something other than full citizens. According to Aristotle,

> It must be admitted that we cannot consider all those to be citizens who are necessary to the existence of the *polis*. . . . [I]n ancient times, and among some nations, the artisan class were slaves or foreigners, and therefore the majority of them are so now. The best form of *polis* will not admit them to citizenship; but if they are admitted, then our definition of the excellence of a citizen will not apply to every citizen, or every free man as such, but only those who are freed from necessary services. The necessary people are either slaves who minister to the wants of individuals or mechanics and laborers who are the servants of the community.[32]

Aristotle removes any doubt concerning this narrow and exclusive reading of the concept in book 7 of the *Politics*, where he distinguishes the citizens "properly speaking"—whom he identifies as the "parts" of the *polis* and who discharge the properly political functions of defense, religious worship, and deliberation—from the "conditions" of the *polis*, whose responsibility is to meet its physical needs by engaging in farming, craftsmanship, and commerce.[33] He concludes,

> Since we are speaking here of the best form of government, that is, the one under which the *polis* will be happiest, it clearly follows that in the *polis* that is best governed and includes only men who are just absolutely, rather

than just relative to the principle of the constitution, the citizens must not lead the life of artisans or tradesmen, for such a life is ignoble and inimical to excellence.[34]

Thus, the belief in the exclusive and exclusionary nature of the term "citizen" was apparent from the very first extensive conceptualization of citizenship. Stemming from this was the need to further define the others who resided within the society, and these others were classified as something other than those eligible to rule. These individuals became the subordinate members of the democracy.

In his limiting view of citizenship, Aristotle went on to address the peripheral categories that would complicate a search for a universally acceptable definition.[35] These peripheral categories included the resident aliens, who had the right to access to a state's courts; the disenfranchised citizens; the young, who were "undeveloped" citizens; and the aged, whom he called "superannuated."[36] Women were another subordinate group within the Greek structure and were considered noncitizens who had access to some sort of religious and legal resources of the *polis* and its protection.[37]

Another group was the *periokoi* (meaning "those who live around"), who were the free noncitizens in Sparta and may have actually outnumbered Spartan citizens.[38] The *periokoi* were integrated into the Spartan hoplites (heavily armed infantry soldiers), and some garnered great influence.[39] From time to time, the Spartan state rewarded noteworthy battle conduct by non-Spartans and sometimes granted them a subordinate citizen status.[40] *Metics* were another grouping of what amounts to resident foreigners, but even they were distinguished into several categories, i.e., at least seven in Athens.[41]

The ancient Greeks lived richly in the practices of membership and exclusion and had a varied lexicon for identifying the outsider within Greek society, including the "*xenos*," "*metoikos*," and "*barbaros*."[42] These major distinctions between the Athenians and other inhabitants included the foreigners (*xenoi*), resident aliens (*metoikoi*), and slaves (*douloi*).[43] These marked "others" suffered disadvantages during their lives in Athens. For instance, the *xenos*, unlike citizens, could not hold public office, own Attic land, or marry an Athenian woman.[44] Also, if a *xenos* wished to trade in the public marketplace, he had to pay a *xenika* tax.[45]

Also, any foreigner who desired to settle in Attika as a *metoikos* had to be sponsored by an Athenian citizen.[46] Once the *xenoi* converted to a *metoikos*, he had to pay a yearly tax on his inferior status.[47] Nevertheless, once the conversion was registered, a *metoikos* gained certain legal advantages over other foreigners.[48] The *metoikoi*, however, also continued to suffer exclusion at the hands of the Athenians, as they could not act as prosecutors in public indictments and, unlike citizens, they could be exposed to torture in order to extract judicial testimony.[49]

Another category of "other" consisted of the *thuraios* (derived from the Greek word "*thura*," meaning door to a house),[50] who were people "at or just outside the door."[51] This metaphorical use of a door describes concepts of citizenship in ancient Greece quite appropriately. On one side of the theoretical door were the citizens—the inhabitants of the proverbial house—endowed with special powers and obligations. On the other side were all the other members of Greek society with limited rights yet significant obligations.[52]

In addition to categories of various groups who were not considered citizens, there were also differentiations within the class called citizens. As one historian recently described, "Throughout centuries, whether codified by legislators such as Draco, Solon, and Clesthenes in Athens, or remaining latent in many other *poleis*, or becoming deeply entrenched as in Sparta, various classes and categories were devised and contested that differentiated citizens according to their wealth, status, descent, or some combination."[53] For instance, in Athens during the seventh century B.C., the *geomoroi*, largely a peasant class of farm holders, were freemen and were higher in class than the *demiorgoi*, who were artisans. Both *geomoroi* and *demiorgoi*, however, were lower in social and political class than the *eupatridae*, who were the aristocrats.[54]

Despite his early recognition of categories of members within a society (or, at least, individuals who engaged each other within a society), Aristotle was particularly interested in the category of individuals who were the actual full participants within a city-state. It is perhaps for this reason that when Aristotle's writings are referred to in the context of democracy and citizenship, little emphasis is placed on his views concerning the outsiders of a society. Only recently has literature recognized the differentiated nature of the construct during its creation in classic times. As one writer recently described the phenomenon, "That the body of citizens itself was a differentiated group and that there was a difference among its ranks was mostly obvious to the Greeks themselves though it seems much less so to the moderns, given our insistence on referring to "Greek citizenship" as a unified concept.[55]

Much of the modern literature conflated Aristotle's writings concerning the citizenship class with writings that allegedly concerned all members who were formally a part of the society. For Aristotle, equality among the citizenry was not only a deeply rooted component of citizenship;[56] it was also a basis for the citizenship ideal.[57] Aristotle likened political and social citizenship to the communitarian structure aboard a sailing vessel—although all sailors (citizens) were specialized in their tasks aboard ship, all were indispensable members of a whole, without which the community could not function.[58] Yet even Aristotle, who sought the good order of a city, recognized that "[n]ot only is the city composed of a number of people; it is also composed of different kinds of people, for a city cannot be composed of those who are like one another."[59] He concludes, "a city, by its nature, is some sort of plurality. If it becomes more of a unit, it will first become a household instead of a city, and the individual more of a unit than the household. It follows that, even if we could, we ought not to achieve this object: it would be the destruction of the city."[60]

While there was considerable discourse early on concerning equality among the citizenry as being essential to a democratic state, not all who actually resided within the state merited the title of an equal. As Pocock observed, "This account of human equality excludes the greater part of the human species from access to it."[61] Citizenship's exclusionary aspect, though containing substantial historical support, is largely unexplored in legal literature and decisions.[62] Yet, the roots of citizenship's dual nature are well established. For example, in *Politics*, Aristotle championed equality among members in one passage, but in another passage he observed,

> Is he only a true citizen who has a share of office, or is the mechanic to be included? If they who hold no office are to be deemed citizens, not every citizen can have this virtue of ruling and obeying; for this man is a citizen. And if none of the lower class are citizens, in which part of the state are they to be placed?[63]

Aristotle later declared,

> For [if these individuals] are not resident aliens, and they are not foreigners . . . may we not so reply, that as far as this objection goes there is no more absurdity in excluding them than in excluding slaves and freedmen from any of the above-mentioned classes? It must be admitted that we cannot consider all those to be citizens who are necessary to the existence of the state. . . . Since there are many forms of government there must be many varieties of citizens and especially of citizens who are subjects.[64]

Citizenship's classical construction, as evinced by Aristotle's works, equated the ideal of citizenship with virtue, in that "the good man and the good citizen are the same. . . ."[65] Virtue, in this case, was strictly reserved for those members of society who participated in the polity as "statesmen," i.e., men fit to hold political office. Since polity participation was not a virtue present in all Athenian community members, not everyone was entitled to full citizenship.

The ancient Greek political leader Solon, who is credited with institutionalizing and studying the concept of citizenship, divided the citizenry according to their wealth. He is believed to have created levels of participation in order to appease the wealthy. His levels included the 500-bushel class, the cavalry, the rankers, and the laborers.[66] The first three categories—the 500-bushel class, the cavalry, and the rankers—were distributed in major offices. Members of each class were assigned according to their level of assessment.[67] Those in the laborers' class had access only to the assembly and jury-courts.[68] Another historian of classic times, Isin, recently described Solon's four classes of citizens as an example of the differentiated *polis*.[69] According to Isin, the four classes included the *pentakosiomedimnoi*, the wealthiest class; the *hippies*, the cavalry class; the *zeugitai*, the hoplites; and the *thetes*, the class that eventually provided most of the rowers for the fleet.[70] Evidently Solon, who is credited with making movements towards a more inclusive and equal society, did not find a contradiction in those ideals and the creation of classes of citizens with different rights.[71]

Despite dramatically increasing the number of members of society allowed to participate in the political process, Solon maintained the dominance of large landholders by dividing the citizenry into four classes on the basis of wealth.[72] Thus, in ancient constructions of citizenship, the capacity to rule was more a matter of status than of ability.[73] Even Aristotle, who at first presupposed a society of homogeneous free men, ultimately developed a theory based on hierarchy.[74] In this hierarchy, for example, a mechanic would be excluded from the ranks of citizens largely because such an individual typically has little interest in developing his mind.[75] As a result, although the classic vision recognized that the state was a composite of its citizenry and that all citizens were equal, not all within a society were deserving of the status of citizen.

The Romans

The Roman Empire was the other civilization that was instrumental in the classical construction of citizenship. Although Rome may not have produced as much well-known literature on the subject as Greece did, Rome's great contribution lies in its grand application of the citizenship construct. Due to the success of the Roman Empire, its broad territorial expansion, its ideology, including the construction of citizenship as a concept, has affected almost every region of the world.

In many ways, Roman citizenship was dramatically different than that of the Greeks. For instance, in 212 A.D., Emperor Caracalla issued a constitution or edict granting Roman citizenship to all "free peregrine" in the empire.[76] The Roman construct was more malleable and consequently more inclusive than the Greek's vision of citizenship. Nonetheless, much like the Greeks, the Romans instituted citizenship involving different levels of membership. In fact, Roman law developed a precise and complex system of differentiation. The Roman era evidenced a period of public humiliation and subordination of the poor, the plebeian, the peasant, the weak, the artisan, the merchant, the slave classes, and those who lacked property.[77] As Isin points out, this treatment was "prevalent, ritualized, and routinized to an extent unimaginable and inconceivable in the *polis*."[78]

The social order of Rome included the senatorial class, the equestrian class, the curial class, the working freemen, and slaves. Each of these classes had different privileges and social statuses. For instance, the equestrian class consisted of aristocratic citizens who were slightly less dignified than senators because they possessed the aristocratic virtues (a reputable lineage and wealth) to a lesser degree.[79] Members of the curial class were superior to the masses because they possessed three aristocratic virtues: wealth, respectable birth, and moral excellence.[80] The freemen, however, were not citizens at all.[81]

Even the imperial social order was stratified. The leisure class of the empire was made up of the top three orders: senatorial, equestrian, and curial (local town councilors).[82] Ideally, all senators were to be endowed with the three aristocratic qualities (high birth, wealth, and moral excellence), but even within this group, some senators were better endowed than others, creating stratification within the small and elite group.[83] At the bottom of the social hierarchy were the enslaved human chattel, but stratification was found within this class as well, as some even owned their own slaves.[84] Many slave artisans in cities were free to engage in business transactions as long as they paid their masters a part of their profits.[85]

The Romans constructed various strategies and instruments for creating subordinate classes. Among these instruments was the use of the census every five years to identify the citizenry and its property. This accounting was undertaken in order to determine the liability, obligations, rights, and privileges of the citizens in what one writer described as "the most elaborate devices of classification ever invented."[86]

Nevertheless, the Roman model afforded much more access to citizenship than the Greek. For instance, Romans afforded opportunities for slaves to acquire the status of citizenship: a process called manumission, which could be expected for a slave with talent or ability.[87] The Roman model also allowed the title to be attained by a large number of individuals and communities, and eventually by groups and inhabitants of conquered cities throughout the Roman Empire.[88] Nevertheless, a Roman citizen was distinguished from a man who was of a lowly status, enslaved, illegitimate, or foreign.[89] Therefore, the Roman vision of citizenship was more expansive than that of the Greeks, to the point that it allowed for the possibility of mobility from one social and political class to another, irrespective of Italian lineage. Nonetheless, the Roman vision of citizenship recognized the superiority of the citizen over any other member of society.

By creating a theory of universalism associated with citizenship, Rome greatly transformed the concept and helped to explain the inclusiveness of its model of citizenship.[90] Rome eventually managed and ensured the growth of its empire on the basis of a form of universal citizenship of free men and a Stoic notion of universal brotherhood of mankind.[91] In many respects, the universalism inherent in the Roman construction resembles the Greek egalitarian notions that extolled the virtues of equality among the citizenry. The Roman approach, however, perhaps due to the instrumental motivations of expansion, was far more inclusive than the Greek manifestations. One can speculate that this was due to the Stoics' development of natural law as the supreme law of the nation and the world. Although Rome could only pass laws of convention, the notion of being a citizen of the world, and a Roman citizen, was fostered by both Roman law and Stoic ideology. The ideal nation-state was a universal nation-state.

The innovativeness of Rome's developing its citizenship ideal in the natural law context stems from the Romans' understanding of liberty, freedom from involuntary servitude, and freedom to exercise specific rights and assume specific duties. Under this ideal of liberty, the Roman people were their own masters, free from internal domination by a monarch or by a political faction, and free from subjection to any foreign power. Roman citizens were supposed to be free to exercise their sovereignty, free to determine their destiny, and free to follow those laws and customs that represented the Roman way of life.[92]

Typically, as an individual, the Roman was free from the impositions of slavery; as a citizen, he was free from arbitrary exactions of fellow citizens, including magistrates. He was free to enjoy a variety of rights: the right to elect his own occupation, to marry the woman of his choice, to own slaves, and to dominate his wife and children. As a citizen, he was free to participate in the assembly, free to vote, free to hold public office, and free to serve in the army.[93]

Despite this fervently egalitarian ideal, the Romans did not always offer conquered or about-to-be conquered lands full Roman citizenship. In some cases they did, but in other instances, they offered lower levels of membership.[94] As Rome continued to expand, some cities were annexed as integrated parts of the empire, the *civitates liberae*, and others were made allies and controlled by treaty, the *civitas foederata*.[95] Rome also created the *municipia* and *coloniae*, which left the cities to govern themselves with a limited autonomy subject to Roman law.[96] Some cities within this category were granted complete Roman citizenship, some were granted citizenship without voting rights, and others were not granted any form of citizenship.[97]

As a result of the creation of different forms of associations with Rome, and with it, different forms of Roman citizenship, the label "Roman" ceased to be a marker of ethnicity or national origin or an accurate means to describe a "Roman." "[The term Roman] became dissociated from a specific ethnic group and came to connote citizens of the *civitas* irrespective of their ethnic origin and, at the same time, a specific way of life."[98] One writer recently observed, "Roman citizenship, like American or British citizenship today, carried with it certain privileges irrespective of the holder's ethnic origin."[99] The inclusive nature of the Roman form of citizenship made it something that even the humblest provincial could aspire to attain, and probably more than any other factor, this inclusivity contributed to internal stability among the provinces.[100] Unlike the Greeks, who required a common language, culture, and lineage, the Roman Empire created a world state that forbade internal warfare and embraced a large diversity of languages, religions, and cultures.[101]

During the course of the Roman conquests (including that of Latium, a territory to the southeast of Rome), the Romans transformed the concept by two important decisions concerning access to Roman citizenship.[102]

Although the Romans repeatedly granted citizenship, they did not always offer full citizenship to allies or conquered peoples. During the course of Rome's conquest of Latium (the territory southeast of Rome), the Romans made two decisions that had consequences for Roman citizenship. The first was applied in 381 B.C. in the Latin city Tusculum, an independent land surrounded by Rome that had taken a hostile stance towards Rome.[103] Though it could have decided to take aggressive action, Rome offered full Roman citizenship to this land while allowing these people to maintain their own form of municipal government. Also, the inhabitants of the city of Etruscan of Caere (who aided Rome against the Gaulish onslaught of 390 B.C.) were granted citizenship but without voting rights.[104] The second decision occurred in 338 B.C., when Rome created a formal form of second-class or subordinate citizenship.[105] Rome fought a fearsome war with her neighbors of Latium and Compania, the Latin War.[106] At this war's conclusion, the Latin participants in the war were treated differently. The citizens of seven of these towns were granted a new status, "*civitas sine suffragio*," which means "citizenship without the vote."[107] The inhabitants of these Latin cities were granted legal and economic rights but not full political rights.[108] Thus, by the end of the fourth century, this type of limited citizenship was a means to provide the appearance of a grant of rights, but it could also be easily viewed as a means of keeping distrusted populations under strict control.[109] As a consequence, Rome created various forms of membership: the full citizen, the citizen without the vote, or just the Roman ally.

During this pre-Renaissance period, nation-states recognized the concept of citizenship but equally recognized its component of gradations of membership.[110] As demonstrated in this chapter, the very first writings on the subject highlighted the importance of citizenship to the state and even went so far as to equate the citizen and the state. The notion that the citizenry was to be equal was a central tenet of these early writings. However, for both classical civilizations—Greek and Roman—the practice of bestowing citizenship had little to do with being inclusive. The Greeks largely institutionalized the notion of citizenship; many great Greek writers opined on its importance and on how central the notion of equality was to a democracy and its survival. Nevertheless, for the Greeks, there were limits on those who were eligible to be equals, resulting in a quasi-formalized hierarchy. Under contemporary sensibilities, many who should have been eligible for membership, such as women and long-time residents without appropriate lineage, were denied the ability to become citizens. In this early stage of citizenship development, there were several classifications of people, some with full rights but many others with less than equal positioning.

The Romans, for their part, placed notions of citizenship into global practice. Perhaps because it was an effective empire, the Roman Empire was far more expansive in granting citizenship than the Greeks, who limited the granting of citizenship to those men with appropriate lineage and social stature. The Romans did not limit the notion of citizenship to ethnicity and granted it repeatedly to people of (what one would describe today as) foreign lands. On the other hand, the Romans and the Greeks did share similarities in the use of gradations of membership. While the Greeks were more formalistic in their application of their rules for membership, the Romans had a long history of granting one form or another of membership, depending on the circumstances and the perceived threat to or support of the empire.[111]

The depiction demonstrates that the early literature on citizenship focused on equality of membership, yet the application of these concepts suggests otherwise. Interestingly, an assumption of equality was held by all members within a society, even though it was not practiced. In ancient times, at least with respect to the Greeks, there was a belief that a democracy is a representative system of government of the citizenry, and as a result all of the citizenry of that land had a say in that form of government. Today, in contrast, although the classical assumption of equality is central to our notions of citizenship, the belief is that all of the citizenry are the same as all of the legally documented members of society—as opposed to undocumented workers or, as they are more commonly known, illegal aliens—who are the ones entitled to have a say in their form of government.

In other words, the basic flaw of the current belief in the ancient construction is the misperception that the people of a land are the very same people who have the political power to form a government. In ancient times only a small portion of a people of a land had a right to a say in their government, though many assume that by virtue of being part of a democracy all who resided within a society had a say in its rule. That is the fundamental strength of democracy, the notion that all within a society are essentially stakeholders in that society and its government.

At least historically, the reality is that not all within a society are the privileged members endowed with the right to rule and be ruled. From the onset of the term "democracy," there was no pretense that all within a society were stakeholders. The notion of citizenship was a line of demarcation between the privileged and everyone else in society. Despite the current popular belief that a democracy is "of the people, by the people, and for the people," the historical reality was that from the very onset of the concept of both democracy and citizenship, not all the people who legally resided within a land were in fact included in the ostensibly all-inclusive citizenship concept. In other words, the representative form of government that is democracy only represented that small faction of society who were worthy of the label "citizen." Despite the dominant and popular belief in a social contract between the state and the people that make up the state, there has never been any so-called agreement or "social contract," to use a term that would be developed centuries later, for the large portion of society that was excluded from citizenship or equal-member status. In fact, throughout world history, the notion of "the people" or the citizenry was limited to a select few of largely economically privileged white men, a group that formed a number far less than the whole of society.

The following chapters will trace, somewhat briefly, world historical developments that were central to the development of the concept of citizenship. The question to be explored is whether the belief in the equality of citizenship remains a central component of both the concept and the very notion of democracy. If this is the case, the next question to be addressed is whether the notion of gradations of membership or levels of citizens continued to be a basic component of the practice of Western societies. As the following chapters will demonstrate, although the categories and definitions of which groups became the less-than-equals changed, and some former outsider groups were allowed to at least obtain the *de jure* status of citizenship, the practice of maintaining certain groups in a subordinate status, sadly, continues.

Despite his extremely exclusive views concerning the concept, Aristotle is widely viewed as a profound influence on citizenship and democratic theory as well as political philosophy in general. Indeed, as the following chapters will demonstrate, Aristotle's conception of the term, even with its exclusionary overtones, has stood the test of time, though eventually the concept became more inclusive for some groups.

The City-States of the Dark Ages

Since the beginning of the concept, citizenship was a critical element of nation building and the very development of democracy in the Western sense. It is therefore not surprising that citizenship has reflected, in form and content, the historical development of ancient territories into what eventually came to be known as nation-states.[1] The concept of citizenship after the end of the ancient world was at first in jeopardy, as was the Western world itself. In fact, after the collapse of the Roman Empire in the wake of the invasions and control by various Germanic peoples, citizenship was almost lost as a political concept.[2]

Nonetheless, the fall of the Roman Empire did not result in the demise of the construct of citizenship.[3] A somewhat changed form of citizenship continued in Italian cities and slowly spread over continental Europe.[4] In many respects, the enduring nature of citizenship demonstrates the vitality of Roman legal order and influence on Western culture. Despite the fall of Rome and the invasions of the "barbarians"—Huns, Lombards, Goths, Visigoths, and others—Roman notions of membership survived though little else did. This period of foreign invasions and domination, from roughly the fifth to the tenth centuries A.D., along with the rise of Christianity, was crucial in the development of Western and world history.[5]

It was during the medieval era when "European nations as we know them today were formed and solidified."[6] While the end of Rome marked the end of the ancient world and ancient political order, its culture survived in many ways. As previously mentioned, Roman civilization was one of cities, many (but not all) of which were destroyed during the barbarian invasions. Nevertheless, despite the dramatic changes resulting from the fall of the Roman Empire and the fall of many of its great cities as well as the figurative and literal monuments of its power, an individualized notion of the city emerged; it was this development, coupled with the historic power of a new cultural force—Christianity—that dramatically changed Europe. In many respects, both of these phenomena, in their own ways, ensured the survival of the concept of citizenship in a world that was very different from the ancient world where the concept had originated.

The Middle Ages, also referred to as the Dark Ages, was a time of worldwide change and uncertainty. With the fall of the Roman Empire came a time of instability and transformation. This transformation of culture, politics, and social interaction brought change to the construct of citizenship, but the concept nonetheless remained. New powers, such as the Arab nations, had entered the heart of commercialization in the Mediterranean Sea. The desperation of the Dark Ages thrust the need for some form of notion of membership upon the surviving city-states to ensure the survival of the city-state. In other words, a form of loyalty and economic stability was necessary if the city-state was to survive.

The City-State

The type of citizenship created in the Dark Ages started as a necessity for survival of the city-states due to the fall of the Roman Empire and the rise of distinct smaller and initially weak city-states. Max Weber observed that in order for a settlement to develop into a city, it had to be a "nonagricultural-commercial type" of settlement and needed to be equipped with the following features: a fortification, a market, its own autonomous law, an associational structure, and at least partial autonomy.[7] Weber also noted that as a general rule town dwellers were members of professional associations of guilds and crafts with a specifically urban location, and they were members of the urban districts, city wards, and blocks into which the city was divided by local authorities.[8] In such capacities, the town dwellers had definite duties and, at times, even certain rights.[9] The city ward as a collective entity could be made responsible for the security of persons or for carrying out other police duties, and for this reason they could be organized into communes with elected officials or hereditary elders.[10]

Weber regarded the medieval city as an important location for Western democracy because the independent guilds, the decline of slavery, the growth of independent legal institutions, and the creation of an urban militia all favored the growth of social rights.[11] In the towns, merchant and artisan classes arose that were independent of feudal knights.[12] Even so, the notion and practice of citizenship managed to be sustained. This continuity was achieved partly through the agency of the Christian church. The fact is that citizenship evolved in antiquity when religion and politics were but two sides of the same coin.[13]

The harmony and unity attributed by Weber to the ancient *polis* and medieval corporations overlooked the otherness of citizenship, its strangers and outsiders.[14] However, these cities were exceptions in the context of a feudal system that was "overwhelmingly princely and hierarchical." They also enshrined a citizenship that was nonuniversal and hierarchical. Most individuals were excluded as a matter of course. Even citizens' rights varied according to property ownership. Some have argued that it was only with the development of liberalism that citizenship was furnished with an egalitarian logic.[15]

Nevertheless, within the city, there was one crucial requirement for preferred status—ownership of property in the city. An inhabitant of the county or even a foreigner could enter the ranks of the citizens by purchasing a house in that city.[16] As a result, identifying the backgrounds of the formal members of society was difficult. Similarly, qualification for citizenship, as might be imagined, varied greatly from city to city and over time. Nonetheless, as previously noted, it was commonplace to grade citizens into major and minor classes, though some kind of property ownership was usually required as evidence of an intent to commit to the community.[17]

The economic well-being (and at times even survival) of both the individual and the city itself all too often relied on access to citizenship and having enough citizens to defend the city-state. The lands, which later could be characterized as small nation-states, were still run by their kings and emperors, but there were no citizens under this rule—only subjects. However, the kingdoms were spread out by their cities, and within these cities a sort of self-governing took place so that the city itself could survive.[18] This later became more of a reality in Italy when the Peace of Constance of 1189 was passed.[19] In time, each city would exercise its own type of sovereignty under its king,[20] and with that individual sovereignty came the notion of the citizen of a city.

The slowly forming society in these cities became more and more merchant focused; as in many societies, the city required a strong economy for its survival. The economic consequences of this major development—the creation of the urban world—was the evolution of the importance of the modern city and the urban merchant sector. This in turn effectively ensured the continuation of the citizen within the all-important economic engine, fueled by the merchant philosophy that thrived within the city. This development ensured that citizens were those who exerted power and influence within the city and were politically significant. Those who were not among the merchant, religious, or otherwise noble members of the ruling class fell outside the political and economic realm; these individuals were therefore not eligible for the preferred political and legal status of citizenship.

In order to achieve the goal of a city's economic growth, full citizenship was offered to those of certain financial status. Citizenship was a lure to the merchant because with citizenship came certain privileges exclusive to those holding the citizen label. For example, only citizens could open retail shops and price items a certain way.[21] This opportunity was not offered to noncitizens. Through the practice of awarding special privileges to citizens, the city attracted more-successful merchants to reside and seek citizenship within its walls; once this citizenship was achieved, it would be hard for a citizen to move and leave such privileges behind. As a result of this practice, the cities were in a state of constant competition with each other, each exerting great efforts to attract the best merchants. This put the citizen-merchant in a position of great power, and through that power, the merchant was able to advance the civilization of his particular city-state.[22] But insofar as this benefit was constructed for the betterment of the city-state, the advantages were not equally available to all.

The potential for wealth through citizenship created competition that yielded economic benefits to the city-state. However, the city-state met this competition with certain discriminations. For example, literacy and a higher education was a mark of a certain social class, as the merchant aristocracy was among the only classes that could afford it. This marked the beginning of the guilds and from them came the authority to decide who would and would not be a member of the political community.[23]

Again, this process of citizenship formation was necessary to the city-state because the granting of citizenship to certain individuals yielded loyalty. This loyalty to the city-state, in turn, created "services, taxes, and a moral outlook that promoted active participation in its affairs."[24] Citizenship was a benefit, and like most benefits, restrictions and protections were also considered. These restrictions were thought to be necessary in that everyone could not partake in the material benefit merchant privileges offered, and the power of the citizen through political service was not to be shared by all. Only the wealthy and those who attained their status through birth were blessed with the ability to serve their city-state in such a preferred fashion.[25]

Thus, the citizenship that was formed primarily in Italy during the Dark Ages featured a design that, although inspired by the fallen Roman culture, was quite different from Roman citizenship. While it may be argued that there was a hierarchy of citizenship in the Roman culture, this hierarchy was more apparent during the Dark Ages, as class and the role one had within society were more distinct. While in Roman culture the theory existed that no one was higher than a citizen[26] (this theory meeting its closest realization in the third century),[27] this status in the Dark Ages was initially reserved for monks (as churches began to run government) and eventually extended to the wealthy and educated.[28]

During this era, citizenship became not so much a national institution as it was an urban institution. As Max Weber wrote,

> In the middle ages, the distinguishing characteristic [of a city] was the possession of its own law and court and an autonomous administration of whatever extent. The citizen of the middle ages was a citizen because and insofar as he came under this law and participated in the choice of administrative officials.[29]

According to Weber, the medieval city played a central role in developing the foundations for the emergence of modern citizenship.[30] He observed that these cities combined the notions of a fortress and a market. This dual notion bore a similarity to the context in which modern citizenship emerged.[31] Much as in the eighteenth and nineteenth centuries, citizenship in the medieval city since the twelfth century was largely made possible by the economies developed within the cities and "the money economy and industrial activity that provided a tax base upon which a citizenship community could be constructed."[32]

The medieval cities, however, were the exceptions to the feudal system that developed throughout the lands of Europe. Under this feudal system, most inhabitants lived in a society that was both hierarchical and filled with gradations within the members of society.[33] While within and outside a city the clergy enjoyed a privileged status and nobility continued to hold their continuing privileged stature, the bulk of the population, the peasantry, in most of the countryside was reduced to serfdom.[34] Thus, by no means did the entire populace consist of citizens.

The political rights of the citizenry nonetheless fluctuated over the centuries. More often than not there was a small upper stratum of citizens who were much more equal than others. In Florence, for instance, only members of the guilds were citizens; country folk and the city plebeians were excluded from the status.[35] Any citizen could be stripped of his status if he failed to help the city in a crisis. In order to forestall such shortcomings, great efforts were made to instill a sense of civic belonging, loyalty, and patriotism. In these processes, the church was especially prominent.[36] In other words, citizenship was no longer a universal institution as it had been under Roman rule when all free inhabitants were eventually allowed the right of some form of citizenship; in the medieval era citizenship was an urban institution held by city dwellers.[37]

Cities became what have been described as "islands of urban and civic freedom within the sea of feudal society, of landed nobility and half enslaved peasant classes."[38] The city thus became a sanctuary—a place for escape—and a locale for one to change one's station within society. Usually, after a year and a day spent in a city, a fugitive serf gained freedom.[39] Geography thus became a basis for differentiation. Whereas cities were communities with the potential for freedom and privilege, the countryside, which made up most of the landscape, was a place for subordinate inhabitants. A peasant or a serf could not even marry before he paid a special tax, and could not marry a woman outside his village without permission of the lord, who also received a part of the serf's inheritance.[40] Nevertheless, different cities had different arrangements, and even in any one city the constitutional and legal conditions changed over the years.[41]

The European medieval city was not only central to the development of modern notions of community but became a looming physical reality and a political institution. Towards the middle of the eleventh century, significant changes began to develop, all of which had considerable impact upon citizenship.[42] By this period, cities had not only achieved their expected physical significance; they had also achieved crucial social, political, and religious prominence.[43] Related to the development of the city was the importance of the walls that typically encircled the cities. The merchant class was particularly interested in the wall as a basis for defense of their property.[44] In other words, the merchants and their merchandise were such a tempting prey that it was essential to protect them from pillagers by a strong wall.[45] The city walls—which were costly and required a community effort to erect—had the practical effect of surrounding an urban locale, and those within those walls were members holding a preferred status within the political community.[46] In this merchant society, be one a merchant, notary, artisan, or religious administrator, he regarded himself as a member of a civic whole.[47]

Gradations of Membership

The medieval world that followed the ancient era was dramatically different in terms of political, social, and economic structure—yet the concept of citizenship survived and eventually thrived. The gradation of citizenship also survived as a legacy of the ancient world. A hierarchy of citizenship was considered necessary because it was thought that not all within a city-state could show the loyalty that the preferred citizen class could, perhaps if only through the economic well-being of the city-state. For example, some members of the city were immigrants in the process of naturalization, some were too poor to pay the tax that the wealthy citizen could, and yet others were simply loyal to their native place.[48]

The developed medieval city was, as Weber described, "above all constituted, or at least interpreted, as a fraternal association. . . ."[49] One important consequence of this fraternal society was the stratification of its members, and with that stratification came differing rights and privileges.[50] Accordingly, city society was broken up into groupings of inhabitants. In other words, religious background, citizenship, or modified political status determined, for instance, what political offices were available, what trading opportunities were possible, whether one could become a member of a guild, and whether one could own property.[51] The key determination was whether one was a citizen. Such a status determined whether one could effectively compete in the marketplace and ultimately attain the great wealth that was available in the city.

Gradations of membership were thus readily apparent. For instance, some inhabitants of the urban society were in the process of becoming citizens, some could not become citizens because of poverty, and some simply held their loyalty to another land.[52]

This is not to say, however, that dual citizenship did not exist.[53] The hierarchy of citizenship began with those of the highest social status. These citizens had the ability to exercise the full extent of civil and political powers, which included litigation, the creation of civic policy through voting, and the ability to become a candidate for political office.[54] With this political office came the security of the individual and his family.[55] The citizen, or the *cives*, was the head of the hierarchy, and from the *civis* spawned different classes of members,[56] including the *municeps, incolatus, subditus,* and *habitator*.[57] In this context, being a citizen meant having responsibilities in one's hometown, yet not every citizen lived in his hometown.

As in ancient Greece and Rome, the citizens had equal rights within the cities. However, many of the city inhabitants were not citizens, and there were various classes of noncitizens.[58] The *cives* (the citizens) were found within the city; there also were the *incolae*—permanent residents who paid taxes and had legal duties—and the *habitatores*—the temporary dwellers.[59] The laws that applied to these groups varied, as did their respective rights. The cities of Eastern Europe grew in large part due to their willingness to accept immigrant craftsmen and merchants. These foreigners were admitted and granted citizenship largely because of their skills and the wealth they contributed to the city. Some of these cities were also places of political and religious sanctuary. The religious dissidents were admitted due to the king's tolerance or approval by sections of the ruling class.[60] One example of such tolerance was the case of the Unitarians in Poland.[61]

Generally, the *municeps* were town residents. This was significant because not only was a *municep*'s purse loyal to the city in which he resided but he was rooted and would probably serve his inhabited city through all his responsibilities. Whereas other citizens who were not dwelling in the city were still acting as citizens by paying taxes, these citizens were nonetheless contributing economically to a city in which they resided and not to their native city where their true citizenship lay. The *municeps* were not only considered good citizens in the sense that they carried out their responsibilities, but they were "pure" citizens because they resided within their city and by doing so were in constant service.[62] From this point, it would seem that the more active the citizen was in the community, the closer he reached recognition as the perfect citizen.

The next type of inhabitant, the *incolatus*, was defined in two ways: according to the ease by which he could move to a new town and according to whether he brought property as well.[63] Because it was easy for them to relocate, the *incolatus* were considered to be less loyal to the city in which they resided because they could easily betray allegiance and move again. Accordingly, the responsibilities assigned to an *incolas* were fewer than those assigned to the citizen; by the same token, so were the *incolas*'s benefits. The *incolas* was simply committed to his city voluntarily because he did not need the benefits and protections of the city. Thus, in accordance with its purpose of increasing economic power, the city did not extend full rights to an *incolas*; there was no guarantee that an *incolas* would benefit the city as much as the city would benefit him. In the eyes of the law and society, the *incolas* was inferior to the citizen, and the only way he could overcome this status was through the test of time;[64] if he remained with hopes that the city would recognize his commitment, he possibly could reach the status of a *municeps*.

"*Subditus*," or subject, is an elusive term when discussed in the area of citizenship during the Dark Ages. During the beginning of the Dark Ages, there was a clear difference between subject and citizen. Everyone was a subject of the king/emperor, but not all were citizens. The king did not offer citizenship to his subjects; citizenship was a creation of the city-state. However, by the fourteenth century, the two distinctions were becoming harder to recognize because the responsibilities of each were becoming similar. For example, as military service was being hurled upon them, the sovereign cities treated their citizens more like subjects. The significance of citizenship declined as princes (or the like) began leading the cities, converting republican forms of governments within the city-state to a form of monarchy.[65] The convergence of the subject and the citizen was necessary as the distinctions between their respective responsibilities evaporated.

The *habitator* resided at the bottom of the membership hierarchy. Early on, this term was coined merely to signify residence and was not directly related to a status of citizenship,[66] but because all individuals living within the city had some responsibilities (such as loyalty) and would receive some benefits (like protection), they were in fact a type of citizen or formal member of the city-society. The term *"habitator"* speaks directly to this aspect— one who inhabits a place. The city allowed the *habitator* to have a form of citizenship, albeit a low status, primarily to satisfy its own needs. For example, the city did not need people simply to reside within its walls; the city needed the residents' money and services so that it could remain strong.

Qualifications for citizenship varied greatly from city to city, and as mentioned above, grading citizens into major and minor classes was common practice.[67] The city sector of the medieval city-state was the kernel of the state, encased by agricultural land and, often, many villages. Unsurprisingly, city-states differed in the qualifications they set for citizenship and in the distinction they made (or didn't make) between holding the rights and duties of basic citizenship and eligibility for civic office. There was, however, one crucial requirement: ownership of property in the city.[68] Against this background, citizenship (defined as some form of participation in the political process and/or performance in some administrative capacity out of a perceived sense of duty) did not really exist in Northern Europe, at the level of the kingdom or feudal state. However, it did exist within the city— although probably not with full resonance as the institution was found in Italy and elsewhere in the Mediterranean, where the legacy of Rome was strong.[69]

People of many backgrounds and legal conditions lived in the city: native-born merchants and artisans with the full legal and political capacity of citizenship; persons from the nearby countryside with some legal and political capacity as specified in a treaty or peace agreement; immigrants at some stage in the naturalization process; and aliens, who were perhaps merchants from another city or pilgrims under the protection of the canon law with no intention of returning to their native place, even after years of living abroad. Every one of these groups had some distinctive combination of legal and political powers, but these distinctions did not address questions of social class, *de facto* political importance, and the like.[70] Seen in this way, the medieval city tolerated several citizenships, as had the big ancient towns: these included its own citizenship and the *de facto* citizenship of the group or quarter, which identified and empowered an individual within the community.[71] The medieval city was therefore relatively large not only in terms of overall population but also in terms of differentiated populations that existed within the city complex, along with several forms of citizenship.[72] The period in time that witnessed the organization of townspeople into guilds was also the period during which key decisions were made as to who were members of the political community and what their respective roles in that community consisted of.[73]

Despite the emergence of dramatically different worlds with fundamentally different structures and views, a philosophy consistently remained that endorsed a structure in which some inhabitants held a preferred legal, economic, and political status—full citizenship—and others lived in subordinate levels of membership within the community that affected their ability to participate in all aspects of society. While in the ancient world, as in Athens, the gradations were closely associated with whether one was born in the city that granted citizenship, in the Dark Ages, being born in a city was not as important. Rather, the gradations of membership were more closely aligned with degree of participation in the commercial aspects of city life. In other words, where one was born was less important than one's ability to create wealth or engage in commerce within a city.

Special attention is given here to those countries or regions where economic activity developed most rapidly and most completely during the Dark Ages, such as Italy and adjacent "low countries," whose direct or indirect influence may so often be traced in the rest of Europe.[74] Geography thus became a basis for differentiation. Cities were communities with the potential for freedom and equality, but the countryside, which made up most of the landscape, was a place for subordinate inhabitants. A serf could not marry before he paid a special tax, and he could not marry a woman outside his village without permission of the lord.[75] Nevertheless, different cities had different arrangements, and the constitutional and legal conditions in any one city even changed over the years.[76]

During this period, numerous writings concerning citizenship also existed. In Italy, the *Corpus Iuris Civilis* were the classic laws and made distinctions among various kinds of citizenship.[77] In terms of the law, inhabitants of the city were defined by their legal status. For instance, religious background, citizenship, or modified political status determined what political offices were available, possibilities of trade, guild membership, and the ability to own property.[78] The key determination in all these instances was whether one was a citizen. Such a status determined whether one could effectively compete in the marketplace and ultimately attain the great wealth available in the city.

The Role of Christianity

As mentioned above, over time the notion of citizenship changed and was influenced dramatically by a changing world. It was a European world with a new political, economic, social, and cultural order. Whereas during the Greco-Roman era of citizenship, the social and political order required loyalty to the city-state, during the Dark Ages, more complex social, cultural, and political relationships evolved, which included divided loyalties between the nobility and the church. The inhabitants of what was to become Western Europe now had to be accountable to the local lord, who was typically an agent of the prince or king, as well as loyal to the representative of the church, who usually was a bishop or his agents. The development of these divided local loyalties had the effect of inhibiting the development of a state-centered notion of citizenship.[79]

The actual cause of the Dark Ages can probably be attributed to many things, and many scholars have diverse theories about what brought Western Europe into these dark times: whether it was the fall of the great Roman Empire and the resulting instability from such a dramatic political shift,[80] the growth of Islam,[81] the prominence of Christianity,[82] or even climate change.[83] One thing that is certain about the Dark Ages is that economic despair was an initial result, and from this fact came the need for a new form of membership within societies grouped together by cities.

Though the fall of Rome was a change of considerable historical magnitude, the cultural unity and economic dealings of the territory had not been completely disrupted. In fact, trade and lines of communication among many nations in the Mediterranean basin and commercial engagements with Western Asia and Northern Africa, though initially developed at a slower pace, continued between the regions.[84] The continuity of culture was kept alive more than anything else as a result of the rise of the influence of Christianity, especially the Romanized form of Christianity.[85] During the Roman Empire, trade and communication were fruitful due to the availability that the Mediterranean basin offered. The Muslim invasions of the seventh and eighth centuries, however, brought an end to the Mediterranean's availability, and the clashes of religion and culture were too great for either side to willfully assimilate for the sake of financial stability.[86] This resulted in the slowing of economic progress through the use of the Mediterranean.

This economic downfall brought despair, causing poverty throughout Europe. With this phenomenon came the notion of the Christian citizen, which also helped stabilize Europe by converting pagan Romans and Germans.[87] The new institution that replaced the Roman Empire was the church, headed by a bishop. The church became not only the religious authority but a consequential form of political authority as well.[88] Because, under this belief system, man's highest loyalty was to be given to G_d,[89] loyalty was transferred to the city's bishop and saint and hence to the city itself.[90] Under the rule of Charlemagne, the practice of church and state acting as one became a formal obligation.[91] Coupled with economic self-interest, the city needed the loyalty of its citizenry if it was going to survive. In Italy, this form of loyalty to the city was called *campanalismo*;[92] under this concept, the affairs of the city were the affairs of the individual. This practice was born in Italy, and Northern Europe would later follow suit as its tribal regions grew into their own city-states.

Based on Roman and Latin traditions, the church in many respects inherited the Roman Empire.[93] As one writer described it, "the Holy Roman Empire stepped into the tradition of imperial Rome."[94] A new economic, social, and political system—the feudal system—had developed.[95] It was one that melded with ancient classic traditions. Society had become very different. Under feudalism, rural and even post-tribal communities prevailed and cities, with the exception of the early Italian cities, at first were of lesser significance. Under the new feudal system, new institutions related to it were introduced, and they in turn developed considerable importance. Perhaps above all was Christianity in its importance to the new legal, economic, and social order.

In sharp contrast to the classical era, in the Dark Ages Christianity introduced to the Western world the concept of a universal religion. Christianity hence had a profound effect on the Western world and changed, but in some respects ensured the survival of, citizenship. In terms of citizenship during this period, Western culture witnessed two significant developments—the importance of the urban world, described above, and the importance of the world beyond this world—the focus on one religion. In terms of the emphasis on religion, the primary effect of this development was a shift in both individual and collective focus away from the public order, in contrast with the emphasis the Roman and Greek cultures put on that subject.

As Christianity grew and became more influential, the concept of citizenship changed radically from its classical-period development. By 55-135 A.D., Epictetus answered the question "What is a man?" with the answer that he is one who is a part of a civic community (*polis*).[96] He was more specific in dividing one's loyalties between two communities, thereby presaging what was to become a conflict in values. Allegiance first belonged to the community of G_d and men, and then to the civic community.[97] These changing attitudes suggested a dramatic change in the view and role of the members of the community. Whereas during the classical period there was a division of loyalty between family and civic responsibility, Christianity proposed a new focus on the kingdom of G_d in place of a focus on the secular world.[98] Religious leaders became civic and political leaders. For instance, the great Greek Orthodox theologian St. John Chrysostom wrote the "Homilies on the Statues to the People of Antioch," in which he explained the responsibilities of Christian citizenship.[99]

Other instances of this sort of leadership include St. Jerome, in Palestine, and St. Ambrose, in Italy, who pronounced the willingness of the Holy Fathers to accept the concept of Roman political universalism and Christian spirituality.[100] Besides writing on worship, organization, authority, history, and theological questions, Augustine emphasized that "true Christian citizens are those who in spiritual development . . . model their lives on Christ and the Apostles."[101] Augustine's interpretations and formulations of Christian and Platonic thought finally give Christianity its powerful stance:[102] "out of this mix of theological messages, imperial authority replaced individual citizen participation and the growth of the monastic movement began. The development of the bishopric and the powers relegated to the bishop increased."[103] The political and religious powers merged, and loyalty became relegated to the "city through the bishop and saint."[104]

The central figure in the "Christian cultural-political development was the bishop."[105] As the influences of the bishop increased, the importance of citizenship and civic virtue waned. The bishop's main interest was in creating Christians out of pagans rather than converting the pagan public to active civic citizenship. Interest in the public domain became equivalent to having interest in pagan ideas.[106] The creation of this monastic form of citizenship effectively did away with ancient notions of citizenship, albeit temporarily.[107]

During this period, the notion of citizenship managed to be sustained partly through the Christian church. However, in order for citizenship as Western democracies now know it to have flourished once again, it was necessary for individuals not just to passively submit to the church's command but to actively participate in the affairs of the state. The church considered this to be heresy.

Christian theologian St. Thomas Aquinas nevertheless significantly contributed to the revival of the concept of citizenship.[108] With his commentaries on Aristotle, *Politics* and *Summa Theologica*, Aquinas began to revive the idea of individual participation in civic affairs. He posited that a good citizen could be someone who was also not a good man.[109] Despite these radical ideas, Aquinas remained revered as an accomplished theologian in the Roman Catholic Church, and his ideas helped create a separation between the church and secular political life.[110]

The writings of Marsilius of Padua advocated and hastened the separation of the church and civic affairs. His ideas were considered heretical by the church because he believed that the state should be a self-sufficient entity with no divine guidance or judgment from the church.[111] He stated that his ideas were derived from the writings of Aristotle. However, he believed that the citizenry, as a whole, was too large for direct representation and supported the idea of a representative government—that the laws should be consequent to the will of the people.[112] As a result, the Christian church was a highly stratified organization and did not provide a hospitable environment for such ideas of equality.[113]

Therefore, by the end of the fourth century, the writings of Aristotle and Cicero had lost considerable influence largely because the environment they had assumed no longer existed.[114] Citizenship developed during antiquity when religion and politics were part and parcel of the same institution. However, religion now supported small cities that served as shrine sites—the bishop's seats. In these cities, the concept of citizenship survived and provided coherence by making Christian "citizens" out of the pagan Romans and Germans.[115]

Thus, the basis for early medieval citizenship was a localism dependent upon religion.[116] Christianity demanded a loyalty to something different than or, at best, in addition to, the traditional source of power. Instead of loyalty to the community or service to the state, Christianity emphasized loyalty to oneself and to the church community.[117] With respect to membership, unlike its universal availability under the Roman Empire, citizenship in these new social constructs was not available to all free inhabitants of the land. Citizenship, much like what had been its first permutation under Greek notions of gradations of membership, became limited to urban institutions of city dwellers.[118]

Any citizen could be stripped of his status if he failed to help the city in a crisis. In order to forestall such shortcomings, city leaders took great steps to create a sense of community and loyalty to the city. The church was especially prominent in these processes.[119] In other words, as it had been under Roman rule where all free inhabitants were eventually allowed the right of some form of citizenship, citizenship was no longer a universal institution; in the medieval era, citizenship was an urban institution where the city dwellers were essential to the political and economic security of the city.[120]

Inclusion thus became a matter of necessity. For instance, in 1293, the Standardbearer of Justice, enrolled new citizens. Foreigners and typical residents in the Contadino were welcomed into the ranks of the citizenry if they were willing to help reduce the city's debt. When this occurred, it became much more difficult to justify exclusion from the community, which was now defined by its exercise of the powers of government and by its immunity or freedom from interference from higher authorities within a definable locality. Since it was notoriously the practice of the Italian urban elites to restrict political participation as much as possible, the die was cast for nearly two centuries of civic turmoil.[121]

Thus, the European medieval city was not only central to the development of modern notions of community. These medieval cities became looming physical realities and political institutions as well. Significant changes began to develop towards the middle of the eleventh century, all of which had considerable impact on citizenship.[122] By this period, cities had achieved not only an expected physical significance; they had also achieved crucial social, political, and religious prominence.[123]

The Merchant Class and the Dawn of a New Era

The opportunity for great wealth was a common phenomenon in all centers where trade was developing.[124] Religion may very well have spurred many within the merchant class to achieve fortune, which they intended to dedicate a good portion of to the service of G_d.[125] These *nouveaux riche*, who were the leaders of the bourgeois class, also developed as a legal class with its own particular tendencies and needs.[126] The interests of this group became so incompatible with the traditional organization of Western Europe that it aroused violent opposition. The interests of this merchant class ran counter to the interests of a society that had been dominated spiritually by the church and by owners of large amounts of land.[127] Eventually, in the ninth and tenth centuries, conflict arose between the church and its subjects, particularly the merchants. The guilds—organizations of merchants—began to desire the rights of self-government.[128] These guilds, as organizations of artisans, functionaries, and merchants, existed in Northern Europe from the eighth century; in Southern Europe, forms of corporate organization had never ceased to exist. Geographical factors, particularly the presence of a trade route, in addition to the presence of a town or fortified burg, were apparently essential for the creation of what has been called a colony of merchants.[129]

The tenth century was part of a commercial European revival led by the efforts of merchant colonies that were enjoying a period of uninterrupted growth.[130] Perhaps as a result, from the tenth century on, townsmen grew in self-appreciation and came to desire rights of self-government. The result was the novelty of urban politics as the traditional authorities (bishops and counts) faced new interest groups in the forms of the petty nobility, merchants, and a new urban professional class composed of lawyers, notaries, and other administrators. As these groups struggled with each other over taxes and fines, the unity of the body politic was further established through this very conflict over control of city government and its spoils.

In terms of citizenship, two points relating to the guilds should be noted. First, the major guilds, except for some short periods, enjoyed more privileges and exercised more power in government appointments than the minor ones did. Second, even the members of the minor guilds were so jealous of the citizenry status of those in major guilds that they helped block any attempt by the large numbers of men employed in the flourishing woolen industry from forming guilds and thus achieving the rank of citizen. The leading members of the government were called "*priors*," a majority of whom were elected by the major guilds.[131] In Florence, a man by the name of Guiccardini declared that "a republic oppresses all its subjects and allows only its citizens a share in power." In Florence, only the members of the guilds were citizens; country folk and the city plebeians were excluded from the status.[132]

The guilds are key to understanding the elitist nature of citizenship during this time. Weber regarded the medieval city as an important location for Western democracy because the independent guilds, the decline of slavery, the growth of independent legal institutions, and the creation of an urban militia all favored the growth of social rights.[133] In the towns, the merchant and artisan classes that arose were independent of feudal knights.[134] Even so, the notion and practice of citizenship managed to be sustained. This continuity was achieved partly through the agency of the Christian church. The fact is that citizenship evolved in antiquity when religion and politics were but two sides of the same coin.[135]

Eventually, there was in a sense a revival of Roman culture in early European states. The restoration of the concept of citizenship as a political role, consequent upon the renascence of Aristotle's political theory in the thirteenth and fourteenth centuries, was soon followed by a broadening of the concept through a quickening of studies in Roman law and history. The most notable names in each of these fields are Bartolus of Sassoferrato and Niccolò Machiavelli, respectively. Bartolus, who lived in the first half of the fourteenth century, was a distinguished professor of law. The key to Bartolus's work was a synthesis of the ancient Roman status of the citizen, and Bartolus found it necessary to define a person's eligibility for this status. He thus distinguished between citizenship acquired by birth and that acquired by legal conferment. In defining the second category, he conceded the status (in a limited sense) to women by asserting that, upon marriage, a foreign woman becomes a citizen of her husband's state.[136]

Bartolus gave a vital boost to the revivification of Roman law as an underpinning for citizenship. He reasoned that the Roman status of citizenship, together with the principles of Roman law, justified the idea that the people as a whole should be considered to hold the sovereign power of the state.[137] As Bartolus was a lawyer, it is no surprise that he wished to define those who were eligible for the citizen status.

The Non-Italian Cities

Though the focus of this chapter is on the development of citizenship in the great cities of Southern Europe, specifically in Italy, there were also developments in terms of citizenship in Northern Europe. In particular, in France, England, and the Rhineland, great cities developed—in terms of size, economic power, and political and architectural accomplishment.[138] In the history of Northern Europe, the development of citizenship was not vivid. It existed, but not as one of the principal institutions by which a political way of life—civic republicanism—was defined and carried out. Cities and towns existed in this world, to be sure, but as special constitutional and social units that were allowed certain governmental functions by their legitimate lords.[139] The citizenship of the north was then a localized, limited institution, practiced within town walls by the burghers, who lived there, and limited largely to their concerns. But all this politics and administration were carried on within the political constraints of the feudal world, in which urban life, even at its oligarchic level, constituted a sort of second-class existence.[140]

Citizenship in the north was not as independent as in the Mediterranean model, being more closely tied to royal or feudal command.[141] In this region, the cities could construct a precisely defined space in which peace was guaranteed and the merchants gained a personal freedom enabling them to calculate their commercial activities.[142] Within the city, the ideal of equal burghers had long been dismantled. The fights between different factions and corporations against the supremacy of the city councils show that the citizens did not feel that they had the same possibilities for political participation as the urban elites. Apart from this, the urban population was far from enjoying a common legal status. It often contained bondmen and bondwomen, notwithstanding the theoretical guarantee of personal freedom after one year of uncontested residence within the city walls. The clergy and the members of the rising universities were other groups exempt from urban legal status—a form of coexistence that often ended in conflicts.

Nevertheless, if historians were forced to recognize that there was a conglomerate of different social and legal layers within the medieval city, and that the idea of a community of equal burghers could not be maintained, at least one element seemed to survive this assessment. Although not every inhabitant of the city had the status of a burgher, and although there were differences among the citizens, at least the fact that the urban law guaranteed equal legal status to the burghers could be taken as an extraordinary feature of medieval history.[143] In contrast to Roman- and canon-law systems, the enjoyment of rights in England in this period did not arise from grant by superior authority but from membership of the community, which was the offspring of the feudal community of the twelfth century.[144]

Before there could be citizens of London or York, a legal framework within which men might organize as citizens first had to exist. From the twelfth century forward, the English monarchs provided those charters, which were in fact negotiated contracts by which each party gained. The king assured himself of loyalty, money, and men on a regular basis. The townsmen won many rights of self-organization and government, all of which were based on royal comprehension of the special nature of their way of life and willingness to allow it legal recognition.[145]

In London and other English cities, control of the town corporation came under the control of the guilds. Guild membership soon became a prerequisite for citizenship, and by the middle of the thirteenth century citizenship became a political issue. What made it so was the constant preoccupation of townsmen with privileges. In England as well as in Italy, merchants and artisans cared more for the enjoyment of the legal and economic benefits of citizenship than for the exercise of political rights. Participation in town assemblies, to say nothing of parliament, meant time away from money making and a public commitment to a person or cause that might bring economic disadvantages.[146] In general, the rules were restrictive and the lower ranks of artisans were excluded. Given the economic uncertainty of the period, it is not surprising that guild members were concerned to protect the privileges of citizenship against dilution through any extension of citizenship.[147]

In terms of status, those clamoring for citizenship saw it as a means to wealth and higher social status. The push for citizenship in London is analogous to that in Florence: for members of the lesser guilds it seemed to be the prerequisite for political and economic power.[148] In England effective citizenship status was acquired by means of a city or town obtaining a charter, which listed the rights and degree of independence conveyed by the king or the local lord.[149] Full citizenship, that is, the franchise or freedom of the municipality, gave the individual an array of rights and duties: to elect and stand for the various offices from mayor downwards; to serve on the juries; to maintain law and order by "keeping watch and ward," suppressing disorders; and to ensure the upkeep of the town's fabric of roads, bridges, and walls.[150] The Magna Carta was a self-styled charter of liberties granted to the kingdom. The barons who forced King John to grant them had become used to granting similar liberties to their own towns and other communities within their dominions. In 1215 they applied that logic to the king himself and his kingdom. Now, in terms of legal logic the Magna Carta establishes something new in treating the kingdom not as a collection of subjects but as the subject of rights, just as churches had been collective recipients of grants and privileges, just as towns had been.[151]

Thus, as the preceding pages illustrate, with the end of the Roman Empire came an end of the ancient world. With the end of the ancient world came an end to classical constructions of citizenship. What ended, at least for a time, was a universal vision of citizenship and with it a universal vision of the importance of good civic life. In the place of these views came the importance of urban life within the cities that survived and eventually thrived after Rome's fall. In this new world, there were citizens within the city walls, although the cities themselves were only autonomous in a limited sense. In fact, the cities were still subject to the rule of the kings of the respective lands.

The importance of the citizens during this period was more a function of their economic potential than of where they were born, as was the emphasis during the ancient period. The ability of the members of the merchant class to ensure the economic strength of the city was central to the creation of a form of citizenship within the city that gave these members of the all-important business sector certain privileges over noncitizens.

The other significant development as it relates to citizenship during this era was the growth in importance of Christianity. This development initially limited the impact and actually threatened the viability of the construct of citizenship in that Christianity ushered in a focus on matters aside from the material world. This in turn threatened the importance of being a good civic participant. One's loyalty shifted from the community to individual salvation. Eventually, influential Christian writers reconciled the role of the church with the importance of civic responsibility. As a result, citizenship survived. Interestingly, throughout this period of transformation of citizenship, what remained intact was the notion that there was a need for levels of membership. During the Dark Ages, there were stratifications of membership both within the city walls and between the citizens within the cities and the largely feudal countryside.

Therefore, though citizenship was threatened during this era and eventually regained its importance, what did not change was the notion that some members within a society needed special privileges and those privileges were bestowed on these people on the basis of their citizenship status. Many within the cities and outside the cities, although all being subjects of the king and the church, were less fortunate. Largely because of their lack of wealth or inability to conduct trade, they were merely subjects and had little or no ability to participate in civic life or play a part in the manner or form of city governance.

The Movement toward Nascent Nation-States

As the previous chapter illustrated, the fall of the Roman Empire and the coming of the Dark Ages ushered in a new time and place for citizenship. Long gone was the notion that one had to be from a particular city in order to reap the benefits of citizenship. Also gone was the great Roman Empire that could, with little pause, bestow the status of citizen on the inhabitants of conquered lands. A European world emerged, which had to regroup after the fall of what was arguably history's greatest empire. In many respects, it was a world in disarray. Not unlike what occurs after a forest fire, small pockets of life emerged, which eventually grew into major populations. The city-state, in some respects the vestige of Roman trade and culture, was the soil upon which the citizenship construct could once again revive itself, not unlike what was occurring with the notion of democracy and the idea of civilization during the period. The literature concerning the movement toward the development of the nascent nation-states, however, is not as detailed as the creation of the concept or the existence of citizenship during the Dark Ages. As a result, this chapter serves to describe the transitional period from the ancient world to the modern one.

In this important transitional period that would eventually lead to the democratic notions and the citizenship construct that we are familiar with today, a form of citizenship nonetheless existed. Perhaps stemming from the morphed version of the concept that emerged during the Dark Ages, a form of urban citizenship based on the importance of the merchant class emerged. This class became the key citizenship class, and like the ancient citizens, those within this group within a particular city were generally equals. The economic vitality of the city itself existed in this class. Though the notion of citizenship was no longer focused upon geography, at least in terms of where one was born, it was geographically tied, specifically to the medieval city. As it evolved, Christian ideology also maintained some sort of idea of membership, which in turn evolved into a form of political membership much later during this period and eventually established itself during the European Renaissance.

However, the idea of levels of citizenship remained constant from the ancient world to the Dark Ages. During the late Dark Ages, the label of citizen existed, as did other labels for subordinate inhabitants. Many who fell within the strata of subordinate members nonetheless held some forms of rights and obligations. Thus, there continued to exist, not unlike in the ancient world, various forms of membership and even citizenship. However, the thrust of equality as a central component of democracy (and therefore citizenship) was not a force, and notions of democracy were replaced with feudal and monastic structures of rule. This chapter will explore the development of citizenship during the period that witnessed the evolution from the European city-state to the modern notion of the nation-state. As one historian recently noted, citizenship survived in the early modern period, but it was quiescent.[1]

Before its eventual revival—with the coming of the Renaissance, the growth of the large nation-state, and the influence of philosophers from the Enlightenment—citizenship, in the modern sense of the word, almost disappeared. This was in part due to the initial despair that had arisen during the Dark Ages and the eventual development and bureaucratization of the centralizing state during the early part of the modern age.[2] In order for the prerequisites of the modern notions of citizenship to blossom during the modern age, medieval ideas of municipal citizenship had to be transformed. This in part was made possible through the liberation of the concept from the complications and limitations of Christianity and the role it had in government and through a revival of the views concerning citizenship associated with Roman law.[3]

St. Thomas Aquinas attempted to manage the association between the rise of Christianity and the need for some form of citizenship.[4] As a leading thinker of his day, he had great influence. Aquinas believed that all life was an expression of G_d's purpose, including politics. Aquinas is credited with a masterful analysis and revitalization of Aristotle's *Politics*.[5] As a result, Aquinas placed Aristotle's works firmly in his Christian model of the universe. However, his concepts and the writings of Aristotle in particular did not fit neatly within Christian thinking of the time. Moreover, because he was primarily a theologian, Aquinas did not detach citizenship from the Christian context.[6]

The theorist Marsilius of Padua took Aquinas's views a step farther, and perhaps more than anyone else, restored citizenship to its secular Aristotelian interpretation. For Marsilius, the state was a self-sufficient entity, and the citizens who conducted its affairs were not in need of divine guidance or intervention of any kind.[7] Much as in earlier writings, though modern in tone and perhaps even modern in practice, Marsilius's writings expressed hesitation about allowing the lower orders of society full citizenship rights.[8]

The theoretical foundations of secular citizenship were further developed by subsequent early modern theorists. Prior to the grand development of democratic thinking, Enlightenment philosophers, and permanent large nation-states, a movement known as "civic humanism" began in modern-day Italy.[9] During the fourteenth and early fifteenth centuries, writers like Bartolus of Sassoferrato and Niccolò Machiavelli greatly influenced contemporary notions regarding citizenship and democracy. As mentioned in the preceding chapter, Bartolus, a professor of Roman law, is credited with creating in his writings a synthesis of Roman law, Roman citizenship, and the Roman concept of customary law.[10] Like Marsilius, Bartolus noted the need for elected representative forms of government, and since the citizen was the central figure in such a system, he felt it necessary to define eligibility for such a status of citizenship. In doing so, he noted the need for levels of membership, drawing a distinction between citizenship acquired by birth and that acquired by legal application. In defining this second category, he conceded that women could hold a limited form of membership and asserted that upon marriage a foreign woman would become a citizen of her husband's state.[11] Thus, Bartolus, in redeveloping the importance of democracy, also found it necessary to define a person's eligibility for the status of citizen.

Bartolus gave a vital boost to the revivification of Roman law as an underpinning for citizenship. He reasoned that the Roman status of citizenship together with the principles of Roman law justified the idea that the people as a whole should be considered to hold the sovereign power of the state.[12]

Another keen example of the revitalization of the ancient notions of active citizenship lies in Leonardo Bruni's *Funeral Oration*, tracking Pericles' own oration, where he provided a defense and definition of citizenship:

> Equal liberty exists for all [save for the lesser guilds and labourers] . . . the hope of winning public honours and ascending is the same for all, provided they possess industry and natural gifts and lead a serious minded and respected way of life; for our commonwealth requires *virtus* and *probitas* in its citizens. Whoever has these qualifications is thought to be of sufficiently noble birth to participate in the government of the republic. . . . This, then, is true liberty, this equality in a commonwealth; not to have to

fear violence or wrong-doing from anybody, and to enjoy equality among citizens before the law and in the participation in public office. . . . But now it is marvelous to see how powerful this access to public office, once it is offered to a free people, proves to be in awakening the talents of the citizens.[13]

Bruni, seen as a key figure in the revivification of citizenship, is credited with accelerating the transition from the ideal of studious contemplation to an ideal of active civic participation.[14] He is also credited with moving the contemporary thinking of the day "from a belief in hierarchical society to an egalitarian polity; and from an acceptance of tradition to faith in the possibility of controlling in some measure one's own destiny."[15]

Yet despite his consequential role in reinvigorating the dormant notion of active citizenship, Bruni did not depart in his vision of active citizenship from the classical vision of exclusionary citizenship. By merely examining his oration, one can see the central theme of this book: extolling equality and at the same time calling for the exclusion of some members from access to equality. Bruni calls for active membership and equality, but he also calls for gradations of membership. Take, for instance, his first sentence (representing the classic notion of inclusiveness), which declares that equal liberty exists for all, yet in the very next clause, he appears to set forth the caveat that noble birth is required in order for a person to participate in the government. This dichotomy is emblematic of the classical vision of citizenship as well as the contemporary practice of selectively granting citizenship.

The ideas in the writings of these early Renaissance or pre-Renaissance theorists were put into practice in Florence during the 1400s, in the bedrock of the revival of both the theory and the practice of ancient notions of active citizenship.[16] Florence became the breeding ground for what was to become the Renaissance, and the influence of the Enlightenment writers during that period had a profound effect on citizenship and democratic theory.

Florence was virtually and literally isolated in its devotion to the republican state and played a remarkable role in the recovery of the classical ideal of citizenship.[17] Unlike the surrounding Italian cities, where tyranny prevailed, Florence retained a constitutional form of government. Men in the city enjoyed the rank of citizen, and laborers, along with members of the lesser guilds, were excluded. Evidently, even when active citizenship was under serious threat, gradations were still nonetheless apparent.

In fact, a potentially historically significant event caused an increased interest in and practice of active membership. The monastic land of Milan was prepared to mount an invasion of republican Florence. But for the death of the duke of Milan, Florence would have replaced its representative principles with administration by a princely state. The happenstance of, or perhaps the providence associated with, the duke's death allowed Florence to survive and even flourish. As a result, Florentine businessmen, notaries, lawyers, and other intellectuals were able to recast the narrative of their history that otherwise would have prevailed.[18] They reemphasized their links to an ancient republican Rome, and in the works of Cicero found the model for active citizenship.[19] Almost immediately, the example of the monk was replaced by that of the citizen.[20]

Just as they were of considerable importance in the Dark Ages, the guilds were terribly important to citizenship in Florence. In fact, they were central to understanding citizenship in Florence. Only members of guilds were citizens; those who lived in the countryside or city plebeians were excluded— this being another example of graded citizenship. Moreover, in the Florence of this era, there existed the major guilds and the minor ones. Eventually these guilds controlled the government, and though many writers of the era, such as Francesco Guiccardini, boasted about the city's form of republican government and the equality of the citizenry, not all inhabitants were equal. For instance, though the guilds controlled Florence until approximately 1530, the members of the major guilds enjoyed more privileges and had more power than the members of the minor guilds.[21] Those who were not part of a guild were merely excluded from public life.

Thus, the potential overthrow of Florence and its resulting revival were the turning point not only for revisiting the classic notions of citizenship but also for a more or less permanent implementation of the classic vision of citizenship, and along with it the notion of levels of membership.[22] While the complete adoption of this view of citizenship had to await well over a century of further development by the Enlightenment philosophers of the Renaissance, the writings of the early humanists as well as the practice and writings stemming from Florence had an irreversible effect on the concept.

As historian Peter Riesenberg points out in describing this important yet slowly developing transition in the development of the theory,

> An event like the Visconti threat [to Florence] is important; it may inspire writers, artists, and musicians; it may make their inspirational creations, their stimuli to action and resistance, more comprehensible and acceptable. But alone, without the existence of objective institutions and situations through which such values and goals may enter history, they do not

go far enough to explain the acceptance and success of the active worldly life, which had, in fact, been part of Italian life for centuries. It so happens in history that rationalization and rhetorization come long after the fact. Such was the case with civic humanism. The reality of the active life *and* its formal defense by lawyers and other apologists came at least a century before the elegant stylists of the Renaissance appeared in the salons of Florence.[23]

The result of this early period when Western Europe began to move away from the Dark Ages was that citizenship began to regain its luster from the classical period. The eventual adoption of what is known as the modern notion of citizenship in a democracy took time to develop, well over a century in fact, but it did develop. The key Enlightenment philosophers of the next chapter permanently changed the way the world would view citizenship. Though their theories differed significantly, each in his own way contributed mightily to modern notions of democratic theory and to citizenship theory.

Thus, during this transitional, post-Dark and premodern period, the notion of the importance of the citizen in society was renewed, and with this renewal came the importance of equality among the citizenry. What also existed during this transitional period was the belief in the classical construction of the term and with it the notion of an exclusionary vision of the concept. As a result, the practice of denying some members of a society, who arguably should have been eligible for citizenship, the ability to become citizens was a practice that would stand the test of time, despite the popular rhetoric extolling the virtues of equality of all members of a society.

The Philosophical Influence of the Enlightenment

Contemporary domestic citizenship theory was mightily influenced by the Enlightenment over and above the continuing pull of ancient Greco-Roman constructions, the legacy of the Dark Ages, and the writings of early pre-Renaissance theorists. Modern rhetorical constructions of citizenship followed Western notions of equality and focused on the mutuality of rights and obligations of citizenship. The contribution of the Enlightenment theorists was a remedy to the dearth of ancient and medieval writings on the importance of equality of membership. The following pages will examine these important theorists and the role they played in our contemporary notions of democracy and citizenship theory.

Toward the end of the Dark Ages, the so-called Enlightenment Renaissance philosophers began writing on government and the role of the citizenry within a governmental structure. This chapter will review the views of many of these theorists and their writings, and will address their impact on the United States' views on democracy and citizenship theory. Often referred to as the Enlightenment thinkers, each of these theorists—Niccolò Machiavelli, Thomas Hobbes, John Locke, Charles Montesquieu, and Jean-Jacques Rousseau—significantly contributed to Western liberal thought. Somewhat surprisingly, the views of these giants championed the virtues of democracy but equally often championed treating some within a society as less than equal members of society. It is unfortunate, but perhaps not surprising in light of their views on certain disfavored groups, that these theorists, who greatly contributed to the structure and focus of the United States Constitution, did not have a similar impact on dismantling or at least challenging the less-recognized practice of subordinating the membership of disfavored groups within the United States.

This less noteworthy aspect of their writing and influence is highlighted here to demonstrate a consistent pattern: since the very inception of democratic thought, the virtues of democracy and the central postulate of equality have simultaneously supported the practice of treating disfavored groups as subordinate members of society. As this chapter will demonstrate, even the greatest champion of equality among these Enlightenment thinkers, Jean-Jacques Rousseau, agreed with treating women as inferior, dependent members within a society. Others, such as Hobbes and Locke, though acknowledging man in his natural state as born in a state of freedom and equality, granted too little importance to the equality of membership for all within a civilized society. Charles Montesquieu, who was a great champion of democracy and a central figure of the theory behind the separation of powers, nonetheless used what would now be viewed as not only peculiar theories concerning global climates but also arcane and bigoted views to justify the imposition of slavery against African members of Western countries. He also used odd, temperature-based global views to justify the subjugation of women and their relegation to inferior status within Western societies. The following pages will briefly review the central and better-known aspects of these thinkers' theories and also examine their support of something other than equality for all members of society.

Niccolò Machiavelli

Perhaps the earliest as well as the transitional Enlightenment philosopher was Niccolò Machiavelli. Though his theorizing on civic humanism may have started with the works of Leonardo Bruni, it was Machiavelli's works that had a significant impact throughout Europe. In the fifteenth century, through his writings such as the *Prince* and the *Discourses on the First Ten Books of Titus Livy*, Machiavelli was the most influential humanist of the period. It was in his works on the *Discourses on Livy,* which reflected on the greatness of ancient Rome, that he commented on citizenship.[1]

He was one of the early European writers influencing modern constructions of democracy, and he reemphasized the need for active citizenship as extolled during the classical era. Peter Riesenberg noted that Machiavelli "is so important in the greater history of citizenship because it is his reformulation of the concept and issues surrounding it that plays a big role in later history."[2] Machiavelli was thus the most distinguished of all the Florentine writers.

His works were written roughly a century after Milan's threat to invade Florence and the impact said thwarted effort had on republican governance and active citizenship. Machiavelli drew upon the Roman and the Greek experience to supplement his own views, though he drew upon Rome more than Athens. His ideal of civic behavior, as opposed to monastic edict, is found in his writings on Livy. In his *Discourses on Livy*, he regarded Livy as the most famous—as well as the most controversial—defender of civil liberties. Inspired by the ideal of civic virtue as practiced by the Romans, Machiavelli called for a new ethos of devotion to the political community, sealed by a practice of collective self-rule and self-defense.[3] He was interested in the freedom of a people and in the political and military arrangements needed to assure that freedom.[4]

Needless to say, Machiavelli's conception of the citizen-body remains emphatically patriarchal, as is the case, with rare exceptions, for the entire political theory tradition until recent times. Therefore, Machiavelli may have been interested in freedom and the nature of rule that could allow for such freedom, but the freedom he was focusing on was apparently not available to all within a society. As in the classical period, his discussions of citizenship were focused on the men who were eligible to hold such title. In fact, much of his writing focused on the need for successful citizens to protect the government through military engagement. Indeed, military service, which obviously was available only to men throughout world history until just recently, was essential for the state to achieve political success and greatness.[5]

Understanding the internal and external challenges to the survival of the "free state" led Machiavelli to recognize that the duties of successful leadership of a free state would necessitate actions that would, at times, contravene the precepts of conventional morality.[6] Nonetheless, he praised republics over principalities, for it was only through collective self-rule that the greatest number could guarantee their personal autonomy and independence and thereby achieve a more lasting and glorious state.[7]

Machiavelli played an important role in the history of citizenship because of his reformulation of the concept. He "organized discussions of liberty, citizenship, and republicanism as they had developed in the previous century and passed them on as a corpus of interconnected issues or problems."[8] By liberty, Machiavelli meant two related values: first, independence, or self-rule; and second, freedom from aggression that could destroy independence.[9] He believed in the superiority of republics over monarchies and agreed with Aristotle on the ultimate superiority of the judgment of the majority of the citizenry.[10] Machiavelli rejected the soft or inactive citizenship of the Dark Ages because it was premised upon Christianity's message of peace.[11] He preferred a religion that would not weaken a state by weakening its citizens, as he believed Christianity did; he favored a belief system that would stimulate the citizen's appetite for conquest.[12] He did not believe in passivity, but in active exercise of *virtue* by the citizen-soldier, which would allow a regime to survive, expand, and flourish.[13]

Thomas Hobbes

The seventeenth century was essentially the period of genesis for the development of the nation-states of Europe. Enlightenment philosophers of the time began to develop theories on what form of government was best suited to govern a nation-state. Their writings necessarily and naturally had a substantial impact on democratic theory.

One of the earliest and best known is the English philosopher Thomas Hobbes. In his book *The Leviathan*, the main character was a mythological, whale-like sea monster that devoured whole ships. Hobbes began his book describing the "state of nature" where all individuals were naturally equal.[14] Hobbes said that in the state of nature there were no laws or anyone to enforce them. The only way out of this situation was for individuals to create some supreme power to impose its rule on everyone.[15]

Hobbes borrowed a concept from English contract law: an implied agreement. Hobbes asserted that the people agreed among themselves to "lay down" their natural rights of equality and freedom and give absolute power to a sovereign. The sovereign, created by the people, might be a person or a group. The sovereign would make and enforce the laws to secure a peaceful society, making life, liberty, and property possible. Hobbes called this agreement a contract concerning who shall have dominion, though subsequently writers have argued that he was referring to some sort of "social contract." Hobbes believed that a government headed by a king was the best form that the sovereign could take. Placing all power in the hands of a king would mean more resolute and consistent exercise of political authority.[16] Hobbes also maintained that the social contract was an agreement only among the people and not between them and their king. Once the people had given absolute power to the king, they had no right to revolt against him.

At the beginning of his treatise on the citizen, *De Cive*, Hobbes noted that his method dictated that he begin his treatment of civil behavior with a consideration of how men are fit or not fit to engage in civil government. Beginning at "the very matter of civil government," Hobbes discussed man as a political component of civil government, not as an entity that precedes civil government.[17] Hobbes wanted to distinguish between the discussions of men as men and discussions of men as citizens because he believed that a science of human political behavior is impossible apart from a consideration of human nature as it appears within the framework of the structure of civil government.[18]

As one writer recently observed, though Hobbes did not focus his analysis on the citizen within a governmental structure, and ultimately supported an all-powerful sovereign as the preferred choice for ruling, he nonetheless focused his treatment of the natural state of man-as-citizen on the organization of interaction of individuals related by civil law. This, in turn, appears to have demanded that men be considered as equals, at least within the civil system. This theory also appears to demand that their civil relationships be based on a universally reliable and effective calculus—namely, that of gain and fear.[19] This approach, as well as his support for a supreme sovereign, did not lend itself to the sort of detailed discussion of equality of citizenship that has driven contemporary constructions of the term. As a result, while Hobbes's theories have been influential and often critiqued, they have not had nearly the profound influence on citizenship studies that the next series of theorists have had on the subject.

John Locke

Subsequent Enlightenment philosophers like John Locke, Charles Montesquieu, and Jean-Jacques Rousseau developed far more lasting and influential theories of government and citizenship. These thinkers significantly contributed to the ideals of both the American and French revolutions and the democratic governments that they produced. Among the most influential of these writers was John Locke. Locke is often cited as a primary influence on the founding fathers because Thomas Jefferson, in drafting the Declaration of Independence, admitted to drawing liberally from Locke's *Two Treatises on Government*.[20] In particular, the famous assertion that all men are "endowed by their Creator with certain unalienable rights, that among these are life, liberty, and the pursuit of happiness," was drawn from Locke's work almost verbatim.[21] In addition, Locke is often credited as an early proponent of religious tolerance, the importance of a separation of church from state, and the concept that government must be strictly limited in power and function.[22]

Locke's theory of government as a "social contract" provided the colonial citizenry with a justification for revolting against a tyrannical king, and Locke is therefore romantically linked with the spirit of the American Revolution itself.[23] In his words,

[C]ivil society originates when, for the better administration of the law, men agree to delegate this function to certain officers. Thus government is instituted by a "social contract"; its powers are limited, and they involve reciprocal obligations; moreover, they can be modified or rescinded by the authority which conferred them.[24]

In 1690, John Locke published his *Two Treatises of Government*.[25] In the *Second Treatise of Government*, Locke proposed enduring ideas of government and democracy that included the importance of consent for both imposing civil duties on the individual and endowing the individual with the benefits of membership. To this end, Locke posited a primordial state of nature in which individuals possess "natural liberty."[26] In order to escape the brutish ills of an unbounded, universal liberty, individuals consensually enter a social compact whereby they agree to restrict their natural liberty for the benefit of "unit[ing] into a community for their comfortable, safe, and peaceable living . . . and a greater security against any that are not of it."[27] For example, in the state of nature, each individual possesses "a power to punish offences against the law of nature in prosecution of his own private judgment."[28] By entering into the social compact and thereby civil society, individuals have deferred this power to the courts and legislature.

Locke largely agreed with Hobbes about the brutality of the state of nature, but he disagreed with Hobbes on several other significant points. Specifically, Locke disagreed with Hobbes over whether certain inalienable rights, such as those of life, liberty, and property, could be taken away or given up voluntarily. Locke believed that life, liberty, and property were natural rights that all people have at birth. Also reflected in the Declaration of Independence is Locke's argument in *Two Treatises of Government* that the government is formed to protect people's natural rights; that government should have limited power; that the type of government in place should be accepted by all citizens; that government has an obligation to those it governs; and that the people have the right to overthrow government if it fails in its obligations or takes away natural rights.[29] Locke also disagreed with Hobbes concerning the social contract allegedly referred to by Hobbes. Locke argued that the social contract was not just an agreement among the people but one between the people and the sovereign. Accordingly, the rights of individuals limited the power of the king. Therefore, the power of the sovereign was there to enforce and protect the natural rights of the people, and if a sovereign violated these rights, the social contract was broken, and the people had the right to revolt and establish a new government.

For Locke, a basic premise of his theory concerning man is the basic equality of all men.[30] He states, "all men by nature are equal,"[31] and all men are born in

[a] state . . . of equality, wherein all the power and jurisdiction is recipro-cal, no one having more than another; there being nothing more evident than that creatures of the same species and rank, promiscuously born to all the same advantages of nature, and the use of the same faculties, should also be equal one amongst another without subordination or subjection.[32]

For Locke, freedom and independence were linked with equality among men and were commonly simply grouped together, with the assumption that they are implied by each other.[33] Locke repeatedly made these connections, referring to "mankind . . . being all equal and independent" and to the "equal Right that every man hath, to his Natural Freedom," and again to "men being, as has been said, by Nature, all free, equal and independent."[34]

Locke also stresses the importance of equality, as he writes,

Man being born, as has been proved, with a title to perfect freedom, and an uncontrolled enjoyment of all the rights and privileges of the law of nature equally with any other man or number of men in the world, hath by nature a power not only to preserve his property—that is, his life, liberty, and estate—against the injuries and attempts of other men, but to judge of and punish the breaches of that law in others as he is persuaded the offence deserves.[35]

The *Second Treatise of Government* is the best-known account of what was to develop as liberal theory, harnessing the idea of individual rights to a notion of collective sovereignty.[36] According to the Lockean view of the basic nature of man, the point arises: if all men are equal, free, and independent, and all can act to protect their own rights, then the way in which society and gov-ernment can form is by agreement among men for the sake of more eas-ily preserving their own rights.[37] Locke makes that very point, as he writes, "Man . . . seeks out and is willing to join in society with others, who are already united, or have a mind to unite, for the mutual preservation of their lives, liberties, and estate."[38] Thus, the quality of citizenship has often been judged more by the accountability of liberal democratic governments toward their citizenry than by the actual forms and degrees of popular participa-tion.[39] Locke favored a representative government, but he wanted representatives to be only men of property and business. In his view, only adult male property owners should have the right to vote. Locke was reluctant to allow those without property to participate in government because he believed that they were unfit.[40]

Hobbes and Locke viewed the subject of citizens and citizenship in the way the ancient Greeks envisioned citizenship—as the form of civic virtue and civic consciousness of the community.[41] They saw the individual as a moral, thinking being that reflected on society and acted on those demands and needs. Hobbesean thinking focused on the individual and the individual's influence in society.[42] Locke, on the other hand, seized upon the idea of the role of the individual and expanded it to include the individual's role in government and in the acquisition of property.[43]

The far-reaching influence of the idea of exchanging a limited loss of individual liberty for governmental protection runs throughout the jurisprudence of American citizenship. Hence, the 1873 edition of Justice Story's famous *Commentaries on the Constitution* defined a "citizen" as "a person owing allegiance to the government, and entitled to protection from it."[44] Above all these connections, however, the centrality of property rights to his theory of government as a "social contract" has most profoundly endeared Locke to American liberal theorists and their notion of citizenship, citizenship jurisprudence, and the nature of government.[45]

Author David Abraham observed,

> Daily experience reminds us that, when it comes to rights, we still very much live in a Lockean world. Throughout American history we have borne a conception of liberty that is formal, negative, expressed in contract, and dependent on possession of property, which may or (more often) may not bear a connection to labor. In fact, "private property" was and remains the fulcrum for our system of constitutional rights. . . . [D]espite the changes wrought by post–Civil War, New Deal, and 1960s-1970s equal protection/fundamental rights jurisprudence, we in the United States have yet to escape the liberty-property linkage. The result is that American law and politics operate within narrower, less pliant limits than do those of other capitalist democracies while our rights ideology retains its individualist and libertarian cast. Since Federalist No. 10, the first object of government has been to protect the inequalities manifested in and derived from property and its accumulation by individuals of diverse faculties. Property has not been eclipsed by concepts such as "citizenship."[46]

After listing the unalienable rights enumerated in the Declaration of Independence (life, liberty, and the pursuit of happiness), former Republican Speaker of the House Newt Gingrich once proceeded to nakedly expose the hollowness of American egalitarian rhetoric when he declared, "the declaration only guarantees the pursuit, not the outcome."[47] Gingrich went on to express the prevailing theory of the reciprocal rights and responsibilities extant between individuals and their government typical of modern Lockean theory:

> These precious rights have since been eroded as the "welfare state" attempted to guarantee results instead of opportunity. Congress, presidents and courts have loosened the limits on government and have weakened the protection of private property. The courts have allowed the taking of property rights without the compensation guaranteed in the Fifth Amendment to the Constitution. Powers guaranteed to the people and to the states have been assumed by the Federal Government. This has limited the opportunities of the people. It has made them poorer and less free.[48]

Despite this kind of politically expedient commandeering of "Lockean" principles, others have argued that any liberal-theory-based interpretation of Locke is a betrayal of Locke's personal beliefs and intentions.[49] While Locke is generally characterized as a positivist,[50] one author has suggested that a careful reading of Locke's *Essay on Human Understanding* reveals a denial of any real knowledge of the essences or substances of things whatsoever, citing specifically the following passage:

> If you demand to know what . . . real essences are, it is plain that men are ignorant and know them not. . . . From whence it follows that the ideas they have in their minds . . . cannot be supposed to be any representation [of essences or substances] at all. . . . [W]e know nothing of these real essences. . . . It is plain that our ideas of substance are not adequate, are not what the mind intends them to be. Besides, a man has no idea of substance in general, nor knows what substance is in itself.[51]

In his theory of the genesis of legal obligation, Locke's footsteps are dogged by the deficiency in his philosophy of knowledge. In short, while it is the confection of contracts that raises men from the state of nature to the state of citizenship in civil society, there is precisely no reason given, nor could one be given, as to why it might be that such a person ought to be obligated to honor a contract.[52]

Despite his great influence on American jurisprudence and our system of government, Locke is not without his critics, especially in recent times among feminist scholars, who have questioned his social contract theory and its effect of further subordinating women. Accordingly, Locke is another significant influence on citizenship who apparently had little distaste for segregated forms of membership, at least with respect to the female members of society.

According to Donna Dickerson, Locke's social contract had the effect of oppressing women: "[W]omen's deteriorating status during the golden period of liberalism flows from the emphasis on contract, rationality and property in the person of Locke."[53] Indeed, according to this view, the exclusion of women from the political realm was deliberate and explicit in liberal theory. Contract is explicitly egalitarian; however, as Dickerson observed, the theory primary relegates women to the level of subjects of contracts.[54]

In essence, the contrarian individual, in the Lockean model, necessarily is the proprietor of his person, but in Locke's times, married women were incapable of owning their own persons—and if a woman was incapable of being a possessive individual, then she could not enter into a social contract.[55] According to Dickerson, Locke's failure to address women's unequal status during his times was not a mere oversight but was in fact central to his thesis. Gordon Schochet observed that it is hardly news that the participating members of the civil society were the adult males of that society.[56] Though Locke was not explicit about their exclusion, according to Schochet, Locke left no place for women in the public sphere.[57] As a result, women were simply excluded from the compacts or contracts that Locke theorized.

Other scholars have similarly taken issue with Locke's view of women. One author observed that Locke made various distinctions among different groups of individuals, based ostensibly upon their capacity for reason and (a specific form of) industry but implicitly based on gender, race, and class.[58] While class analysis has attempted to examine the economic distinctions among different groups of men in the public sphere, and a second-wave feminist analysis has attempted to examine the gendered role of wives of free men within the private sphere, the explicit divisions, in Western political thought, between *different groups of women* in the private sphere, and the degree to which power is attached to those differences, has been ignored.[59] The groundbreaking feminist analyses of thinkers like Carole Pateman examined not only the gendered division between the free citizen and his wife but also the multilayered divisions within the private sphere among wives, servants, and slaves.[60]

By recognizing the existence of *female* servants and slaves, Locke's theory incorporated not only the diversity among women in the traditional private sphere of Western political theory but also the hierarchy of power that corresponds to that diversity. Moreover, the theoretical and historical distinctions drawn by Locke among other groups of people (both male and female) on the basis of ethnicity, and their different relationships to the private or domestic sphere (for example, African slaves, who were completely submerged within the private sphere, or American "Indians," who were never to be enslaved or incorporated into the private sphere) was not fully explored. These distinctions, according to Pateman, with regard to the private sphere, based on gender, ethnic, and class differences, are the theoretical foundations upon which Western liberal democracies have been built, and continue to be crucial to the way "politics" and power—or, more precisely, empowerment—is defined for different groups.

Whether it is the distinction in the *Two Treatises* between a husband's conjugal authority over his wife, a master's despotic power over his slaves, or the higher levels of authority accorded to wives over servants and slaves, it is clear that free citizens (and their wives, with regard to the human property in the private sphere) have authority different from all of these other groups in Locke's political theory. "Clearly, Locke was not interested in creating a world in which all were equal"; in his view, there would always be differences among individuals.[61] Accordingly, despite such differences in society, women's rights are of an inferior value because, as Pateman reiterates, in contract theory, "'men alone have the attributes of free and equal individuals.'"[62]

Susan Okin has observed that "although women have become legal citizens as defined by Locke and Rousseau, they still do not have political or economic power, a fact that suggests the inability of liberal social philosophy to bring about women's liberation."[63] As a result, democratic philosophies cannot be successfully expanded or revised to include women as citizens because they are predicated on a division between the public sphere of men's activities and a natural, private sphere of family relations to which women are confined.[64] The result is that liberal political philosophy only describes relations among men. Because those relations are predicated on the assumption that women are maintaining households and rearing children in the family, women cannot practically be included in liberal politics.[65] In a similar analysis, Lorenne Clark pointed out an irony, namely, that descriptions of the family tucked away in little-read parts of Locke's *Second Treatise of Government* are in fact the necessary foundation for his projection of a democratic society.[66] As a result, the rights on which Locke bases his civil society require that women be restricted to "monogamous marriage so that male property owners will have heirs."[67]

Nancy Holland argued that empiricists assume that simple impressions are the same for all, but in fact women have different experiences and, therefore, different ideas.[68] Locke's "solipsism," for example, his assumption that "others' mental states are only indirectly knowable, does not take into consideration a pregnant women's experience of the fetus within her."[69] Locke, separated from parenting by social norms, barred from pregnancy by biological fact, had a necessarily restricted male view of personal identity; his mistake as a philosopher was to claim that his limited experience as a man is universal, thus erasing the experience of women.[70]

Charles Montesquieu

Another consequential Enlightenment philosopher was Charles Montesquieu, who published *The Spirit of the Laws* in 1748. A sociologist, naturalist, and advocate of liberty, Montesquieu observed the world around him and attempted to make sense of the differing cultures that inhabited it. He was one of the great political philosophers of the Enlightenment. His two most famous works, *Lettres persanes* (*Persian Letters*; 1721) and *De l'Esprit des lois* (*Spirit of the Laws*; 1748), act as windows to explain and demonstrate his philosophy of government, which is credited with being the inspiration behind the United States' separation of powers. Montesquieu believed that in the world, there were only three types of governments: republics, monarchies, and the despotisms.[71]

Montesquieu constructed an account of the various forms of government and the causes of each that either advanced or constrained their development. He used this account to explain how governments might be preserved from corruption, as the main purpose of government, in his view, is to maintain law and order, political liberty, and the property of the individual. Montesquieu saw despotism, in particular, as a standing danger for any government not already despotic, and he argued that it could best be prevented by a system in which different bodies exercised legislative, executive, and judicial power, all of which were bound by the rule of law. This theory of the separation of powers had an enormous impact on liberal political theory, and on the framers of the U.S. Constitution. Montesquieu opposed the absolute monarchy in his home country of France and favored the English system as the best model of government.

Montesquieu believed that democracies could be corrupted in two ways: "the spirit of inequality" and "the spirit of extreme equality."[72] The spirit of inequality manifested when citizens and the country did not share the same interests,[73] because when the interests were not the same, the citizen will pursue self-interest and lust for power.[74] The spirit of extreme equality manifested when citizens no longer wish to be equal with other similar citizens and instead wish to be equal with public officials; in this spirit, the citizens wish to act as the public officials themselves.[75] Montesquieu's writings stressed the importance of the role of citizen—defining citizenship within the realm of liberty and society as "a life being lived under the rule of law." His popularity and public acceptance gave credence to the ideas of young Rousseau, who echoed Montesquieu's thoughts and proposed his own ideas on the virtuous citizen.

Despite the significant role Montesquieu's theories played in Western democracies and particularly in the United States, he believed (like the other writers on citizenship dating back to the first works on the subject) that certain members of society deserved less than equal membership. According to Montesquieu's view, although all may be citizens and consider themselves to be equal, some citizens are more equal than others.[76] Montesquieu develops this point further by suggesting that the law should ensure equality among nobles and noble families[77] and by making a clear distinction between two different levels of citizenship and corresponding levels of equality: that of the average citizen and that of the noble.

A fundamental component of Montesquieu's musings was his "Climate Theory," which he believed explained how governments and people function. Though Montesquieu's views under this theory are quite arcane and even bigoted to a thinker of modern times, they were the basis for his beliefs in the disparate treatment of racial minorities and women. Climate theory also had the effect of justifying the subordinate treatment of the less-empowered people within a society. Montesquieu argued that cooler climates are more likely to produce republics and monarchies, and warmer climates are more likely to produce despotic governments;[78] he also argued that warmer climates made despotic governments more likely to practice slavery and polygamy.[79] Montesquieu also believed that people who resided in warmer climates experienced a physiological weakness due to the environment.[80] Because of this physiological weakness, Montesquieu argued, slavery was natural and tolerable.[81] Montesquieu also explained that in the warmer climates, the heat rendered men "slothful."[82] As a result, men were naturally unmotivated to work towards the betterment of society, and Montesquieu believed that it was only the fear of chastisement that motivated the citizen to perform laborious tasks.[83]

Furthermore, in the despotic governments of warmer climates, the status of a slave was not much different than that of the despot's subjects. When his advocacy of slavery was inevitably criticized, Montesquieu responded in *Spirit of the Laws*, "In all this I only give their reasons, but do not justify their customs."[84] Interestingly enough, however, Montesquieu's excuse for slavery in his theory did not appear to support the system of slavery that was taking place in the Americas. Montesquieu made it clear that when he was speaking of slavery, he was mostly speaking about slavery in the Orient. When he did address the slavery resulting from the colonization of the Americas, he focused mostly on Spain and conveniently turned to the Orient when questions arose of slavery in French colonies.[85] While condemning the practice of slavery in the Spanish colonies, Montesquieu made only a brief mention of the French colonies: "our colonies in the Antilles are admirable."[86]

Of course, one possible explanation for his oversight is that Montesquieu believed the French colonies should be in climates where "natural causes" and "particular circumstance" made slavery tolerable. Although he arguably condemned the practice of slavery, he nonetheless made troubling statements justifying the enslavement of Africans, such as "because Africans are black from head to toe, it is impossible to pity them; . . . God in all his wisdom would not have placed a soul in a black body; and . . . sugar would be too expensive were it not grown by slaves."[87]

With respect to gender issues, Montesquieu held views that were similarly troubling to contemporary sensibilities. He believed that both sexes had equal rights to life, liberty, and property, and that there was no justification in natural law for one sex to have absolute power over the other.[88] However, Montesquieu also believed that besides what he considered were the obvious natural differences between men and women, other differences existed between the sexes. For example, he believed that wives had a "natural dependence" on their husbands, that husbands were the heads of families because of the "natural weakness" of wives.[89] Although Montesquieu believed that women had greater physical charms and a capacity to resist sexual license, he also believed that women were weaker than men both physically and mentally.[90] For example, he argued that women's menstrual cycle evidenced their lack of reason[91] because evidently, this cycle attacked women and particularly their minds.[92]

Montesquieu also referred to climate theory to explain the differences between the sexes and the practice of polygamy. Montesquieu believed that a natural inequality existed between men and women in southern countries because of the climate.[93] He believed that women in warmer climates tended to mature earlier than women in cooler climates; to him, this maturing was purely physical, not mental, resulting in women becoming physically older more quickly than men.[94] He also reasoned that because women matured earlier, they married earlier. This disadvantaged women because although they were physically mature upon marriage, they were not yet mentally mature and thus were inferior to their much older husbands.[95] However, according to Montesquieu, once a woman mentally matured, she would still be at a disadvantage because by that time she would have lost her physical charm, which was used to influence her husband.[96] He concluded that because women in warmer climates were at a constant disadvantage, their husband dominated them and at times even wed multiple wives.[97] In cooler climates, however, women did not physically mature too quickly; so when women married, they were both physically and mentally mature.[98] In any event, Montesquieu believed that, naturally, women are mentally inferior,[99] making this distinction moot.

Because husbands living in warmer climates were often under despotic rule, the despot considered the wife a form of property and a slave, whose purpose was to perform her duty to her husband.[100] It was Montesquieu's belief that a man must keep his women under strict despotic rule for fear that if he did not, they would be his undoing.[101] Like so many other practices that Montesquieu condemned, he too offered an explanation for this relationship of domestic servitude. He believed that men living in despotic governments had no choice but to treat their wives like slaves because this practice was thrust upon them by the nature of the environment that they lived in; men were biologically superior, which allowed them to enslave women,[102] and the fear of a despotic nation encouraged them to do this because being a subject of the despot and being a slave were not very different.[103] It was Montesquieu's fear of a despotic government that led him to the conclusion that even though men and women should have equal rights to life, liberty, and ownership of property,[104] in the social sphere, women and men should be separate; men should act in the social sphere while the women maintained the home.[105]

Montesquieu believed that virtue was one of the keys that held republics together. In a monarchist government, virtue was not necessarily a key element as much as honor.[106] It was Montesquieu's fear that if a government were to lose its virtue, its structure could collapse and possibly result in a despotic government.[107] For example, in a republic, Montesquieu believed that economic surplus was dangerous because it provided luxuries that enabled people to be overcome with their own personal pleasures and lose their virtue and yet also participate in the collective interest of the society.[108] Montesquieu placed the responsibility of virtue primarily on women, arguing that a violation of chastity was a clear renunciation of all virtue.[109] Although Montesquieu studied the old republics of Greece and Rome, he did not believe that they served as models for the modern republic.[110] However, he did agree with the practice of allowing women a degree of freedom ruled by particular manners:[111]

> In republics women are free by the laws and restrained by manners; luxury is banished thence, and with it corruption and vice. . . . In the cities of Greece . . . such were the virtue, simplicity and chastity of women . . . hardly any people were ever known to have had a better and wiser polity.[112]

Montesquieu's idea of women being "free by the laws and restrained by manners,"[113] however, is not what some readers would recognize as an attempt to replace the word "law" with "manners." Montesquieu did not believe that these restrictive manners were necessarily laws of man so much as they were laws of nature. Montesquieu believed that women were naturally virtuous because they were naturally modest, and the fact that the social nature of the state wished to reinforce this modesty was a subpoint.[114]

Montesquieu also argued that women showed little restraint in monarchies because the distinction of rank called them to the court; in court, they developed a freedom of spirit that was the only behavior tolerated there. Each man uses their charms and their passions to advance his fortune; and, as their weakness does not lead to pride but only to vanity, luxury always reigns there with them.[115] Because he believed in the power of women to get from men whatever women wanted,[116] Montesquieu believed that women should be limited in the social sphere.[117] This meant that although he believed that men and women have equal rights to life, liberty, and ownership of property, he did not believe that women should participate in the politics of men. In fact, he believed that the proper place for women was the home:

> Women must not only be separated from men by the enclosure of the house; they must also be separated within this enclosure, such that they constitute a family within the family. From this derives their whole practice of morality. . . . Women have naturally to fulfill so many duties that are proper to them that they cannot be separated enough from everything that might give them other ideas, from all that is called amusement.[118]

Here, Montesquieu explains that the place for the woman should be in the home; since women have so much work there, including them in the social sphere would spread them too thinly. However, two other factors fueled his belief that women should solely maintain the household—his fear of women corrupting politics and the socioeconomic status quo of the country and his belief that women in this sphere also encouraged effeminacy in men.[119]

Montesquieu feared that if women integrated themselves into the politics of men and retained the same freedom as men, men and women would spend too much time together, and would consequently become the same.[120] This was to be avoided, Montesquieu believed, because women were responsible for the decaying standards of France's monarchy and their political involvement would inevitably lead to a fall of government and possibly to the installment of despotic rule: "It is our social intercourse with women which has brought us to this state, for they are dilettantes by nature. Today there is only one sex left; we have all become women as far as intellectual life is concerned. If one night our features were to change, no one would notice the difference."[121]

Unfortunately, like the other leading thinkers of his day, Montesquieu had very little hesitation about supporting a segregated society, particularly with respect to the treatment of women. It seemed he believed in women's rights only if those rights did not include women interfering with affairs, such as politics, that should be left to men. As with citizenship's little-known exclusionary aspect, sadly, the uneven support for equality by this and other thinkers of his day has not been exposed or examined nearly as much as their laudable pronouncements.

Jean-Jacques Rousseau

A third important seventeenth-century Enlightenment philosopher was Jean-Jacques Rousseau, who wrote that man was naturally good and was only corrupted by society.[122] In 1762, Rousseau published his most important work on political theory, *The Social Contract*. His opening line is still striking today: "Man is born free, and everywhere he is in chains." He described savages in a state of nature as free, equal, peaceful, and happy. When people began to claim ownership of property, Rousseau argued, inequality, murder, and war resulted.

According to Rousseau, the rich stole the land belonging to everyone and fooled the common people into accepting them as rulers. Rousseau concluded that the social contract was not a willing agreement—as Hobbes,

Locke, and Montesquieu had believed—but was instead a fraud against the people committed by the rich. Rousseau agreed with Locke that the individual should never be forced to give up his or her natural rights to a king. The problem in the state of nature, Rousseau argued, was to find a way to protect everyone's life, liberty, and property while maintaining each person as free.

Rousseau's solution was for individuals to enter into a social contract. They would give up all their rights, not to a king but to "the whole community," all the people. He called all the people the "sovereign"—a term used by Hobbes mainly in reference to a king. The people then exercised their "general will" to make laws for the "public good." Rousseau argued that the general will of the people could not be decided by elected representatives. He believed in a direct democracy in which everyone voted to express the general will and to make the laws of the land.

Rousseau is characterized as the champion of democracy because he believed that authority lies with the people. He asserted that man is born free; that controls by a freely formed government are good; that consent to a form of government means that the individual gives up self-interest in favor of the common good; and that when government is by the consent of the governed, the people retain their rights. Rousseau put faith in the general will of the majority. He wrote that the majority should always work for the common good of the people. He hated political and economic oppression and supported revolt. Rousseau influenced thinkers for more than two hundred years and probably influenced the writers of our Constitution.

Not unlike Aristotle, Rousseau envisioned a democracy on a small scale, a city-state like his native Geneva. All political power, according to Rousseau, must reside with the people, exercising their general will. There can be no separation of powers, as Montesquieu proposed. The people, meeting together, will deliberate individually on laws and then by majority vote find the general will, in a manner arguably similar to modern notions of a town meeting or a domestic presidential caucus. Rousseau's view of the general will was later embodied in the words "We the People"—which are found at the beginning of the U.S. Constitution.

Rousseau was rather vague on the mechanics of how his vision of a democracy would work. There would be a government of sorts, entrusted with administering the general will. But it would be composed of "mere officials" who got their orders from the people. Rousseau believed that religion divided and weakened the state. "It is impossible to live in peace with people you think are damned," he said. He favored a "civil religion" that accepted G_d, but concentrated on the sacredness of the social contract.[123]

In his famous work the *Second Discourse,* Rousseau thoroughly develops his idea of man in his "natural state," happy, free, and uncorrupted by the social forces that came with his transition into civilized society. In the opening remarks of the *Second Discourse,* Rousseau asserts that while many philosophers have attempted to describe man in the state of nature, none has actually succeeded.[124] "[A]ll these philosophers talking ceaselessly of need, greed, oppression, desire and pride have transported into the state of nature concepts formed in society. They speak of savage man and they depict civilized man."[125] According to Rousseau, the above mentioned character traits are unnatural; they are the effects of social interaction and property ownership, two things that did not exist in the natural state.

Rousseau's idea of the natural state is essentially that man is just another animal in the wild—unenlightened, and acting only to resolve his immediate needs.[126] "I see him satisfying his hunger under an oak, quenching his thirst at the first stream, finding his bed under the same tree which provided his meal, and behold, his needs are furnished."[127] Rousseau argues that living in this state of nature leaves man healthy, at peace, and happy.[128]

When Hobbes asserts that man is naturally evil and vicious because he has no idea of goodness or virtue, Rousseau answers that it is this same ignorance that prevents the natural man from being evil and vicious, as a man cannot be one without knowledge of the other.[129] Hobbes believes that the notion of *amour de soi,* which he referred to as one's natural or naive love of self, leads to competition among men, each fighting for himself and thus having an aggressive inclination toward one another.[130] However, Rousseau argues that Hobbes takes the notion too far, asserting that rather than aggression, the general attitude is one of indifference, and it is the combination of self-preservation and indifference toward others that keeps man from associating or forming social relationships.[131]

According to Rousseau, it was social relations and property that produced jealousy, pride, and vanity. *Amour de soi* was injected with the seeds of "fatal enlightenment,"[132] producing the notion of *amour propre,* which is a love of self driven by pride and jealousy rather than by elemental self-preservation— sending the natural, peaceful, and happy man on his journey into a society of misery and inequality. Rousseau refers to this transitional period as "nascent society," one in which man has emerged from nature but not yet entered civil society.[133]

For Rousseau, the development of society led to the development of even greater inequality. As he asserted, "Such was, or must have been, the origin of society and of laws, which put new fetters on the weak and gave new powers to the rich, which irretrievably destroyed natural liberty, established for all time the law of property and inequality, transformed adroit usurpation into irrevocable right, and for the benefit of a few ambitious men subjected the human race thenceforth to labour, servitude and misery."[134] The growth of industry led to the growth of property, and the effects of the two brought man from nascent society into civil society's institution of inequality. In contrast, John Locke put forth the idea that man had a natural right to property.

Rousseau believed that the natural man had no concept of property and that its advent led to the downfall of equality. Nonetheless, when it came to property rights as recognized by society, Locke and Rousseau both agree that the right derived from manual labor. "It is his labour alone which, in giving the cultivator the right to the product of the land he has tilled, gives him in consequence the right to the land itself. . . ."[135] While it is unclear exactly when man first started large-scale agriculture, Rousseau does believe that the advent of other industries must have compelled man to apply himself to agriculture, for "as soon as some men were needed to smelt and forge iron, other men were needed to supply them with food."[136] And so it went; the more industries that developed and grew, the more there was the need for food. Mass land cultivation naturally led to land division, and land division led to the first notion of property rights.[137]

Rousseau argued that if there were a constant balance between what each person needed and what each person produced, as well as equality of natural talents among men, things might have remained equal, presumably through a system of sharing and barter.[138] However, this was not the case: "the farmer had greater need of iron or the smith greater need of wheat, and with both working equally, the one earned plenty while the other had hardly enough to live on."[139] This is the initial cause of the unequal distribution of wealth and the development of economic classes. People were ranked not just by the quantity of their possessions but also according to "intelligence, beauty, strength, skill, merit or talents."[140] But one feeds the other, as the stronger or more talented are able to work harder and produce more, just as the intelligent and skilled were able to produce more by working less, and those producing more than others naturally ended up possessing more than others.

Rousseau argued that this first form of society was really a way for the rich to take advantage of the disorder at hand, a way to take control—the creation and expansion of slavery disguised as a society of liberty and rule:[141] "All ran towards their chains believing that they were securing their liberty; for although they had reason enough to discern the advantages of a civil order, they did not have experience enough to foresee the dangers."[142] Rousseau argued that those "most capable of predicting the abuses" of such a society were the same people who were expecting to profit from it: the rich. Nonetheless, Rousseau also argued that once the first of such societies was established, its form quickly spread to all corners of the world, and alas, the natural state was indeed gone forever, and nascent government began.[143]

The first forms of nascent government were without a constant and formalized framework. There were a few generalized conventions that communities agreed to abide by, but the agreement was really among the individuals and there was no real centralized authority that could maintain a true legal order. The "public alone was witness and judge," and as a result, breaking the law and avoiding conviction was not a difficult or uncommon task.[144] This commonality created a cycle of order and disorder, one eventual result being the belief that entrusting certain individuals with public authority was necessary, "committing to the magistrates the duty of securing obedience to the deliberations of the people."[145] This meant people would have to give up (at least some of) their liberty and all agree to be subject to the magistrate's authority. This, of course, leads to the problem of said authority taking advantage of the situation and enslaving its subjects.

Rousseau struggled with the notion of man submitting to such an authority, as he felt that to do so is for man to completely relieve himself of his freedom. "[S]ince the worst . . . that can happen . . . in the relations between [men] is to find oneself at the mercy of another, would it not be contrary to common sense for men to surrender into the hands of a chief the only things they needed his help in order to preserve?"[146] Furthermore, Rousseau questioned whether such a proposition, the relinquishment of one's freedom, is even possible.

Rousseau eventually came to the conclusion that the only way one could submit to the authority of a magistrate without jeopardizing one's freedom is to form a society in which every member is subject to its rules, including the magistrate. Thus, "the establishment of the body politic [is] a true contract between a people and the chiefs that a people choose, a contract whereby both parties commit themselves to observe the laws which are stipulated in its articles."[147] According to Rousseau, the people needed to "unite their wills" to form a constitution, which would become fundamental laws "obligatory on every member of the state without exception."[148] A constitution of this sort would not only establish fundamental laws; it would legitimize them, an important concept indicating that the contract between the people and their government is still valid, and everyone is subject to its laws.

According to Rousseau's views in the *Second Discourse*, it seems that when the state of nature was lost, so too was freedom and equality. Further, the idea that one could be ruled and free at the same time was something that it would seem even Rousseau had not thought of when writing the *Second Discourse*. Indeed, he said that if the legitimate rule of the constitution were to become corrupt, the contract between the people and the government would no longer be valid and "each individual would return by right to his natural liberty."[149] This implies that men, in submitting to that (albeit revocable) contract, were in fact giving up at least some of their freedom. Hobbes believed that "sovereignty must be unified and absolute . . . [and] men must choose: either they were ruled or they were free; they could not be both; liberty went with anarchy and security with civil obedience."[150] In *The Social Contract*, Rousseau said that he believed men could be free and members of a sovereignty at the same time, and it is in this way that *The Social Contract* can be seen as an answer to Hobbes's philosophy.[151]

The basis of the social contract stipulates that "[e]ach one of us puts into the community his person and all his powers under the supreme direction of the general will; and as a body, we incorporate every member as an indivisible part of the whole."[152] Two important concepts are integrated in this theory: the sovereign and the general will.[153]

With respect to his focus on equality, it would only seem natural for Rousseau to reject slavery, and in fact he did reject it. "Man was born free, and he is everywhere in chains. Those who think themselves the masters of others are indeed greater slaves than they."[154] From the discussions on equality and the social contract above, it should be clear that the right to slavery has no place in Rousseau's social theory. On numerous occasions, Rousseau addresses the issue of slavery, always asserting that while one can be forced into slavery, one can only remain enslaved by one's own volition. As Rousseau asserted, men are born "free and equal" and will "surrender their freedom only when they see advantage in doing so."[155]

Despite the consistency of his theory of equality on troubling issues of his day, such as slavery, Rousseau was not so kind to women, often using traditionally narrow views that were all too prevalent during that era. In other words, in the case of women, the great champion of equality had little problem with advocating structural inequality. Specifically with respect to women, Rousseau wrote, "The man should be strong and active; the woman should be weak and passive; the one must have both the power and the will; it is enough that the other should offer little resistance. When this principle is admitted, it follows that woman is specially made for man's delight."[156]

Rousseau's depiction of women in his works has been the subject of much controversy. Paul Thomas adequately summarizes the overall sentiment when he asserts, "The question is not whether he [Rousseau] should be identified as a sexist. He should."[157] Perhaps the best-known (and most oft-cited) critic of Rousseau's sexist views is Mary Wollstonecraft in her 1791 work *A Vindication of the Rights of Woman*.[158] Her harsh criticisms focused on the same text from which the excerpt above has been pulled: Rousseau's *Émile*.

Generally speaking, most of Rousseau's work depicts women as inferior to men. As mentioned above, the *Second Discourse* contains what many would argue reflects a biased view: the idea that women have not been equal to men since the natural state.[159] In fact, women are hardly mentioned at all in the *Second Discourse*. In *The Social Contract*, men are exclusively considered to be full citizens—as woman's role in society is confined to the private sphere.[160] As a citizen, man is to go out and exercise political power in the name of the general will, retaining freedom and "equality," while woman is destined to remain within the household.[161]

In *Émile*, perhaps his most criticized work in terms of sexism, Rousseau discusses the upbringing of a boy named *Émile* and the process by which he is educated in each stage of his life as he grows to be a citizen.[162] While the first four books of *Émile* are about Émile's education, divided by the stages of his life (infancy, childhood, adolescence, manhood), the fifth and final book focuses on the education of Émile's counterpart, Sophie.[163] Sophie is destined to marry Émile, and her education is in stark contrast to his; while Émile's education is focused on creating a citizen, Sophie's education focuses on domestic training, child rearing, and pleasing her man.[164]

Finally, Rousseau wrote a tragic love story in *La Nouvelle Heloise* (*Julie; or, The New Heloise*), one in which we see the gender roles identified in *The Social Contract* played out.[165] The story, written as a series of correspondences, is about Julie, the daughter of a nobleman, who falls in love with her tutor, Saint-Preux.[166] When the love is forbidden by Julie's father, Saint-Preux moves to Paris and Julie marries another man named Wolmar. While Julie remains in love with Saint-Preux, she eventually settles into a marriage in which she and Wolmar exemplify Rousseau's mandated gender roles: Wolmar as the ideal citizen and Julie as the dedicated, passionate wife—confined to her home.

Rousseau does not generally include women in the terms "citizen" and "equality" in his work. It is quite easy to make the argument, based on his asserted gender roles and treatment of them in his writings, that Rousseau did not think too highly of women. However, there are also those who argue that Rousseau's gender roles are misunderstood, or that the sexist charge is altogether overstated.

Paul Thomas, for example, makes the argument that while he would confine women to the household, Rousseau is not saying that they are powerless, as many assume.[167] To the contrary, Thomas argues that Rousseau believes women have so much power over men that it must be contained within the household, from where it should be utilized to help man in his political endeavors.[168] Lori Marso agrees with Thomas in that women have a lot of power in Rousseau's eyes, but Marso has a very different basis for her argument.[169]

Marso references *The Social Contract, Émile,* and *La Nouvelle Héloise,* agreeing that Rousseau, textually, appears to be extremely sexist with his gender roles.[170] However, through an analysis of *La Nouvelle Heloise,* Marso argues that Rousseau shows by example that the gender roles he claims are necessary for civil society must be reexamined if society is going to succeed.[171] Marso focuses on the fact that while Julie, Saint-Preux, and Wolmar all adhered to the gender roles that Rousseau had laid out, Julie still dies in the end, showing that "Rousseau has failed to sustain community in the way he set out."[172] Marso argues that this ending is a message directly from Rousseau challenging the way people think of his views, arguing that a reexamination of such gender roles is necessary in order for society to succeed.[173]

To summarize, of all the Enlightenment thinkers, Rousseau was the great champion of equality. He was the great advocate for a government made up by and run for the people. He called for direct and active participation by the populace. He rejected the top-down approach of Hobbes and was generally skeptical of the rich and their ability to manipulate the masses in order to achieve their own desires. Despite his egalitarian focus and inclusive themes, Rousseau was not kind to women, believing that they should hold a subordinate role to men in society and in their private lives. It is somewhat ironic that such an advocate for equality would fall in the same trap as the other Enlightenment thinkers and ultimately advocate for subordinate membership. Though credited with prompting the all-important language of "we the people" in our own founding documents, he evidently believed the "we" only consisted of men.

The Enlightenment Thinkers' Influence on the U.S. Constitution

The four Enlightenment philosophers discussed in this chapter had a lasting and significant impact on the structure of and points of emphasis in the U.S. Constitution. The Constitution, in many respects, was an attempt by our forefathers to create a government that executed all of the principles that were put forth by the Enlightenment thinkers.[174] During their respective periods of scholarly productivity, these philosophers wrote numerous consequential and ultimately lasting works explaining how governments and their citizenry should rule and be ruled.

Thomas Hobbes, John Locke, Jean-Jacques Rousseau, and Baron de Montesquieu each influenced the Constitution by writing "social contracts" in which they explained how the government must relate to its people.[175] Thomas Hobbes could receive the credit for initiating the discussion that would influence the structure of the Constitution.[176] He wrote the first social contract in his book *Leviathan*. The works of the other Enlightenment philosophers were arguably based on, or least written in response to, this book.[177] Although Hobbes may not have had direct influence on the founding fathers with his book, which was largely based on the principles of monarchy, he seems to have had influence on its structure.

Hobbes's other major contribution to the Constitution was his ideas of the elements of laws, and, more specifically, civil laws.[178] He defined these laws as those rules that the government uses for the distinction of right and wrong in society. This is in direct correlation with the ideas set forth in the first article of the Constitution,[179] which gives Congress the power to create laws. Another of Hobbes's contributions was the idea of judicial review, which is also put forth in his chapter "On Civil Laws."[180] He states that all laws need interpretation, for no one can ever truly define a law without it. The Supreme Court in *Marbury v. Madison* interpreted this power as being implied even though not explicitly set forth in the document.[181] The final contribution Hobbes made to the Constitution was the belief in the illegality of *ex post facto* laws.[182] These laws are ones that are created after an offense is committed in order to punish the offender. Hobbes essentially stated that if there is no law, there cannot be a crime.[183]

John Locke also wrote several important major documents on government: his *Letter Concerning Toleration* and his *Two Treatises of Government*. He is arguably the most influential of all the Enlightenment philosophers. In fact, the framers of the United States Constitution followed many of Locke's ideas on tolerance, along with his thoughts on liberty and civil rights.[184] The first and foremost place in the Constitution where Locke's effects can be felt is the Preamble.[185] Locke reinforced what Hobbes stated about the creation of laws by the legislative branch but also added the idea of federal supremacy.[186] Locke also addressed the notion of a civil magistrate, defined as the governing body, or the executive branch of government. The creation of our presidency is based on Locke's idea of a magistrate.[187]

Another major contributor to the Constitution is Jean-Jacques Rousseau. In his book *The Social Contract*, he sought to bring transparency to government, and effectively he brought about the resurgence in popularity of the republic. "Since he was a citizen he believed in his right to have a fair say in the government. This led to the idea of the general will. The general will can be expressed as the idea that every man has the right to have and express an opinion."[188] This is the idea of the republic, which is evident in every article of the Constitution.

Besides addressing the lawgiver or, in modern terms, the legislative branch, and of the prince or, in modern terms, the executive branch, Rousseau added the importance of the general will in determining sovereignty and laws. In order to prove that this was the best way, he demonstrated that the general will cannot err. For if people were informed, they could always make the best choice for themselves. This was the major change from Rousseau's peers. Everyone before him had been of the view that man must submit without input.

The last of the four great political philosophers to influence the Constitution was Baron de Montesquieu. Montesquieu tended to focus specifically on the laws and structure of government. In his book *The Spirit of Laws*, Montesquieu is credited with the unique idea of the separation of powers. This is made very clear in the United States Constitution by the three separate articles for the three individual branches of government, not to mention the strong implication of checks and balances in our government.

All philosophers of the period basically agreed that the legislatures of Western democracies may make laws, but Montesquieu further examined the subject by devoting books to this topic. In fact, the powers given to the legislative branch in the Constitution are nearly all directly quoted from some part of *The Spirit of Laws*. A few of these powers include the collection of taxes, the regulation of commerce, the control of armies, and the right to declare war. These ideas were all incorporated into our system of government and have, accordingly, enabled us to more firmly define the final aspects of our legislative branch of government.[189]

Accordingly, each of the Enlightenment philosophers addressed in this chapter had tremendous influence on liberal thought, democratic theory, and even this country's form of government. To varying degrees, these philosophers also contributed to contemporary thinking on citizenship. Interestingly, though largely credited with championing democratic theory, and presumably the importance of the tenet of equality within that construct, at least three of these theorists suffer from the same criticism that is echoed throughout this book, namely, being known for advocating the inclusive virtues of democracy and equality but harboring biased beliefs that keep some members of a society in a subordinate position and on an unequal footing. In other words, citizenship's dark little exclusionary secret is perhaps a function of the lesser-known, but equally damning, bias held by its great philosophical champions.

6

The *De Jure* Subordinates

As the preceding chapters demonstrate, Western societies have followed the pattern set by the ancient world concerning the citizenship construct. From the classical period to the Renaissance, influential theorists and politicians repeatedly extolled the virtues and necessity of equal citizenship within a democracy. Though the dominant discourse focused on equality, the practice of granting citizenship was far more exclusionary. This pattern was practiced with zeal in the United States' development of the construct.

In fact, little of the modern domestic discourse on citizenship questions the concept of equality, let alone accepts that there exist differentiated levels of membership for subordinate social or ethnic groups. Indeed, Congress as well as the Supreme Court has repeatedly addressed the importance of the citizen in a democracy but has never admitted to endorsing gradations of membership. Despite this fact, many American citizens to this day fail to enjoy equal rights.

These inferior rights are vividly evidenced in the U.S. Supreme Court's creation of legal fictions when racial and ethnic minority groups sought equal and full membership rights. In fact, the role that constructions of subordination, including those based on national origin and race, have played in excluding members from the U.S. body politic at the very least calls into question the sincerity of domestic citizenship rhetoric. American citizenship has unfortunately all too often been a tool for including Caucasians and excluding African Americans,[1] indigenous people,[2] and other non-Whites.[3] For instance, the legal doctrines created over a century ago to maintain African American slave status[4] and to deport and exclude legal immigrants still maintain inferior citizenship status for millions of United States citizens, such as the inhabitants of this country's island colonies and the indigenous people of this land.

Despite this reality, the concept of citizenship in the United States Constitution is based on equality. The primary source for citizenship, the Citizenship Clause of the Fourteenth Amendment, is a post-Reconstruction amendment specifically aimed to provide former slaves—African Americans—with political rights associated with citizenship. Although this clause centers on the notion of equality, in practice Congress and the Supreme Court have repeatedly denied people of color the benefits of equal treatment.[5] Many of the inconsistencies in the treatment of these groups stem from century-old constitutional doctrines that gave the political branches of government complete or plenary power over these groups and established disparate treatment for these less favored citizens.[6] Those whom the United States government exercised complete power, in effect, were deemed by that same government not to be true citizens, but "outsiders."[7]

The Supreme Court addressed the repeated pleas for equality of racial and ethnic minority groups by deferring to the plenary power of the political branches of government. This so-called plenary powers doctrine forms the central constitutional basis for the disenfranchisement of millions of Americans. The disparate treatment of these groups provokes this criticism of the citizenship jurisprudence's rhetoric concerning equality. The period from the early nineteenth century to the second decade of the twentieth century is the key juridical period when the Supreme Court and Congress attempted to define what groups were true American citizens eligible for full and complete citizenship rights.[8]

The Supreme Court's response to claims for equal treatment was that each and every member of every statistically significant racial minority group was not eligible for full citizenship rights and therefore could be treated in an unequal and often repugnant manner.[9] Between 1823 and 1922, the Supreme Court reiterated the importance of citizenship in a democracy but endorsed a model of differentiated levels of membership.

The Supreme Court responded to actions by racial minorities seeking citizenship by removing the issue from the courts and into the political branches through the plenary powers doctrine. In matters of citizenship, Congress's acts were effectively unreviewable because its constitutional power on these questions was plenary. As a rationale for avoiding a more strict level of judicial review, the plenary powers doctrine was used as a means to defer questions about the nature of citizenship to Congress and its wisdom. Limited judicial review and broad congressional discretion resulted in a citizenship matrix with different classes of citizens enjoying discrepant rights to participate in the body politic: some were full citizens, but others were subordinate citizens.

In the 1800s, the U.S. Supreme Court began articulating and defining the contours of the plenary powers doctrine. The Court defined this doctrine as meaning that the Court would defer to the full and complete power of Congress when faced with certain types of challenges to official conduct brought by certain groups.[10] The Supreme Court relied upon the plenary powers doctrine to justify turning a blind eye to government actions that subordinated certain groups, such as indigenous peoples, inhabitants of the United States' overseas possessions, and immigrants. The doctrine was and continues to be used as a weapon to disenfranchise those groups universally recognized as the most vulnerable.[11] The plenary powers doctrine and a similar doctrine applied to African Americans form the central constitutional basis for the disenfranchisement of millions of Americans.

In a series of decisions dealing with immigration, national security, and overseas expansion, the Court endorsed the unequal treatment and inferior status of various groups that should have been considered citizens or legal residents of this country. These cases include decisions addressing African Americans, in the infamous *Dred Scott v. Sandford*[12] and *Plessy v. Ferguson* cases;[13] indigenous peoples, in *Elk v. Wilkins*,[14] *United States v. Kagama*,[15] and *Lone Wolf v. Hitchcock*;[16] Asian immigrants, in the Chinese Exclusion Cases;[17] and inhabitants of the island conquests, in the Insular Cases.[18]

In each of these decisions, racial and ethnic minority groups were challenging the propriety of governmental action that discriminated against them. In each decision, the Court used similar racial and xenophobic justifications to uphold the disparate treatment. With the exception of the treatment of African Americans, when certain groups challenged violations to their constitutional rights, the Supreme Court justified deference to the political branches of the government by relying upon the plenary powers doctrine it extracted from the Constitution.

The plenary powers doctrine developed as an extension of the inherent powers doctrine during U.S. colonial expansion in the nineteenth century. Beginning in 1822, the Supreme Court upheld the federal government's doctrine of inherent plenary powers over indigenous nations, the inhabitants of the island colonies, and immigrants in entry and exclusion proceedings. The decisions that established and first applied the plenary powers doctrine to various outsider groups include *United States v. Kagama*,[19] *Chae Chan Ping v. United States*,[20] *Jones v. United States*,[21] *Nishimura Ekiu v. United States*,[22] *Fong Yue Ting v. United States*,[23] *Stephens v. Cherokee Nation*,[24] *Cherokee Nation v. Hitchcock*,[25] *Lone Wolf v. Hitchcock*,[26] *De Lima v. Bidwell*,[27] *Downes v. Bidwell*,[28]

Goetze v. United States,[29] *Dooley v. United States,*[30] *Fourteen Diamond Rings v. United States,*[31] *Hawaii v. Mankichi,*[32] *Kepner v. United States,*[33] *Dorr v. United States,*[34] *Huns v. Porto* [sic] *Rico S.S. Co.,*[35] *Balzac v. Porto* [sic] *Rico.*[36]

In each of these cases, the United States Supreme Court concluded that even the most basic liberty protections, as a matter of a constitutional law, did not apply to these groups. The Court based these holdings on international law principles and found that because Congress was primarily responsible for national security, issues that touched upon the status of individuals from sovereigns within and without the physical boundaries of the United States should be addressed primarily by the political branch of government and not the judicial branch.

The doctrine that ultimately became the plenary powers doctrine evolved over a series of decisions that purportedly based their determinations upon national security, but it was also used to espouse racist and xenophobic principles. The doctrine is perhaps more widely recognized in the immigration arena and was first developed in the immigration setting in the so-called Chinese Exclusion Cases. In *Chae Chan Ping*, the Court upheld the exclusion of legal Chinese residents and concluded that courts would not interfere with the government's action because it derived from the government's authority over national security.[37] Three years later, in *Nishimura Ekiu v. United States*, the Court upheld an exclusion of a Japanese immigrant without a hearing,[38] invoking the "accepted maxim of international law that every sovereign nation has the power, as inherent in sovereignty, and essential to self-preservation, to forbid the entrance of foreigners within its dominions, or to admit them only in such cases and upon such conditions as it may see fit to prescribe."[39] As it subsequently explained in the 1936 decision of *United States v. Curtiss-Wright Export Corp.*,[40] the theory of inherent plenary powers was premised essentially upon concerns over international law principles that recognized a nation-state as having the inherent power to take its place among the sovereign nations of the world despite being a government of limited and enumerated powers.[41]

These subordinate members of society, in turn, fell into two categories: those enjoying formal equality but continuing to suffer from the badge of exclusion (*de facto*) and those subordinated as a matter of law (*de jure*, the subject of this chapter). The original members of the citizenry, in name but not in effect, derived their citizenship from the Fourteenth Amendment. Their descendants now derive their citizenship in the same way that other citizens do, but the dynamics of transgenerational subordination raise questions as to whether they are equal members of society. The ancestors of most members of this group once held *de jure* subordinate status, but such inferiority was, at least formally, remediated by constitutional and statutory reforms. Nevertheless, members within this group, including African Americans and certain other racial and ethnic minorities, may still question whether they are full or first-class citizens. This form of *de facto* subordination will be the addressed in the next chapter.

The following pages tell the story of the *de jure* subordinates, whose inferior status was inscribed on the very face of the statutes and Supreme Court cases in question. The first section describes how the limited review available under the plenary powers doctrine led to a patchwork of conditional rights for the indigenous people of the United States. The cases in this section reflect an explicitly racist construction of indigenous people and deep ambivalence about the recognition of their rights, which often depended on contextual variables like the impact of the right on state-federal relations. The subsequent section considers the special legacy of the Insular Cases, which, like the islands whose inhabitants these cases classify, created an archipelago of inferior rights, far from the shores of mainland citizenship. Although the plenary powers doctrine also provides the foundation for the subordinate status of these island people, the cases follow a different pattern. Unlike the construction of the plenary powers doctrine used with respect to indigenous people, the version of the doctrine used for island people does not reflect the federal-state wrangling for power. Instead, the doctrinal issues tend to revolve around the Territorial Clause, as developed in the judicial standards of territorial incorporation.

The Indigenous People

If one of the primary means of acquiring U.S. citizenship is to be born on U.S. soil, it would stand to reason that indigenous people ought to be considered at the apex of citizenship, because they were the first born on this soil. However, they were initially excluded by the U.S. Constitution and then by the plenary powers doctrine.[42] As a first move, the United States considered indigenous tribes as sovereign nations within the United States—sovereigns to be subordinated. In the context of these indigenous people, the plenary powers doctrine rested—and continues to rest—on the notion that the political branches of the federal government are responsible for the nation's security and for its relations with other sovereigns.[43] Then, the United States, in addition to taking their land and declaring war on them as one sovereign could do with another under the public international law of war, used the indigenous people's foreign sovereign status to classify them as a foreign threat from within the United States.

The ongoing subordinate status of indigenous nations would be based on notions of their natural inferiority.[44] Indigenous membership was also premised on notions of inferiority. The group was characterized as existing in a state of "ignorance and mental debasement." For instance, in *United States v. Ritchie*, the Court declared, "From their degraded condition . . . and ignorance generally, the privileges extended to them in the administration of the government must have been limited; and they still, doubtless, required its fostering care and protection."[45] These demeaning characterizations and classifications reflect the United States' deep dislike of, or at best ambivalence towards, its indigenous people. They also illustrate the contingent nature of politically determined citizenship when a judicial power abdicates its role in questions of nationality: a doctrine developed for foreign sovereigns came to be used to justify the continued subjugation and mistreatment of the original inhabitants of this land.

The plenary power over the indigenous nations stems from a series of Supreme Court decisions that began in 1823.[46] In these decisions, the Court upheld repeated abuses of indigenous people's rights, including the continuous breaches of their treaties with the United States and the theft of their inhabited lands.[47] Congress exercised powers over indigenous people in a manner that the Court would not have upheld against a constitutional challenge if similarly asserted by other U.S. citizens.[48] However, given the Court's deference to the political branches, the Court effectively sanctioned virtually all congressional acts. In membership terms, the plenary powers doctrine justified the Court's imposition of limited membership and property rights. Perhaps more importantly, at the same time, the Court used racist stereotypes to maintain paternalistic "guardianship" over the indigenous people that justified their mistreatment.[49]

Chief Justice John Marshall illustrated this attitude: "The tribes of Indians inhabiting this country were fierce savages, whose occupation was war, and whose subsistence was drawn chiefly from the forest. To leave them in possession of their country was to leave the country a wilderness."[50] The Supreme Court assumed indigenous people to be an "other" in America: "the Court's treatment of tribal sovereignty [was] premised on an underlying conception of Indian identity that assumes Indian peoples are the 'other.'"[51] Hence, the Court indicated the "otherness" of the indigenous people through the type of language it used in several judicial opinions, which emphasized the distinctness and inferiority of the indigenous people.

The History of Subordination

In the first case of what resulted in the development of the plenary powers doctrine, *Johnson v. M'Intosh*,[52] the Court in 1823 began to justify the taking of indigenous lands by looking to the international law principle of discovery.[53] Under that doctrine, the first Western power to "discover" new lands had the exclusive right to that land against other Western powers and had the power "to acquir[e] the soil from the natives, and [establish] settlements upon it."[54] The self-professed "discoverers" created the label or mark of the subordinate Indian, and as a result, only the United States government could participate in land dealings with the indigenous people.[55]

In a dispute over whether indigenous people could convey land subsequently deemed by the United States to be U.S. property, the M'Intosh Court reasoned that the tribe in question had occupied the land but had no ownership rights to it. The Court's language indicates the inferior status of Indian title to the property.[56] Although at the time of the case, indigenous people were not U.S. citizens, the Court began to show that the United States' power supersedes that of the indigenous people yet subjects them to the laws of the United States. In doing so, the Court began regarding the indigenous people as distinct subjects within the United States.

After the *M'Intosh* decision, the Supreme Court in *Worcester v. Georgia*[57] addressed a similar issue of indigenous rights over land and the existence of indigenous sovereignty. Unlike the decision in *M'Intosh*, the *Worcester* Court seemed to recognize indigenous sovereignty and the indigenous people's right to hold and convey land. In that case, the Cherokees drafted and adopted a written constitution in 1827, declaring the Cherokee Nation an absolute sovereign over tribal territory. During the next three years, Georgia law attempted to abolish the Cherokee Nation's sovereignty.[58]

The Supreme Court reviewed the historical treatment of the Cherokee tribe as a nation in several treaties. The Court found that the United States had regarded the Cherokee tribe as a nation. The Court noted, "all these acts . . . manifestly consider the several Indian nations as distinct political communities, having territorial boundaries, within which their authority is exclusive, and having a right to all the lands within those boundaries, which is not only acknowledged, but guaranteed by the United States."[59] As a result, the Court reasoned that Georgia's attempt to manage Indian affairs was unconstitutional because the issue had been vested exclusively with the federal government.[60]

The impact of *Worcester* was the apparent recognition of the Cherokee as a nation. Although the decision seems far reaching, subsequent decisions suggest otherwise.[61] *Worcester's* notion of sovereignty was soon unmasked in *United States v. Rogers*, in which the Supreme Court rejected a claim that federal courts did not have jurisdiction over crimes committed on a reservation.[62] In *Rogers*, the Supreme Court held that a mature adult could not become a Cherokee Indian voluntarily without the authorization of the United States government. The Court noted that although a "White man" can choose to belong to an indigenous tribe, he is not of the "Indian race" and, therefore, he remains subject to the laws of the United States.

As a result of the *Rogers* decision, the Court suppressed its prior recognition of indigenous sovereignty and replaced it with notions of inferiority and foreignness. The indigenous nation's power to recognize a person as an indigenous citizen diminished while the United States' power to disregard such status, when it deemed it beneficial for its interests, increased. The Cherokees' acceptance of Rogers as one of them was immaterial to the Court because the United States was the arbiter over whether one was a member of an indigenous nation. The Court was unwilling to recognize the voluntary expatriation of a United States citizen residing within a territory of the United States. Because of the Court's reluctance to accept the power of the Cherokee nation to confer citizenship upon a person not born a Cherokee, the Court to some extent banned the naturalization process for non-Cherokee U.S. citizens who desired to become Cherokee citizens. Thus, less than a decade and a half after *Worcester's* recognition of indigenous sovereignty, the Court had a different vision of indigenous sovereignty—one with limited rights.[63]

Out of the decisions in *Rogers* and *Worcester*, the Supreme Court created a malleable conception of sovereignty as it related to indigenous nations; when convenient for the federal government to assert supremacy over states' rights, indigenous sovereignty was legitimate, but the Court found a diminished form of sovereignty when it came to federal judicial jurisdiction over certain criminal matters occurring on reservations.[64] The Court also continued to subordinate indigenous rights and thereby continued to treat members of indigenous nations as something other than formal members of the domestic landscape. The 1831 case of *Cherokee Nation v. Georgia*, also known as one of the Cherokee Cases, illustrates this point. That case concerned the Cherokee Nation's efforts to prevent the state of Georgia from seizing Cherokee land. Ultimately, Georgia wanted to expel the Cherokee Indians from their territory and eliminate many indigenous rights. Notwithstanding the existence of treaties between the United States and the Cherokees, Georgia attempted to regulate indigenous land.

The Cherokees considered themselves a sovereign nation that could seek judicial relief from such as an injunction, but they were ultimately denied such sovereignty and access to the U.S. federal judiciary. The Cherokees issued a bill to the Supreme Court, challenging several acts passed by the state of Georgia. In the complaint, the Cherokees claimed that the state of Georgia did not have the power or right to interfere with the self-government of the Cherokee tribe. The complaint also alleged that the Georgia legislation in dispute violated several treaties between the United States and the Cherokees, including the Treaty of Hopewell and the Treaty of Houston. The Supreme Court found that it lacked jurisdiction over the case, and as a result, it did not address the issues raised by the complaint. The majority reasoned that the Cherokee did not constitute a foreign state, as the word was used and intended in the Constitution. In this landmark case, the Court made troubling proclamations concerning the status of the indigenous people. In the Court's words,

> The condition of the Indians in relation to the United States is perhaps unlike that of any other two people in existence. In general, nations not owing a common allegiance are foreign to each other. The term foreign nation is, with strict propriety, applicable by either to the other. But the relation of the Indians to the United States is marked by peculiar and cardinal distinctions which exist nowhere else. The Indian Territory is admitted to compose a part of the United States.[65]

In dismissing the Cherokees' claim, the Court found the indigenous territory was part of a domestic dependent nation that the United States nonetheless held title to, irrespective of the Cherokees' will. This decision not only crippled the Cherokee Nation's ability to sue in U.S. courts; it also placed indigenous people, as Professor Sarah Cleveland recently observed, "in a 'no-man's land' status of being neither citizens of the United States nor aliens of a sovereign foreign state."

This language makes it clear that as early as 1831, the Supreme Court implicitly created an alien-citizen paradox applicable to indigenous people. In this paradoxical state, the individuals within this group are neither full citizens (with all the rights associated with the status), nor are they completely foreign because they enjoy some form of formal (in this case custodial) relationship with the United States. As Chief Justice Marshall explained it in *Cherokee Nation*, indigenous nations (and their people) were considered "wards" of the United States "guardian."[66]

In *Elk v. Wilkins*,[67] what would become the most significant indigenous citizenship case, the Supreme Court formally established the *de jure* inferior membership status of the indigenous people. The *Elk* Court concluded that despite being born in the United States, an indigenous person was not a member of the U.S. political union. In *Elk*, the petitioner (an indigenous man) renounced his tribal membership, became a Nebraska resident, and sought to register to vote.[68] He satisfied all of the statutory requirements to register to vote and cast a ballot,[69] but before the election day, the state of Nebraska (through Wilkins) rejected Elk's application because he was not a citizen—despite the passage of the Fourteenth Amendment.[70] Elk brought a cause of action against Wilkins before the Circuit Court of the United States for the District of Nebraska for depriving him of his right to vote in the elections.[71] The defendant filed a general demurrer, the court entered a judgment for the defendant, and Elk sued out a writ of error to the Supreme Court.

The *Elk* Court ruled that the Fourteenth Amendment established that citizenship was available only to persons who, at birth, were completely subject to U.S. jurisdiction.[72] Because indigenous nations were "distinct political communities" "within the territorial limits of the United States," they were not completely subject to U.S. jurisdiction.[73] The Court affirmed the holding in *Cherokee Nation v. Georgia* that indigenous nations were not entirely foreign and that indigenous people existed in a dependent condition. The Court noted,

> The alien and dependent condition of the members of the Indian tribes could not be put off at their own will without the action or assent of the United States. They were never deemed citizens of the United States, except under explicit provisions of treaty or statute to that effect, either declaring a certain tribe, or such members of it as chose to remain behind on the removal of the tribe westward, to be citizens or authorizing individuals of particular tribes to become citizens on application to a court of the United States for naturalization and satisfactory proof of fitness for civilized life.[74]

Noting the exclusive (as well as exclusionary) nature of U.S. citizenship, the Court concluded that "no one can become a citizen of a nation without its consent" and that because indigenous people "form[ed] no part of the people entitled to representation," they "were never deemed citizens."[75] The Court held that Elk was not a citizen of the United States, and as a result, he could not claim a deprivation of rights secured by the Fifteenth Amendment.[76]

The *Elk* Court further declared that the *Scott v. Sandford*[77] decision did not imply that indigenous people had the right beyond other foreigners to naturalize, and become United States citizens, without the consent of and naturalization by the United States.[78] In *Scott*, Chief Justice Taney, writing for the majority, stated that the Indian tribes were similar to subjects of any foreign government and could become United States citizens through the naturalization process. Despite *Scott's* language, the *Elk* Court clarified that any emigrant, including an indigenous person, who formally renounces his or her tribe does not become a U.S. citizen unless the United States accepted the renunciation.[79]

Thus, even after the government ratified the Fourteenth Amendment (which specifically provides that all persons born within the United States are citizens), the Supreme Court concluded that indigenous people were not citizens by birthright.[80] In an effort to protect the perception of what was an American, courts became resolute in not diluting citizenship with an "inferior" class of people. The government used the pretext that the indigenous people were part of a "distinct political community" within the United States, and they had never engaged in the social compact to swear allegiance to this country.[81] Indeed, the subordination of indigenous people in earlier decisions like *Johnson v. M'Intosh*[82] facilitated the alternative models of subordinate citizens.[83]

In 1909, the Court in *United States v. Celestine* further confirmed the limited nature of the citizenship of indigenous people. The *Celestine* Court held that granting citizenship to "Indians" did not grant them the "privileges and immunities" of U.S. citizens. On December 23, 1873, the boundaries of the Tulalip Reservation were established in the territory of Washington. On August 30, 1906, Bob Celestine, a tribal member, allegedly murdered Mary Chealco, another tribal member, with an ax on the Tulalip Reservation. In May 1908, the Circuit Court of the United States for the Western District of Washington indicted Celestine. Celestine made a special plea, claiming that the court lacked jurisdiction because both he and the victim were U.S. citizens. He claimed that he was subject to the state law, not the federal law.

The Supreme Court noted that "[t]he act of 1887, which confers citizenship, clearly, does not emancipate the Indians from all control, or abolish the reservations." Moreover, both the Indian defendant and his victim were subject to the laws of the United States, and the federal courts had jurisdiction over the indigenous people. "[I]t cannot be said to be clear that Congress intended, by the mere grant of citizenship, to renounce entirely its jurisdiction over the individual members of this dependent race." The Court reasoned that although the defendant and the deceased had become citizens, they "remained Indians by race" and consequently the murder was committed by one Indian upon another. By asserting that citizenship does not eliminate a person's alleged inferior and dependent race, the Court found that the facts of the case fell within the Act of 1887 and the U.S. district court had jurisdiction over the case. [84]

In the 1913 case of *United States v. Sandoval*, the Court similarly concluded that "citizenship [was] not in itself an obstacle to the exercise by Congress of its power to enact laws for the benefit and protection of tribal Indians."[85] *Sandoval* was an appeal from a criminal prosecution for the introduction of intoxicating liquor into the Indian country called the Santa Clara Pueblo in New Mexico. The indictment was based upon a congressional act that made it a crime to introduce intoxicating liquor into the Indian country.

In a demeaning manner, Justice Van Devanter, in an all-too-often-used, Anglo-Saxon, messianic tone, observed that "as a superior and civilized nation," the United States was obligated to protect "all dependent Indian communities within its borders," and this was particularly appropriate in that case because the Pueblo people were an "ignorant" and "degraded" people. Justice Van Devanter also noted that Congress, not the judiciary, had the power to determine when the nation's guardianship over the Pueblo people shall terminate.[86] In 1916, Van Devanter, in *United States v. Nice*, concluded that "citizenship is not incompatible with tribal existence or continued guardianship, and so may be conferred without completely emancipating the Indians or placing them beyond the reach of congressional regulations adopted for their protection."[87]

Shortly after the United States government marked indigenous people as people other than citizens, it entered into treaties with tribes in order to maintain a relationship that would purportedly afford each side a sense of sovereignty. Not long after the United States created euphemisms of sovereignty and entered into treaties with the indigenous people, the U.S. government ceased to use treaties and simply told the indigenous peoples what they could and could not do, and where they could do it. As a result of its perception of indigenous people as part of their own sovereign tribes and subject to tribal law, the United States took the position that it could dismiss them as a separate people living in certain sections of America who could be controlled and had no recourse.

Although the U.S. government had entered into treaties with the indigenous nations, it subsequently passed legislation that disregarded the terms and procedures stipulated in such treaties. For instance, in 1867, the Kiowa and Comanche tribes entered the Medicine Lodge Treaty Act of 1867 with the United States. Article XII of the treaty established a procedure for the cession of a tract of land of an Indian reservation to anyone, including the United States. The procedure required three-fourths of all adult male Indians of the reservation to agree with signature to cede the land. In an agreement made on October 6, 1892, the Kiowa and Comanche tribes surrendered their rights of reservation land to the United States. The agreement provided for the allotment of land to the indigenous people and the conveyance of a fee simple title to them and their heirs after twenty-five years.

In the 1903 case of *Lone Wolf v. Hitchcock*,[88] Lone Wolf and other tribal members challenged an agreement between the United States and 456 male Indians that allowed for the allotment of tribal land and compensation. Lone Wolf and the other petitioners challenged the agreement (and a congressional act that carried it into effect) as violating the Medicine Lodge Treaty of 1867; they argued that because the indigenous people's assent was obtained by fraud and less than three-fourths of the males on the reservation signed the agreement, the conveyance of land was invalid. On June 6, 1901, Lone Wolf filed a complaint that sought an injunction against the secretary of the Interior, the commissioner of Indian Affairs, and the commissioner of the General Land Office. The complaint was filed in the equity side of the Supreme Court of the District of Columbia for Wolf himself and the tribal members of the Kiowa, Comanche, and Apache Indians in Oklahoma.

On June 21, 1901, the Supreme Court of the District of Columbia denied Wolf's application for an injunction and a demurrer was sustained. A few weeks later, the president of the United States proclaimed that the lands ceded by the Indians were to be opened for entry and settlement in August of 1901. Wolf appealed the lower court's judgment for the defendant. The court of appeals affirmed that judgment. He appealed again and the Supreme Court accepted the case.[89] Wolf claimed that the United States took property without just compensation, therefore violating the Fifth Amendment of the Constitution. However, the Court found that the tribes did not have a fee simple title and Congress could divest the land without following the procedure required by a prior treaty.[90] As in its conclusion in *M'Intosh*, the Court used the plenary power doctrine as a tool to justify the naked taking of indigenous land. The Court explained, "Congress possessed full power in the matter; the judiciary cannot question or inquire into the motives which prompted the enactment of this legislation."[91]

The Court also used a landmark immigration case to justify Congress's power to deal with so-called foreigners living within the United States. In its decision, the Court analogized the status of the indigenous people in the United States to the status of the Chinese immigrants seeking entry into the United States. The Court cited the Chinese Exclusion Cases as primary authority in order to support the congressional agreement that conflicted with a prior treaty. Hence, the Court emphasized the foreign status of the indigenous people and stated that the tribes could seek relief by appealing only to the Congress and not to the Supreme Court. In doing so, the Court reaffirmed the dependent status of the tribes by stating that the indigenous people were wards of the federal government.

Scholars have compared the impact of *Lone Wolf* on indigenous nations to the impact *Dred Scott* had on African Americans. *Lone Wolf* further diminished indigenous rights regarding treaties and land, and further affirmed Congress's absolute power over Indian affairs, including the abrogation of treaties. During this era, the Court used tortured logic in its decisions to justify the subordination of indigenous people, as well as other racial and ethnic minorities.

These decisions not only formally declared the subordinate membership of the original people of the United States; they also facilitated the *Dred Scott*[92] decision. This case, among others, denied rights for African Americans and facilitated other forms of subordination—including the exclusionary treatment of people of color seeking to be naturalized and the denial of rights to the inhabitants of this country's overseas colonial conquests.[93]

Robert Porter recently observed that "Indians today have the status of a minor— acknowledged as citizens but not fully recognized as being able to care for one's own affairs."[94] The indigenous people of America *are* United States citizens for the simple fact that they have been born on American soil; nonetheless, they are only regarded as part of their tribal communities and are afforded rights and immunities subject to their tribal governments.[95] The application of the plenary powers doctrine constitutionalized the inferior citizenship status of indigenous people, and as Professor Saito observed, in practical terms, this resulted in Indian nations losing ninety million acres of reservation land—more than two-thirds of their former holdings.[96]

Although indigenous people today have the right to vote,[97] they have historically received a second-class citizenship; the government,[98] both federal and state, has discriminated against them with regard to their rights.[99] In times of war, many indigenous people fought on behalf of the United States as Americans to support the right to self-determination abroad; regardless, the U.S. government has repeatedly denied this basic human right and has instead supplanted it with an identification marker of inferior membership for the indigenous people of the United States.[100] Though they effectively enjoy the rights of other citizens, because their tribal nations are subject to the U.S. government's plenary power, the rights of indigenous people are constantly subject to question and limitation.

The Territorial Island Inhabitants

The plenary powers doctrine is also the basis for the subordination of island inhabitants who were colonized after the Spanish-American War and World War II.[101] The island people who live under U.S. control are not full members of the body politic and reside in the island groups of Puerto Rico, American Samoa, Guam, the Northern Mariana Islands, the United States Virgin Islands, the Federated States of Micronesia, the Marshall Islands, and the Republic of Palau.[102] These island groups fall into two categories: the unincorporated United States territories, and the newly created sovereign, yet dependent, island groups of the South Pacific.

The islands of Puerto Rico, the Northern Mariana Islands, Guam, the U.S. Virgin Islands, and American Samoa fall into the first category and are so-called unincorporated territories.[103] The Supreme Court concluded, in a series of decisions known as the Insular Cases, that these island groups are dependent lands and are neither "foreign" countries nor "part of the United States."[104] Unincorporated territories should undoubtedly be classified as those existing under a subordinate, dependent, and colonial regime for three reasons: first, the U.S. Congress has plenary or complete power to govern the territories, including the ability to nullify local laws and enact federal legislation dictating the rights of the inhabitants of those territories; second, not one of the territories is fully incorporated as a state of the union or considered a sovereign nation; and third, although all inhabitants born in the territories are U.S. citizens (nationals in the case of Samoans), they do not enjoy similar rights as citizens on the mainland, cannot vote, and have no representation in the federal government.[105] In light of this, it appears that the U.S. citizens who reside in these lands have attributes that resemble both citizen and alien.[106]

They also represent the classic modern-day picture of the subordinate members of this society. Because they are born on U.S. lands (although colonial), these individuals should be considered full U.S. citizens in accordance with the constitutional standard set by the Fourteenth Amendment; however, due to arcane and often bigoted justifications created well over a century ago, they remain subordinate or inferior members of the American body politic. As another consequence of having inferior citizenship, island inhabitants do not receive the same amount of aid or other government largess provided to similarly situated citizens on the mainland, nor do these people have the ability to vote for president, vice-president, or any member of Congress.

The second category of subordinate members consists of inhabitants from the Federated States of Micronesia, the Republic of the Marshall Islands, and the Republic of Palau. Although in international circles these lands are considered to be autonomous nation-states, they are included here because of their similar history of annexation and the existing issues concerning their sovereignty as well as their subordinate or quasi-member status.[107] Although residents of the first group, the unincorporated territories, have obtained a form of U.S. citizenship (and a status as nationals for Samoans), each membership differs from traditional Fourteenth Amendment citizenship. For example, they are not entitled to participate in the national political process;[108] they have no representation in Congress; and, as residents of the territories, they cannot vote for president and vice-president, and their respective territories bear no electoral rights.

Consequently, the U.S. government provides inhabitants of the unincorporated territories with substantially less aid than that given to citizens of the fifty states. Furthermore, these citizens are not entitled to full constitutional protection, and Congress could also conceivably strip their status at any time.[109] Therefore, their status as citizens is not only inferior; it is also elusive in that no other citizen group can potentially have their member status stripped, modified, or removed in one congressional act.

Though citizens born or naturalized in the United States derive their civil rights from the Fourteenth Amendment, these islanders have been granted limited civil rights through the Territorial Clause of Article IV in the Constitution.[110] Under the power granted by this clause, Congress implemented the Treaty of Paris[111] (signed after their acquisition at the end of the Spanish-American War), which provided the United States with the power over the "civil rights" and "political status" of the inhabitants the post–Spanish-American War acquisitions.[112] Consequently, the U.S. citizenship held by people living in these islands is a legislated and colonial concession; it is not a constitutionally derived right, and it could possibly be revoked altogether.[113]

The territories in the second group of dependencies (including Micronesia, the Marshall Islands, and Palau) became U.S. dependents after World

War II. Although these territories are now deemed in international circles as autonomous, they are nevertheless still largely controlled by the United States. In fact, the Office of Insular Affairs—the federal agency responsible for administering the territories of the United States—includes the Republic of the Marshall Islands, the Federated State of Micronesia, and the Republic of Palau within its jurisdiction. Despite the international perception of sovereignty stemming from labels such as "republic" or "federated state," the Office of Insular Affairs classifies these lands as territories where the United States maintains the responsibility for administering and providing assistance.[114]

In essence, the method of U.S. control over these three "sovereign" nations mirrors the controlling efforts over the unincorporated U.S. island territories. The unique history of Palau, Micronesia, and the Marshall Islands closely resembles the stories of the unincorporated U.S. territories of Puerto Rico, the Northern Mariana Islands, Guam, the United States Virgin Islands, and American Samoa.[115] While the newly sovereign status of these three lands may in fact exclude them from the analysis raised in this book, they are included here in part to promote continued debate over their somewhat-American and somewhat-sovereign status. Their treatment and status exemplify the fact that colonialism is not always easily identified or labeled.

The History of Subordination

The United States began its overseas expansion during the period of the Spanish-American War, which resulted in several Spanish territorial concessions. In the Treaty of Paris, Spain officially ceded "to the United States the island of Porto [sic] Rico and other islands now under Spanish sovereignty in the West Indies."[116] Consistent with the Constitution's grant of Congress's plenary power under the Territorial Clause, Article IX of the Treaty of Paris granted Congress the power over "the civil rights and political status" of the territories and its people.[117]

The Treaty of Paris endorsed the United States' imperialistic venture, as it was among the first times in American history that a treaty acquiring territory for the United States contained no promise of American citizenship.[118] In addition, the treaty contained "no promise, actual or implied, of statehood."[119] As a result of the war, the United States acquired Puerto Rico, Guam, and the Philippines, and maintained effective control over Cuba.[120]

The United States later purchased the Virgin Islands from the Danish government in 1907.[121] As a result of these acquisitions, the inhabitants of these lands became part of the United States. However, it was far from clear how and in what way these new Americans would be treated. Though they could have fairly easily been treated as U.S. citizens, much like the inhabitants of the ceded lands following the U.S. victory over Mexico after the Mexican-American War, the inhabitants of the overseas territories were not accepted as members of the body politic. They eventually were granted some form of membership, but to this day, they do not have full constitutional membership and are accordingly not full citizens.

In 1901, the U.S. Supreme Court began deciding what is now known as the Insular Cases, some of which further defined the parameters of the United States' territorial colonial relationship. In the first insular case, *De Lima v. Bidwell*,[122] the Court held that the Treaty of Paris—the document whereby Spain ceded Puerto Rico, Guam, and the Philippines to the United States—established Puerto Rico as an unincorporated (but not organized) U.S. territory that should not be treated as a state. The Court in *De Lima* upheld Congress's unfettered power over Puerto Rico and its people, stating that Congress

> may organize a local territorial government; it may admit it [Puerto Rico] as a State . . . [and] it may sell its public lands [acquired by treaty] to individual citizens or may donate them as homesteads to actual settlers . . . when once acquired by treaty [because the territory] belongs to the United States, and it's subject to the disposition of Congress.[123]

The Territorial Clause touched upon the disagreement over the future development of the unsettled territories by providing that Congress shall have the power to regulate the territories of the United States.[124] The debate ultimately reached the Supreme Court in the Insular Cases.[125]

Political leaders and legal protagonists had distinctly different views on how to treat the territories and their inhabitants. One perspective held that the United States had the constitutional power to expand, as did the European powers. But the expansion did not mean colonialism; it meant the acquisition of territories that would eventually become states.[126] The Supreme Court decisions in the Insular Cases, which settled the issue, sided with the exclusionary colonial perspective. They remain today the most influential decisions in territorial doctrine even though their values and premises now seem arcane and bigoted.[127]

The leading insular decision, *Downes v. Bidwell*, arose at the turn of the century.[128] In *Downes*, the collector of customs attempted to collect duties on trade between Puerto Rico and the states on the grounds that Puerto Rico was a "foreign country" within the meaning of the tariff laws.[129] The controversy centered on whether territorial tariffs could differ from tariffs in the states.[130] Subsequent to the passage of the Foraker Act, Samuel Downes, the plaintiff, was doing business under S. B. Downes & Company and paid $659.35 in duties under protest for oranges transported to the port of New York from Puerto Rico in November of 1900.[131] Downes sought back pay through a cause of action in the circuit court. The district attorney demurred and the court sustained it, dismissing the complaint.[132] Downes sued out a writ of error to the Supreme Court.

The issue before the Supreme Court was whether the territory known as Puerto Rico became part of the United States within Article I Section 8 of the Constitution of the United States, which declares that duties shall be uniform throughout the nation.[133] The Court answered this question in the negative: "the island of Porto [sic] Rico is a territory appurtenant and belonging to the United States, but not a part of the United States within the revenue clauses of the Constitution."[134] As a result, the Court found that the Foraker Act constitutionally imposes duties on imports from Puerto Rico. The *Downes* Court upheld Congress's plenary power over the territory. The Court reasoned that Congress has the power to determine the status of Puerto Rico and Puerto Ricans.[135]

Consequently, Congress could pass legislation that imposes duties upon the transportation of merchandise from Puerto Rico to a port in the United States. The Court in *Downes* essentially concluded that the U.S. Constitution did not "follow the flag."[136] Writing for the Court, Justice Brown explained, "The power to acquire territory by treaty implied not only the power to govern such territory, but to prescribe upon what terms the United States will receive its inhabitants, and what their status shall be in what Chief Justice Marshall termed the 'American Empire.'"[137] The plenary power of Congress arose from the inherent right to acquire territory, and the Territorial Clause of the Constitution endorsed the United States' treaty-making power, and the power to declare and conduct war in other lands. Accordingly, the Constitution applied to the territories only to the degree that it was extended to them by Congress.[138]

If Puerto Rico was considered to be a part of the United States in *Downes*, then territorial tariffs would have to comport with the Uniformity Clause of the Constitution, which requires that "all Duties, Imposts, and Excises shall be uniform throughout the United States."[139] "The issue raised by the Insular Cases centered on whether the constitutional restrictions on Congressional authority applicable to the states serve as a check on the exercise of federal power with respect to the territories."[140] The Insular Cases also addressed the extent of the applicability of the U.S. Constitution to the inhabitants of the newly acquired territories. Despite authority from both the *Loughborough* and *Scott* decisions, which suggested that the territories should be treated equally as states, "Justice Taney's language in *Scott v. Sandford* was dismissed [by the *Downes* Court] as dicta . . . and, therefore, not binding as a precedent."[141] "Justice Brown's opinion [in *Downes*] was interpreted by other members of the Court as permitting [a broad] power by Congress."[142] The decision made clear that Puerto Rico, as a territory, was merely a possession of the New Empire.[143] Justice Brown concluded, "We are therefore of opinion that the Island of Porto [sic] Rico is a territory appurtenant and belonging to the United States, but not a part of the United States within the revenue clauses of the Constitution; that the Foraker Act is constitutional."[144]

There is little question that at its core, the basis behind treating the territories differently was that these territories were inhabited by so-called uncivilized savages. Justice Brown wrote, "If their inhabitants do not become, immediately upon annexation, citizens of the United States, their children thereafter born, whether savages or civilized, are such, and entitled to all the rights, privileges and immunities of citizens. If such be their status, the consequences will be extremely serious. . . ."[145] He added,

> It is obvious that in the annexation of outlying and distant possessions grave questions will arise from differences in habits, laws and customs of the people, and from differences of soil, climate and production, which may . . . be quite unnecessary in the annexation of contiguous territory inhabited only by people of the same race, or by scattered bodies of native Indians.[146]

Justice Brown further elaborated upon the prevalent nativistic thought:

> If those possessions are inhabited by alien races, differing from us in religion, customs, laws, methods of taxation and modes of thought, the administration of government and justice, according to Anglo-Saxon principles, may for a time be impossible; and the question at once arises whether large concessions ought not to be made for a time, that, ultimately, our own theories may be carried out, and the blessings of a free government under the Constitution extended to them. We decline to hold that there is anything in the Constitution to forbid such action.[147]

The *Downes* Court concluded that the territories were different than the states.[148] Therefore, the Constitution did not apply to inhabitants of the territories in the same way it did to inhabitants of the states.[149] The Court concluded that Puerto Rico was "a territory appurtenant and belonging to the United States, but not a part of the United States within the . . . Constitution."[150]

In his concurring opinion, Justice White contributed significantly to the United States' expansionist modality.[151] Quoting from an earlier opinion, Justice White wrote, "The Constitution confers absolutely on the government of the Union, the powers of making war, and of making treaties; consequently, that government possesses the power of acquiring territory, either by conquest or by treaty."[152] He continued, "If it . . . be ceded by the treaty, the acquisition is confirmed, and the ceded territory becomes a part of the nation to which it is annexed, either on the terms stipulated in the treaty . . . or on such as its new master shall impose."[153] Justice White opined that the scope of constitutional protection given to the inhabitants of the newly acquired territories depended on "the situation of the territory and its relations to the United States."[154] Under this approach, Congress did not have to "'extend' the Constitution, but it could extend the United States."[155] Full constitutional protection was reserved for territories that Congress had incorporated into the United States, as opposed to those merely acquired.[156] The line of acts necessary for demonstrating an intent to be incorporated was never clearly settled.

Nonetheless, Justice White's concurring opinion and subsequent Supreme Court decisions recognized the constitutional principle that a conquering country could take several approaches with a new territory.[157] Possible approaches included (1) admitting the territory as a state; (2) incorporating it into the United States as an integral territory; (3) leaving it as a territory appurtenant; (4) leaving it foreign by foregoing acquisition; or (5) pursuing other seemingly appropriate alternatives.[158] Justice White justified this discretion by maintaining that the "evil of immediate incorporation"[159] would open up the borders to "millions of inhabitants of alien territory" who could overthrow "the whole structure of the government."[160] Under Justice White's approach, only through incorporation could alien people attain the rights that peculiarly belong to the citizens of the United States.[161]

Thus, incorporation became a political decision.[162] This principle allowed the United States to expand its empire without being constitutionally compelled to accept as citizens populations that might be part of an "uncivilized race."[163] Otherwise, incorporation could trigger "the immediate bestowal of citizenship on those absolutely unfit to receive it."[164] The question the Insular Cases failed to address is how these decisions comport with this country's democratic principles and its representative form of governance.

As a result, for this group of Americans, there has never been any pretense concerning the Fourteenth Amendment's applicability or equality, for that matter.[165] The inhabitants of the newly acquired overseas territories have never received citizenship through the Fourteenth Amendment, the vehicle used to grant or impose such status on virtually all other groups who have attained it. They became associated with the United States by being inhabitants of lands conquered by the United States. Because they were acquired in this manner, the United States Supreme Court concluded that the Territorial Clause in Article IV of the Constitution, and not the Fourteenth Amendment, determined the rights of this group.[166] As interpreted, this provision endowed Congress with complete or plenary power over these people.[167] In turn, the Court and Congress have kept this group in a subordinate and disenfranchised status.[168]

As Professor Neuman eloquently observed in his book *Strangers to the Constitution,*

> For the federal government to acquire total governing power over new territories—more complete, in fact, than in the states—without the consent of the local population and without according them . . . the rights reserved under the Constitution raises starkly the question of how the exercise of such governing power can be legitimated.[169]

Despite the case's legal and logical shortcomings, the U.S. Supreme Court followed the morally illegitimate constitutional principle announced in *Downes.*[170] In *Dorr v. United States,*[171] a majority of the Court adopted the territorial incorporation doctrine. The *Dorr* Court recognized that the Constitution did not fully apply to an acquired territory if Congress had not incorporated the territory.[172] As Puerto Rico had never been "incorporated" by Congress, the limited form of U.S. citizenship that the Puerto Rican people eventually received was consistent with this constitutional doctrine. Two decades later in *Balzac v. Porto* [sic] *Rico,*[173] The Court reaffirmed the unequal citizenship status of the Puerto Rican people. The *Balzac* Court held that the citizenship status given to the Puerto Rican people under the 1917 Jones Act did not alter the constitutional status of its inhabitants.[174]

As a result, the residents of Puerto Rico had no right to demand a trial by jury under the Sixth Amendment to the U.S. Constitution.[175] Once again, the Court justified its denial of this right by declaring that "the jury system postulates a conscious duty of participation in the machinery of justice which it is hard for people not brought up in fundamentally popular government at once to acquire."[176]

As a result of *Downes* and its progeny, Congress can pass legislation that affects Puerto Rico and the other overseas territories regardless of certain constitutional provisions. Consequently, the rights of Puerto Ricans could be limited by congressional legislation. The *Downes* Court nonetheless did note some basic rights: "Even if regarded as aliens, they are entitled under the principles of the Constitution to be protected in life, liberty and property."[177] Ironically, the Court's use of the term "aliens" for Puerto Ricans indicates an outsider or foreigner status—not unlike the outsider and foreigner status conferred upon the indigenous people on the U.S. mainland. As a result, the Supreme Court recognized the inhabitants of Puerto Rico as different from citizens on the mainland, yet subjected them to Congress's plenary power. This recognition occurred and continues despite the 1917 grant of U.S. citizenship to the people of Puerto Rico.

The *Downes* Court also established the parameters of the doctrine of "territorial incorporation." Under the doctrine, incorporated territories included areas that would become states and would have all parts of the U.S. Constitution applicable to them, while unincorporated territories were not intended for statehood and were subject only to fundamental parts of the U.S. Constitution. Because the *Downes* Court concluded that Puerto Rico was an unincorporated territory belonging to the United States, it held that the U.S. Constitution did not fully apply to it. Consequently, inhabitants of an unincorporated territory of the United States are not entitled to all of the constitutional guarantees granted to U.S. citizens on the mainland.[178]

More recently, the Court has held that U.S. citizenship for the territorial people did not mean full constitutional rights.[179] In 1957, the Court in *Reid v. Covert*[180] endorsed the incorporation doctrine, noting that certain constitutional safeguards were not applicable to the territories.[181] In describing the territories under the jurisdiction of Congress, the Court specifically observed that these territories "had entirely different cultures and customs from those of this country."[182] In 1971, the Court in *Rogers v. Bellei*[183] recognized that Congress had the power to revoke the citizenship of those granted citizenship by statute.[184] The Court held that Congress could impose a condition subsequent on citizenship for those not falling within the Fourteenth Amendment's definition of "citizen"—an individual born or naturalized in the United States.[185]

As a result of their subordinate status, residents of Puerto Rico and the inhabitants of the other overseas territories receive less favorable treatment than the mainland citizens under a number of major federal benefits programs. For the residents of Puerto Rico, federal payments under Aid to Families with Dependent Children (AFDC), Medicaid, and food stamps are made at lower levels and are subject to an overall cap.[186] Similarly, the Supplemental Security Income program (SSI) does not apply to Puerto Rico.[187] Benefits under a similar program are capped and are made at lower levels than SSI payments made to eligible citizens residing in the States.[188] Benefits for needy children are likewise provided at appreciably lower levels.[189]

Similarly, the inhabitants of the unincorporated territory of Guam have received this same form of subordinate American citizenship. On August 1, 1950, President Truman signed H.R. 7273—the Guam Organic Act, extending U.S. citizenship to the native inhabitants of Guam.[190] The Organic Act of 1950, however, only established a local government structure and granted statutory U.S. citizenship similar to the diluted form of citizenship granted to the people of Puerto Rico.[191] As a result, it failed to provide autonomy because it maintained the trappings of foreign control by denying Guamanians the right to elect federal representatives. Moreover, Congress still retained final power over the Guamanian judiciary and the legislature.

In 1970, the people of Guam received a form of quasi representation similar to that afforded to the people of Puerto Rico, which entails the election of a nonvoting representative who exercises a lobby-like role in Congress.[192] However, the inability of the Guamanians to participate in presidential elections remained unaltered. This inequity was further heightened when the U.S. Supreme Court dissolved the Guamanian Supreme Court.[193] This action was consistent with the Court's previous pre-acquisition confirmation of Congress's unconditional authority over the territories, which is "an incident of sovereignty and continues until granted away."[194]

Guamanians were not satisfied with the effectiveness of nonvoting congressional representatives, and the desire for greater independence from the federal government of the United States persisted. "In 1976, Congress passed legislation that authorized the legislature of Guam to hold a constitutional convention and draft its own constitution. Pursuant to this legislation, a delegation of thirty-two individuals drafted a constitution and submitted it to the people of Guam for their approval."[195] Public opposition to the adoption of this constitution was in large part rooted in the indigenous Chamorro people's desire for greater rights as an indigenous majority. As a result, the proposal to adopt this constitution was overwhelmingly defeated.[196]

Although Guam does not cast any electoral votes for president, much like Puerto Rico, it does elect delegates to national party conventions, as does Puerto Rico. Local delegates were irritated when Guam and other territories came up only at the end of the otherwise alphabetical roll call at the Democratic Convention in 2000. "Even with the parties, the hurt doesn't stop. You're not even included in the alphabet."

An example of the often unsubtle rancor that exists was captured in the 2002 edition of the *Almanac of American Politics:*

[When] California Republican Dana Rohrabacher called Guam and other territories "economic basket cases" that are "backward and economically depressed," Guam's Governor Gutierrez attacked "this ignorance and lack of sensitivity which run counter to our country's democratic traditions and which ensures the continuation of our status as second-class citizens in the American family."[197]

Similar to the grant of citizenship to the residents of Puerto Rico and Guam, the residents of the Virgin Islands were granted U.S. citizenship in 1927.[198] However, as with Guam and Puerto Rico, the United States did not grant these people voting rights in national elections. Shortly thereafter, in 1931, the military governor was replaced by a civilian governor, but one that was appointed by the president of the United States and approved by the Senate. The Virgin Islands operated under Danish laws until the summer of 1936, when Congress passed laws that "swept away virtually all of the Old Danish laws and practices."[199]

The new Organic Act "gave the vote [in local elections] to all citizens without regard to race or sex who were 'able to read and write the English language,'" but "there was . . . no outpouring of voters when the first elections under universal suffrage were held in 1938."[200] In that election, "[o]nly a few more than 2,500 went to the polls of the more than 7,000 who were eligible to register."[201] However, Virgin Islanders soon began to increase their participation in politics. Republican and Democratic organizations soon sprang up, but since the islanders could not vote for president and had no representation in Congress, national party affiliation was essentially meaningless.

In 1954, Congress "revised the Basic Act and set up a unicameral legislature to serve the islands as a whole. To the islanders' displeasure, the law did not give them all they wanted—specifically, the right to elect their own governor and to have a nonvoting delegate in Congress."[202]

Approximately a decade later, the United States changed the local government status of the United States Virgin Islands when Congress passed the Elective Governor Act of 1968.[203] The Elective Governor Act provided that the Virgin Islands governor would be locally elected, and it also eliminated a number of federal controls, namely, (1) supervision by the secretary of the Interior of the executive branch of the Virgin Islands; (2) the secretary of the Interior's appointment of acting governors; (3) the requirement for approval by the secretary of the Interior of new departments and other agencies of government; (4) the establishment of certain annual salary rates for the executive branch of the Virgin Islands by the secretary of the Interior; and (5) presidential veto of local legislature.[204]

Today, the United States Virgin Islands remains an unincorporated territory, governed under the Territorial Clause of the Constitution. Although Congress has seen fit to grant the residents of these islands control over the election of their local government, Congress has the power to take this right away. Like Puerto Rico, Guam, and American Samoa, the United States Virgin Islands, as unincorporated territories, are governed by the Supreme Court's holdings regarding the Insular Cases, and their inhabitants are only guaranteed fundamental rights. It should not be surprising, however, that there are virtually no Supreme Court cases addressing the territorial status of the U.S. Virgin Islands. By the time the Virgin Islands were acquired by the United States, the Insular Cases had long been decided, and the proposition that the Constitution did not necessarily follow the flag was well settled.

In 1986, the inhabitants of the Northern Mariana Islands attained a form of American citizenship similar to that granted to the residents of Puerto Rico, Guam, and the Virgin Islands.[205] The people of the Commonwealth of the Northern Mariana Islands (CNMI) were granted United States citizenship in 1986, but under the terms of the covenant establishing these rights, citizens of the self-governing commonwealth are not allowed to vote in U.S. presidential elections.[206] Although the covenant provides for U.S. sovereignty over the Islands, it also specifically calls for the Islands to retain a degree of local self-government. Section 101 of the covenant states,

> The Northern Mariana Islands upon termination of the Trusteeship Agreement will become a self-governing commonwealth to be known as the "Commonwealth of the Northern Mariana Islands," in political union with and under the sovereignty of the United States of America.[207]

Section 103 provides that the Islands have "the right of local self-government in accordance with a Constitution of their own adoption." The CNMI maintained that limited sovereignty was transferred to the United States only in the areas of foreign affairs and defense. "Moreover, the CNMI asserts that the Islands retained any sovereignty not expressly transferred in the covenant."[208] Section 105 of the covenant contains a principle highly sought after by other territories of the United States: the mutual consent principle. The principle provides that the fundamental provisions of the covenant may not be modified without the approval of both the United States and the CNMI.[209]

However, section 105 of the covenant also provides that the United States may enact legislation affecting the Islands' right to local self-government, with two stipulations. First, the United States cannot enact legislation over the Islands unless the legislation also applies to the several states. Second, the United States will limit its legislative authority over the Islands to ensure that the covenant's fundamental provisions are not modified without the consent of both the United States and the Islands.[210]

Unlike Puerto Rico and Guam, the CNMI did not become a territory of the United States under a treaty pursuant to negotiations with a former colonizer. Instead, the Islands' status as a "commonwealth" was reached through direct negotiations between the island inhabitants and the United States. Pursuant to these negotiations, one writer concluded,

> Congress agreed not to alter the Covenant's fundamental purpose unilaterally. The Islands decided that the commonwealth relationship provided assurances of local self- government and a permanent political union with the United States. Consequently, the mutual consent provision specifically names the sections of the United States Constitution that apply to the Islands; therefore, any other laws would have to be mutually agreed to by both parties. . . . As it is currently interpreted, the mutual consent provision is a one-sided agreement through which the Islands have effectively "self-determined their way into bondage." [211]

The mutual consent provision under section 105 of the covenant has, in essence, locked the CNMI into the American political system with only one way to get out: obtaining the approval of the United States. This requirement arguably violates the covenant's mutual consent provision under section 105 because it is effectively no longer mutual but unilateral. In agreeing to the commonwealth status, the citizens of the CNMI did not intend to surrender their sovereignty; at most, they intended to give up only a portion of their sovereignty. The CNMI inhabitants were willing to have limited sovereignty in order to retain their right to local self-government.

The U.S. government has given the residents of the unincorporated territory of American Samoa even less in terms of autonomy and citizenship rights.[212] As nationals, Samoans have even fewer rights than those held by the other territorial inhabitants. The United States granted these inhabitants a title that suggested power in the political process, but in actuality they received little more than a label, coupled with a perception on their part that they were attaining something of consequence.[213]

Though American Samoa may elect its own local government, these governmental employees operate at the discretion of the U.S. secretary of the Interior, who can remove any government employee at will.[214] The struggle for Samoans to assert their will in the international legal and financial spheres is paralleled in the realm of domestic culture and politics. Samoans are among the last of the Polynesian peoples to make widespread use of their traditional architecture, and the Samoan determination to apply traditional methods of land dispute resolution and traditional forms of government have been reviewed in federal court.[215]

The case *Corporation of the Presiding Bishop v. Holdel* illustrates the Samoan desire to retain real property in the hands of ethnic Samoans through the use of the traditional *matai* system.[216] The *matai* system is based on oral traditions, which recognize ethnic Samoans' superior land rights compared to non-Samoans. In a dispute over title of land, the High Court of Samoa ruled against the appellant church, which argued that it had purchased the land in question. The appellant then sought the U.S. secretary of the Interior and then the D.C. Circuit Court to overturn the Samoan decision. While both refused to do so, the federal court specifically noted both the authority of the secretary of the Interior and its own power to resolve the dispute pursuant to the plenary powers doctrine.[217] Equally as significant, *Presiding Bishop* illustrates that a lower standard of constitutional guarantees is afforded to citizens governed by the Territorial Clause. Whereas under federal case law discrimination based on race would have to withstand "strict scrutiny," that is, a state would have to demonstrate a "compelling interest" to uphold a law that discriminates on the basis of race, in possessions governed by a territorial clause, Congress needs merely a "rational basis" for the court system of a given territory to undermine fundamental constitutional rights, in this case, equal protection. In *King v. Morton,* similar reasoning was used to determine that the Seventh Amendment right to a trial by jury is not guaranteed in possessions governed by the Territorial Clause. Professor Thornbury summarizes the absurdity of this hybrid system, saying, "this is not a tenable situation for either culture."[218]

The Samoan customs are still subject to overrule at any time and the common law system of the United States does not apply in full. Again, the political result has been a civilian government that, although "American in appearance . . . [was and remains] illusory."[219] Samoa's government is illusory because it does not have full legislative authority. Its enactments and resolutions have no binding authority since they are simply recommendations made to the governor, who is subject to removal by the U.S. secretary of the Interior.[220] The secretary of the Interior holds appointment and removal power of judges on the Samoan high court. The secretary of the Interior also appoints the chief justice and an associate justice, who are assisted by four Samoan associate judges.[221] The secretary holds the power to overturn decisions rendered by the high court if he or she determines there was an abuse of judicial discretion. The Samoan system does not provide for an appeal to the federal court system because the Administrative Procedures Act does not apply to the secretary's decisions regarding the territories.[222]

The only governing matter that Congress has withdrawn from the secretary is the ability to amend the Samoan constitution, a limitation imposed by Congress in 1983. American Samoa has been represented in the U.S. House of Representatives by a nonvoting delegate since 1981. "The 103rd Congress gave the delegates from those Outlying Areas represented in the House of Representatives the right to vote in the Committee of the Whole, but not on matters before the entire House."[223]

Today, American Samoa is an "unorganized unincorporated territory" of the United States. Not unlike in the other unincorporated territories, the second-class, or arguably third-class, citizenship created by this legal status reveals a contradiction in the American federation of states. Much like the residents of Puerto Rico, Guam, and the United States Virgin Islands, pursuant to the Insular Cases the residents of Samoa, an unincorporated territory, are only entitled to the fundamental rights of the U.S. Constitution. The reverence displayed for the separation of powers and fundamental constitutional rights of citizens of the fifty states is inconsistent with the near-absolute authority of the unelected secretary of the Interior and the lack of constitutional guarantees afforded to American Samoans.

The colonial relationship between the United States and American Samoa is purported to be one that preserves indigenous culture. However, a substantial indigenous population has no relevance with respect to the protections to which "persons" within the jurisdiction are entitled. As described by Professor Thornbury, "though United States in appearance, the government of Samoa is actually a fiefdom, under the nearly unbridled control of a political appointee."[224] The United States places high value upon constitutional guarantees and the separation of powers and professes a policy of self-sufficiency for the Samoans, yet we have allowed this system of government to continue for (more than) a century.

In conclusion, the inhabitants of the unincorporated territories were granted a title that suggested equal rights and power in the political process but, in actuality, they received little more than a label, coupled with a perception on their part that they were attaining something of consequence. For the United States, the effect of these grants was that "[t]hose at the helm of all branches of the metropolitan government saw as fit that citizenship be granted for particular political and strategic reasons without effectuating a change in the political condition of the territories."[225] For the residents of these island territories, their disenfranchised status has not only caused inequality of political and civil rights but also manifested itself through unequal economic treatment.[226]

Relying on the territorial incorporation doctrine, the Supreme Court repeatedly upheld this unequal economic treatment of the people of the United States overseas territories. The justices have concluded that as long as there is a rational basis for the discrimination, the Court will uphold the acts. Resting on Congress's power under the Territorial Clause, the Court in these decisions summarily found a rational basis for disparate treatment, thereby justifying Congress's discriminatory action.[227] Thus, the United States has denied the inhabitants of most of the islands it has conquered or controlled the citizenship status enjoyed by their mainland counterparts under the constitution and federal law.[228] Island people's membership, simply stated, violates foundational conditions of United States citizenship law.

The Subordinate Status of Women

Though not fitting neatly within the structure of a chapter focused on the way legal constructs under the plenary powers and related doctrines were used to keep racial and ethnic minorities in this land in a formal inferior status, the treatment of women throughout this country's history mirrors the formal relegation to inferior status placed on racial and ethnic minorities. For women, there were not many decisions speaking to their formal inferior status. Nevertheless, there were two important decisions that arose during the same period as did the decisions addressed earlier in this chapter that formally recognized women's subordinate status in the United States. The historical judicial view of women is evidenced by the paternalistic view that women are caretakers, dependent on men for economic support and protection. Although this paternalistic view may have evolved through the social and familial expectation of a woman's role, judicial opinions have echoed this paternalism, as is evidenced in *Bradwell v. Illinois*[229] and *Muller v. Oregon*.[230] In 1872, in the case of *Bradwell v. Illinois*, the Supreme Court of Illinois denied Myra Bradwell the right to practice law on the basis that she was a married woman. The U.S. Supreme Court upheld *Bradwell v. Illinois* on the basis of states' legal right to regulate the practice of law. Even though the majority opinion did not focus on Mrs. Bradwell's gender, the concurring opinion by Justice Bradley follows the classical as well as the so-called Enlightenment thinkers' view toward women and dwells on the idea that women's role differs from that of men, expressing the belief that women are better fit for motherhood:

> The natural and proper timidity and delicacy which belongs to the female sex evidently unfits it for many of the occupations of civil life. . . . The paramount destiny and mission of women are to fulfill the noble and benign offices of wife and mother. This is the law of the Creator.[231]

The denial of equal treatment to women by barring them from the practice of law, along with Justice Bradley's concurrence opinion, is proof of judicial paternalism—the presumed need to protect women from professions deemed to be unfit for them. Accordingly, although a woman may be qualified to practice law, as was the case with Mrs. Bradwell, her desire to enter a profession dominated by males is outweighed by the societal interest in limiting women to the role of motherhood.

A similar bias was evidenced in 1908, in *Muller v. Oregon*, where the Court decided an issue guided by the paternalist view that women's physique and social role rendered them incapable of self-protection. Although three years earlier the Court, in *Lochner v. New York*, rejected a similar paternalistic view toward men in upholding the right to contract, thereby invalidating a state law restricting the number of hours that men could work, the Court in *Muller* noted that the physical differences between the two genders distinguished *Muller* from *Lochner*, requiring for the Court in *Muller* to protect women. In upholding a state law limiting women's right to work to ten hours a day, the Court focused on the child-bearing physiology and the effect that long working hours can have on a woman's body, and thus, her ability to have vigorous offspring. Additionally, the Court in *Muller* noted that women's dependence on men, and men's superior physical strength, had led women to rely on the Court for judicial protection.

These cases should not be surprising as this practice in the United States mirrored what had been occurring throughout world history. Take, for instance, the Renaissance philosophers discussed in previous chapters. They championed the value and virtue of equality in a democratic state, yet time and time again they relegated women to an inferior role within society. Women throughout history have been the largely forgotten group even within groups writing about discrimination and inferiority. It has largely taken the efforts of women to remind the world of the disparate treatment they have faced throughout time.

Women in the United States were no different. They were treated in the common law as possessing no legal character and were merely possessions of their husbands or fathers.[232] In the political arena they were treated as non-members and had little say in anything related to citizenship or its rights.[233] Accordingly, they possessed no power to vote. Unfortunately, liberal thinking and theory, which was so influential in developing this country's political and legal framework, had little impact on any notion of equality associated with this group.

It largely took the women's suffrage movement to slowly begin a change in their formal inferior status. Many today would argue that they still are *de facto* subordinates, and evidence of that fact could be demonstrated by the widely recognized employment data that demonstrates that women in the twenty-first century still earn roughly two-thirds of what men make for essentially identical work.[234] The classic historical example of their inferior status was their lack of political rights and the suffrage movement undertaken for over a century in an effort to provide women a political voice.

Women in this country gained the right to vote nationwide through the adoption of the Nineteenth Amendment to the U.S. Constitution in 1920.[235] The struggle to gain this right was, however, long-standing and difficult, as the American women's suffrage movement officially began nearly a hundred years earlier at the 1848 convention for women's rights in Seneca Falls, New York.[236]

Initial resistance to the exclusion of women from the right to vote probably began as a reaction to the passage of the Fourteenth and Fifteenth Amendments:

> In particular, the willingness of abolitionists to incorporate the word "male" in the Fourteenth Amendment, which extended basic civil rights to blacks and served as the basis for Reconstruction, and exclude women from the Fifteenth Amendment, which extended voting rights to all races, disappointed many women's rights activists. However, these events focused women activists' attention on the question of voting rights.[237]

Thrust forward primarily by fragmented regional organizations and more established organizations like the Women's Christian Temperance Union, the women's suffrage movement gained national attention once it began targeting state legislatures—starting with the western states and slowly moving east-ward.[238] In 1869, suffrage efforts expanded on a national level as the National Woman Suffrage Association (NWSA) and the American Woman Suffrage Association were founded.[239] "On average, in every year between 1870 and 1890, 4.4 states considered legislation giving women the vote."[240] Although the ways in which these efforts were unsuccessful varied, efforts in state leg-islatures consistently fell short. "The large majority of these bills stalled in legislative committees or failed to pass at least one house of the state legis-lature. Moreover, eight state woman suffrage amendments were rejected by voters in referenda."[241]

In light of these shortcomings, resistance efforts became more multifac-eted, as women adopted a number of methods to attract national attention to the cause. Some shifted their focus to the streets and adopted a more indirect and sensationalist style:

> Working within the WCTU and the two suffrage organizations, activists campaigned in state legislatures and among the electorate for the right to vote. In addition, during the 1870s NWSA activists tried a number of con-frontational tactics such as attempting to vote, running women candidates, and protesting the lack of suffrage at public events. The NWSA also sup-ported attempts to enfranchise women through judicial challenges to the Constitution during the early 1870s. However, these activities were short-lived and none resulted in any additional voting rights for women. Other-wise, suffrage activists continued to use the same methods they had uti-lized in the earlier women's rights movements: petitioning legislatures and testifying before committees to convince lawmakers to consider woman suffrage bills, and giving public speeches and conducting referendum cam-paigns to rouse public support for the enfranchisement of women.[242]

Wyoming first granted women suffrage in 1869, and when the Nineteenth Amendment was ratified, fifteen states had granted women full suffrage.[243] These successes placed heavy pressures on Congress to pass the Nineteenth Amendment. The Nineteenth Amendment was finally passed in 1919, and was forwarded to the states for ratification. "It took 15 months and 19 hard-fought state campaigns to ratify the amendment."[244]

Before these efforts, women were excluded from democracy and any for-mal power in U.S. politics. Accordingly, women were relegated to exist only in the private sphere and in the home, and much as in ancient Greece, any sort of public identity was available only for men. As Ruth Schwartz Cohen writes in *More Work for Mother*, the identity of women was relegated to a unique social status—the concept of which does not evade the American consciousness to this day—housewifery:

> Etymology can illuminate some of the murkier realms of social history. *Housewifery* has had a long history; in English the word can be traced back as far as the thirteenth century. Women have always cooked, laundered, sewed, and nursed children; but it was not until the thirteenth century, when the feudal period was ending and the capitalist organization of society was just beginning, that some of the women who did these chores were given the name, and the very special social status, of "housewives." Housewives were the spouses of "husbands" . . . both derived their status from the existence of their house and its associated land—the man because he had some title to it, and the woman because she was married to him.[245]

Housewifery encapsulated the political identity of women—which extended to the boundaries of the home and not much farther. Consequently, and for hundreds of years, women were not citizens but, instead, were the housewives of citizens.

Thus, until the passage of the Nineteenth Amendment, the political process and the concept of citizenship itself were exclusively male. However, after women gained the right to vote,

> Women were moving into traditionally male domains, and the social order between the sexes began a transformation. The growing presence of this new woman in the public sphere—in factories, offices, universities, and the professions—gradually weakened the widely held nineteenth-century assumption that women's appropriate place was in the home. Not only did such changes create a growing population of independent women who were often predisposed to suffrage arguments, but the blurring of this public/private distinction helped persuade the population more generally, including male political decision-makers in state legislatures and the electorate, of women's ability to participate in the public sphere, including politics.[246]

Yet, this extension of women into the public sphere was undeniably colored by racial differentiation. Although Black women had a significant presence in the fight for the passage of the Nineteenth Amendment, the cross-section of racism and sexism manifested itself most strongly in the case of

Black women: "for middle-class white women, the movement's victory ended battles that had begun over seventy years before. For Black women, however, the struggle to maintain the vote continued for two generations after the passage of the woman suffrage amendment as most were robbed of their ballots by the success of white political supremacy in the South."[247]

It is not difficult to envision—the victory of the Nineteenth Amendment was a superficial one, as the onset of Jim Crow had already nestled into its place in the minds of White Americans: *The Birth of a Nation*, for example, was released just a few years before the Nineteenth Amendment was ratified and was the best-selling film of its time—when adjusted for inflation, it is still one of the highest-grossing films in American history. Women gaining the right to vote amid the landscape of Jim Crow left Black women with a much larger battle to fight ahead of them—although Black women could vote *per se*, the political participation of Black women changed little after the passage of the Nineteenth Amendment. Although many scholars disagree precisely when the full actualization of Black women suffrage took place, it is arguable that Black women ended their *de facto* subordinate citizenship status when the Jim Crow era ended in the early 1960s. Even since that time, many writers—many of them feminist—continue to argue that Black women still have not acquired equal treatment and equal protection of the law.[248]

The story of women suffrage in the United States paints a telling picture of the ways in which political processes have excluded—and continue to exclude—individuals from the full enjoyment of citizenship. Women were excluded from political participation for thousands of years in world history and for hundreds of years during the annals of this country's history. And even when women began publicly and actively resisting this exclusion, it took over seventy years for women to obtain the right to vote. And even then, White supremacy continued to delineate who were privy to the benefits of citizenship and who were not. Thus, the often silent minority—women—fit squarely within the group of *de jure* subordinates examined in this chapter, particularly because their subordination was so prevalent and taken for granted that it largely evaded Supreme Court or congressional challenge.

As this chapter has illustrated, this country has had a long history of relegating certain groups into formal inferior categories of subordinate citizens. While in the case of some within this group, such as African Americans and women, the formal markers of inferiority were eviscerated by constitutional amendment, the Fourteenth for African Americans and the Nineteenth for women, their struggles for equality did not end with these important legislative directives, and in fact continue to this day. Many could argue that for these two groups their status of subordinates is now merely one of *de facto* subordination, an issue that will be explored in the next chapter in the context of ethnic and racial minorities.

Despite the formal termination of political inferiority for some of the *de jure* subordinates addressed in this chapter, i.e., African Americans and women, some of the *de jure* subordinates still exist in their inferior status. This shameful and unfortunate fact applies to the millions of citizens and nationals who are residents of the United States' overseas possessions. What is perhaps more shameful is the fact that so few know of this fact that it is rarely even discussed in law schools where future lawyers, judges, and legislators first receive their formal training in the law. Despite the provocative nature of the basic premise of this book—that the citizenship construct has always included, and arguably supported, an exclusionary aspect—there is little doubt that in the world's leading democracy there are still millions of inhabitants who are formally unequal citizens. This fact should be abhorrent to advocates of democratic thinking and champions of freedom. The fact that there still exist millions of subordinate citizens is one that is still unfortunately largely unknown and frankly largely without any champions. Even U.S. presidents, when speaking of the inhabitants of this country's overseas territories, fail to or refuse to characterize them as U.S. citizens. More often than not the United States citizens of these lands are referred to as our "our friends" or "our neighbors" instead of "our fellow Americans."[249] For instance, in response to protests concerning U.S. military bombing on the island of Vieques, one of the islands that are part of Puerto Rico, on June 14, 2001, President George W. Bush said, "My attitude is that the Navy ought to find somewhere else to conduct its exercises for a lot of reasons. One, there has been some harm done to people in the past. Secondly, these are our friends and neighbors and they don't want us there."[250] These people are not only our friends; they are our fellow American citizens, albeit through conquest. Why after more than a century does the world's great champion of democracy still support the practice of having citizens with unequal rights?

The *De Facto* Subordinates?

This chapter examines the second, and more controversial, component of the theory of citizenship as it pertains to the United States. Specifically, the question posed here is whether there are in fact *de facto* subordinate citizens in the United States. In other words, this chapter questions whether certain groups in American society, such as African Americans, remain subordinate members of society despite being granted formal legal membership. While other former *de jure* subordinates, such as women, fit within this inquiry, issues addressed here will be whether certain racial and ethnic minorities, such as African Americans and Mexican Americans, continue to exist in an inferior citizenship status despite the formal grant of citizenship to these groups.

It is well known that African Americans were once formally inferior inhabitants in the United States by virtue of their status as slaves and then by virtue of their atrocious treatment during the Jim Crow era. African Americans only became *de jure* full members after a civil war and a constitutional amendment that declared them to be citizens. Despite this grant, the question persists for many whether they still are less than full citizens. Though the Fourteenth Amendment ostensibly granted all African Americans the right to full citizenship, as the brilliant words of W. E. B. Du Bois cautioned in his prophetic book *Black Reconstruction*, there is an important difference between the granting of a theoretical political right and the ability to exercise it as well as all other rights and privileges available to the majority members of society.

This belief is still held by many people of color notwithstanding recent significant events such as U.S. Senator Barack Obama's ascendency to become the first African American president of the United States. Despite this great achievement, such proud moments may not dramatically change the lives of people of color in their day-to-day interactions. As many fellow progressive people of color mentioned the day after the 2008 presidential election, they all awoke from a night's sleep so proud of his victory and had renewed hope for the future of America. Unfortunately, by the end of the day, there was some disappointment in that many may have expected the world to have changed overnight. Time will tell if recent events like President Obama's tenure become transformative moments in U.S. history. Many people of color, however, are skeptical about whether Obama's victory will guarantee that all citizens will be treated equally in every way. Despite the 2008 presidential election and societal efforts at political correctness, many doubt whether racially biased behavior, such as police officers unduly targeting young African American automobile drivers, will end. In other words, racial profiling and similar undermining acts will probably not end with one election, despite how monumental the victory may have been and the hope it probably instilled in millions.

Even if the cynics are proven wrong and a thrilling revelation arises that overt racism (and even the more pernicious form of racism known as the bias of low expectations) ends, the fact remains that when one examines the United States' history of citizenship, one is inevitably forced into a realization. This realization is that despite the formal granting of citizenship to many outsider groups, such as African Americans and Mexican Americans, it will continue to take time for such groups to be treated equally and made to feel like full members of society.

Even for the most cynical, few can argue against granting a degree of importance to the 1954 *Brown v. Board of Education* decision and its elimination of the "separate but equal" paradox from *Plessy v. Ferguson*. Yet, even though it was impactful, one should question the progress of even iconic decisions like *Brown*. For example, *Brown* occurred almost a century after African Americans were granted full citizenship under the Fourteenth Amendment. Moreover, the second *Brown* opinion compromised the integration mandate by calling for *Brown*'s remedy to be implemented with "all deliberate speed,"[1] which resulted in slow and only partial efforts at forcing integration, and effectively led to an end of state-mandated integration. Given *Brown*'s social consequences of "White flight" and its devastating impact on the tax base that supported federal funding of public schools, many can still question just how beneficial was the iconic *Brown* decision.

For other groups, such as Mexican Americans, the struggle for acceptance and equal rights also continues. One does not have to look much further than the hateful rhetoric associated with the recent immigration debates to witness the demonized status of undocumented workers and every Latino and Latina American citizen who is presumptively treated as a foreigner or outsider as a result of the sweeping nature of the anti-immigrant attacks. This chapter will examine the transition of various American racial and ethnic minority groups from their once-held *de jure* (formal) subordinate status to their eventual grant of citizenship. This examination will necessarily expose the specter of inferiority that exists despite these formal grants of full membership: *de facto* subordination.

African Americans

African Americans, without question, fall into a category of individuals who were once subordinates in law. Since this *de jure* subordination, the question remains, at least in the minds of some, whether African Americans are still subordinate, despite attaining citizenship status with the passage of the Thirteenth, Fourteenth, and Fifteenth Amendments to the United States Constitution.

While African Americans were finally granted U.S. citizenship by constitutional amendment after the Civil War, questions persist, over a century after that grant, as to whether they truly enjoy full citizenship rights. African Americans and other groups identified here, though having attained official Fourteenth Amendment citizen status (a status not attained by the territorial island people), have still been repeatedly treated unequally. In other words, although they may no longer be subordinates in law, African American minorities may still qualify as subordinates in fact.

Malcolm X poignantly expressed the depth of the frustration, estrangement, and alienation of this citizen group:

> The Black should be exempt from all taxation . . . we want the federal government to exempt our people from all taxation as long as we are deprived of equal justice under the laws of the land . . . why should you be taxed if you don't get anything in return? How can you be charged the same tax as the White man . . . you have no business in a government, as a second class citizen, paying first class taxes. They should exempt our people from all taxation as long as we're deprived of equal protection of the laws . . . you don't have second class citizenship anywhere on earth, you only have slaves and people who are free.[2]

While the inferior status of African Americans did not derive from the plenary powers doctrine discussed in the previous chapter, it derived from the United States Constitution, interpreted through similarly racist constructions. As originally drafted, the Constitution subordinated, demeaned, and excluded African Americans from membership through the original Article I, Section 2, which counted African Americans as three-fifths of a free person.[3]

In addition, the first Supreme Court decision to address the political status of African Americans, *Sanford v. Scott* (the infamous Dred Scott decision),[4] did not base its decision on the plenary powers doctrine; it did, however, arise during the same period of that doctrine's creation. Accordingly, similar racist and nativist bases were used to subordinate indigenous people, recent Asian immigrants, and inhabitants of U.S. island conquests. Thus, while the case that sanctioned the disenfranchised African Americans was technically not a plenary powers decision, it is analogous in terms of its White-supremacist foundation.

As already mentioned, the Supreme Court defined the contours of American membership and citizenship from roughly the first third of the 1800s to roughly the first third of the 1900s. This period of time was the focal point in determining what groups were to be included within the label of the true American citizen.[5] The Supreme Court and Congress responded to this question by excluding every statistically significant racial minority group from full citizenship status.[6] Between 1823 and 1922, the Supreme Court, consistent with classical notions of the construct, reiterated the importance of equality of citizenship in a democracy but nonetheless endorsed a model of differentiated levels of membership.

In a series of decisions dealing with immigration, national security, and overseas expansion, the Court endorsed the unequal treatment and inferior status of various groups that should have been considered citizens. These cases include the infamous *Dred Scott v. Sandford*[7] and *Plessy v. Ferguson*[8] (affecting African Americans); *Elk v. Wilkins*,[9] *United States v. Kagama*,[10] and *Lone Wolf v. Hitchcock*[11] (affecting indigenous people); the Chinese Exclusion Cases[12] (affecting Asian immigrants); and the Insular Cases[13] (affecting inhabitants of the island conquests).

In each of these decisions, racial and ethnic minority groups challenged the propriety of governmental action that discriminated against them.[14] In each decision, the Court used similar racial and xenophobic justifications to uphold the disparate treatment. When racial and ethnic minorities (with the exception of African Americans) challenged violations to their constitutional rights, the Supreme Court constitutionally justified deference to the political branches of the government by relying upon the plenary powers doctrine. The plenary powers doctrine developed as an extension of the inherent powers doctrine during U.S. colonial expansion during the 1800s. Unlike the pretexts of foreign relations used under the plenary powers doctrine, for African Americans the Court was perhaps more direct or honest with its own racist inclinations and simply declared African Americans unfit for full citizenship as enjoyed by Whites.

In each of the plenary powers cases, the Supreme Court concluded that even the most basic liberty protections, as a matter of a constitutional law, did not apply to these groups. The Court based its holdings on international law principles and found that because the government's political branch (Congress) was primarily responsible for national security, issues that touched upon the status of individuals from sovereigns within and without the physical boundaries of the United States should be addressed primarily by the political branch of government and not the judicial branch. Because African Americans entered the United States as slaves for the benefit of their White owners, the foreign relations justification of the plenary powers doctrine did not seem to fit.

The very nature of the way African Americans arrived in this country strongly suggests that those born here must be citizens, as they could owe no allegiance to any other government than that of their place of birth.[15] Thus, the principles of equality and membership should have always applied to African Americans; of course, they have not. The court-sanctioned exclusion of African Americans is most vivid in the U.S. Supreme Court's decision in *Scott v. Sandford*,[16] where the Court held that African Americans, even those born in a free territory, were not U.S. citizens.[17]

In this case, the plaintiff, Dred Scott, was born into slavery in Virginia sometime around 1800. Scott's master, an army doctor, eventually moved him to Minnesota, which forbade slavery. Scott sued for his freedom, claiming that he was in a free territory and therefore could not be a slave in that land. After engaging in an extensive discussion surrounding the meaning of citizenship, Chief Justice Taney, writing for the Court, denied his claim, concluding, "we think the Negroes are . . . not included and were not intended to be included, under the word 'citizens' in the Constitution, and can therefore claim none of the rights and privileges which that instrument provides for and secures to citizens of the United States."[18]

The Court refused to recognize citizenship for this group because of their perceived inferiority.[19] Specifically, the Court referenced historical perceptions of African Americans "as beings of an inferior order, and altogether unfit to associate with the white race."[20] By doing so, the Court endorsed gradations of membership established in the very first writings on the concept— dating back to the ancient Greek writings of Aristotle.

Writing for the majority, Chief Justice Taney declared,

The words "people of the United States" and "citizens" . . . mean the same thing. They both describe the political body who, according to our republican institutions, form the sovereignty, and who hold the power and conduct the Government through their representatives. They are what we familiarly call the "sovereign people," and every citizen is one of this people, and a constituent member of this sovereignty. The question before us is, whether the class of persons described in the plea in abatement composes a portion of this people, and are constituent members of this sovereignty? We think they are not, and that they are not included, and were not intended to be included, under the word "citizens" in the Constitution, and can therefore claim none of the rights and privileges which that instrument provides for and secures to citizens of the United States.[21]

In his concurring opinion, Justice Daniel observed,

The African . . . was regarded and owned in every State in the Union as property merely, and as such was not and could not be a party or an actor, much less a peer in any compact or form of government established by the States or the United States. . . . [S]o far as rights and immunities appertaining to citizens have been defined and secured by the Constitution and laws of the United States, the African race is not and never was recognized either by the language or purposes of the former.[22]

Justice Daniel further argued that freed Blacks possessed an intermediate membership level akin to that of a "freedman" and not (as Scott argued) of a citizen. Accordingly, as a result of the propriety of membership, Justice Daniel opined that African Americans could not possess citizenship's rights and privileges. Referring to the Roman law system's differentiated inclusion of slaves, freedmen, and citizens, he recommended a comparable system for the United States, further noting,

The institution of slavery, as it exists and has existed from the period of its introduction into the United States, though more humane and mitigated in character than was the same institution, either under the republic or the empire of Rome, bears, both in its tenure and in the simplicity incident to the mode of its exercise, a closer resemblance to Roman slavery than it does to the condition of villanage, as it formally existed in England.

Connected with the latter, there were peculiarities, from custom or positive regulation, which varied it materially from the slavery of the Romans, or from slavery at any period within the United States. But with regard to slavery amongst the Romans, it is by no means true that emancipation, either during the republic or the empire, conferred, by the act itself, or implied, the status or the rights of citizenship.[23]

Ultimately, the *Scott* Court adopted the Roman model of subordinate levels of participation within 1800s American society. Whether labeled a free person or a slave, an African American person could not become a full member of society.[24] As Professor Eric Foner recently observed,

[T]he war . . . held out hope for an even more radical transformation in the condition of the at the time despised black population of the free states. Numbering fewer than a quarter million in 1860, blacks comprised less than 2 percent of the North's population, yet they found themselves subjected to discrimination in every aspect of their lives. Barred in most states from the suffrage, schools, and public accommodations, confined by and large to menial occupations, living in the poorest, unhealthiest quarters of cities like New York, Philadelphia, and Cincinnati, reminded daily of the racial prejudice that seemed as pervasive in the free states as in the slave, many Northern blacks had by the 1850s all but despaired of ever finding a secure and equal place in American life. Indeed, the political conflict between free and slave societies seemed to deepen racial anxieties within the North. The rise of political antislavery in the 1840s and 1850s was accompanied by the emergence of white supremacy as a central tenet of the Northern Democratic party, and by decisions by Iowa, Illinois, Indiana, and Oregon to close their borders entirely to blacks, reflecting the fear that, if slavery weakened, the North might face an influx of black migrants.[25]

In other words, because of the Court's endorsement of state-sanctioned racism and marginalization, non-Whites, like African Americans, were denied equality and full rights under the Constitution. After a long, bloody, and destructive civil war, Congress, led by the Republican party, began to develop the primacy of the national government and the notion of unified national citizenship. As a precursor to the Fourteenth Amendment, Congress passed the Civil Rights Act of 1866, which defined U.S. citizenship and enumerated certain civil rights for all, except unassimilated Native Americans, living in the United States.[26] Eventually, Congress was also able to amend the Constitution to provide citizenship status to "all persons" born in the United States. Nonetheless, after the Civil War, serious doubts persisted as to whether African Americans were free and political persons.[27]

In the words of W. E. B. Du Bois after the Civil War,

> It is clear that from the time of Washington and Jefferson down to the Civil War, when the nation was asked if it was possible for free Negroes to become American citizens in the full sense of the word, it answered by a stern and determined "No!" The persons who conceived of the Negroes as free and remaining in the United States were a small minority before 1861, and confined to educated free Negroes and some of the Abolitionists. . . . Were we not loosing a sort of gorilla into American freedom? Negroes were lazy, poor, and ignorant. Moreover their ignorance was more than the ignorance of whites. It was a biological, fundamental and ineradicable ignorance based on pronounced and eternal racial differences. The democracy and freedom open and possible to white men of English stock, and even to Continental Europeans, were unthinkable in the case of Africans.[28]

Carl Schurz (a German immigrant, intellectual, and idealist who traveled the South extensively in preparing a report on the reconstruction efforts in the Gulf states for President Johnson) found the situation little improved in the years after the war. Du Bois quotes from Schurz's account at length and also finds corroboration from reports from several states to the congressional Joint Committee on Reconstruction. Among Schurz's observations was the following:

> The emancipation of the slaves is submitted to only in so far as chattel slavery in the old form could not be kept up. But although the freedman is no longer considered the property of the individual master, he is considered the slave of society, and all independent state legislation will share the tendency to make him such. The ordinances abolishing slavery passed by the conventions under the pressure of circumstances will not be looked upon as barring the establishment of a new form of servitude. . . . Wherever I go—the street, the shop, the house, the hotel, or the steamboat—I hear the people talk in such a way as to indicate that they are yet unable to conceive of a Negro as possessing any rights at all. Men who are honorable in their dealings with their white neighbors, will cheat a Negro without feeling a single twinge of their honor. To kill a Negro, they do not deem murder; to debauch a Negro woman, they do not think fornication; to take property

away from a Negro, they do not consider robbery. . . . The whites esteem the blacks their property by natural right, and however much they admit that the individual relations of masters and slaves have been destroyed by the war and by the President's emancipation proclamation, they still have an ingrained feeling that the blacks at large belong to the whites at large.[29]

Du Bois also noted that the Fourteenth Amendment emancipates a multitude of people with no political rights. Accordingly, while the perception of many may be that emancipation would immediately evolve to enfranchisement, as Du Bois feared, that conclusion was far from the case.[30] Despite theoretically attaining citizenship and its related rights and anointments of belonging, African Americans were subsequently (and repeatedly) treated in an unequal manner,[31] notwithstanding the enactment of the Fourteenth Amendment, which was supposed to grant them full citizenship status. As a Reconstruction amendment, the Fourteenth Amendment was enacted to specifically recognize that African Americans born in the United States were citizens.

For instance, even after the passage of the Fourteenth Amendment, the Court in the Civil Rights Cases in 1883 struck down the Civil Rights Act of 1875, which prohibited "any person" from denying "any citizen" access to privately owned places of public accommodation on the basis of race.[32] Justice Bradley confirmed the inferior citizenship status of African Americans when he declared,

> There were thousands of free colored people in this country before the abolition of slavery, enjoying all the essential rights of life, liberty, and property the same as white citizens; yet no one, at that time, thought it was any invasion of their personal status as freemen because they were not admitted to all the privileges enjoyed by white citizens, or because they were subjected to discrimination in the enjoyment of accommodations in inns, public conveyances, and places of amusement.[33]

Scholars have long chronicled the pre– and post–Civil War disenfranchisement of African Americans. As Professor Christopher Bracey recently observed,

> Perhaps the earliest expression of this post–Civil War sentiment occurred [during] President Johnson's veto message to Congress denouncing the proposed Civil Rights Bill. For Johnson, immediate bestowal of citizenship

upon newly emancipated blacks, when presumably white "intelligent, worthy, and patriotic foreigners" were required to proceed through standard immigration procedures, was an outrageous proposition because the color line was now made to operate in favor of the colored and against the white race.[34]

These chronicles trace the post–Civil War efforts by White southerners to immediately implement a *de facto* form of slavery through efforts such as the "Black Codes"—designed, in particular, to ban political participation and, more generally, to destroy any pretense of equality.[35] These oppressive efforts operated with the full support of President Andrew Johnson.[36]

The continued disparate treatment of these people, which was often sanctioned by the Court, created the *de facto* inferior citizenship status of African Americans. For instance, despite the passage of the Fourteenth Amendment, in *Plessy v. Ferguson*,[37] Justice Brown, writing for the majority, upheld a statute that required the segregation of White and "colored" persons.[38] Justice Brown based his discussion on a constructed distinction between social and legal equality.[39] He concluded that "[t]he object of the [Fourteenth] Amendment was undoubtedly to enforce the absolute equality of the two races before the law, but in the nature of things it could not have been intended to abolish distinctions based upon color, or to enforce social as distinguished from political equality."[40]

The social and legal distinctions made in *Plessy* replicated the tortured logic of *Dred Scott*, despite the enactment of the Fourteenth Amendment. The *Plessy* Court reiterated that, notwithstanding the amendment's declarations that "all persons born or naturalized" would be citizens, African Americans were not recognized as true citizens: African Americans were citizens in name, not in law. The concepts of equality as applied to rights and opportunity were inapplicable to them. Even after the Fourteenth Amendment's enactment, which was specially passed to acknowledge the freedom and equality of former slaves, the Supreme Court in *Plessy* reiterated that African Americans could be treated unequally. Indeed, they were something less, perhaps even still slaves, to borrow Malcolm X's sentiments. These events highlight that despite attaining a status that is supposed to connote equality, African Americans, at least during the era closely following the Reconstruction amendments of the Constitution, were not full and equal citizens.

Though the Supreme Court decision of *Brown v. Board of Education*[41]—or *Brown I*—specifically rejected the "separate but equal" dichotomy of *Plessy*, even *Brown* failed to lift segregation's stigma in public schools, as evidenced by the *Brown II* decision, which was the Court's determination on how best to implement its order in *Brown I*. Another consequence of *Brown* was the social phenomenon of "White flight." To this day, African Americans must either face unequal treatment or be members of a group that repeatedly faces a series of unfortunate events.[42] Examples of this are found in a variety of circumstances, including racial profiling by police, such as "DWB" (driving while Black)[43] or the more subtle forms of subordination Ellis Close identifies in his book *The Rage of a Privileged Class*; here, Close addresses the way African Americans, irrespective of their academic or financial achievements, are repeatedly reminded of their inequality in society.[44]

A fairly recent manifestation of the debate regarding the subordinate citizenship of African Americans concerns the voting representation of residents in the District of Columbia. Of the over 550,000 D.C. residents, 60 percent are African American.[45] While members of this community pay federal and local taxes, serve in the armed forces, and serve on juries to uphold federal law and policies, these residents have no voting representation in Congress.[46] It was not until 1961, when the Twenty-Third Amendment of the Constitution was ratified by the states, that the residents of the District of Columbia were granted the right to vote in presidential elections.[47]

This event marked the first time that U.S. citizens who were not residing within the political, governmental unit of a state were granted the right to vote in presidential elections.[48] However, that right is effectively their only voice in the political process. Voters in the District of Columbia elect a delegate to the House of Representatives who can vote in committee and draft legislation but does not have full voting rights.[49] Additionally, voters elect two "shadow" senators[50] and one "shadow" representative[51] as nonvoting representatives who lobby Congress on behalf of the District of Columbia and its issues and concerns. Denial of congressional representation to the predominantly African American community in the District of Columbia, to at least some scholars, "not only suggests a belief in the unfitness of the population to participate equally in national life but creates the kind of 'uncomfortable resemblance to political apartheid' that the Supreme Court condemned and invalidated."[52]

More recent "unfortunate events" faced by African Americans are evidenced by their treatment during the 2000 presidential election. In a racially charged national election that was decided by less than seven hundred votes in the pivotal state of Florida (a state where the governor was the brother of the election's eventual victor and where both brothers were strongly disliked by many African American voters due to their positions on matters such as civil rights) the United States Commission on Civil Rights investigated widespread allegations of discrimination against African Americans on election day.

The commission's report found numerous irregularities on election day and confirmed that perhaps thousands of African Americans were denied their right to vote.[53] The report made three findings: first, the most dramatic undercount in the Florida election was that of the uncast ballots of countless eligible voters who were wrongfully turned away from the polls; second, statistical data, reinforced by credible anecdotal evidence, pointed to the widespread denial of voting rights; and third, the disenfranchisement of Florida's voters fell most harshly on the shoulders of African American voters. The report concluded that the magnitude of the impact could be seen from any of several perspectives.

According to the report, county-level statistical estimates indicate that Black voters statewide were nearly ten times more likely than non-Black voters to have their ballots rejected. Estimates indicated that approximately 14.4 percent of Florida's Black voters cast ballots that were rejected, compared to approximately 1.6 percent of non-Black Florida voters who did not have their presidential votes counted. Statistical analysis showed that the disparity in ballot spoilage rates (ballots cast but not counted) between Black and non-Black voters was not the result of education or literacy differences.

Approximately 11 percent of Florida voters were African American; however, African Americans cast about 54 percent of the 187,000 spoiled ballots in Florida.[54]

The commission made more troubling findings concerning the election. For example, there was a high correlation between counties and precincts with a high percentage of African American voters and the percentages of spoiled ballots. The commission concluded that nine of the ten counties with the highest percentage of African American voters had spoilage rates above the Florida average; of the ten counties with the highest percentage of White voters, only two counties had spoilage rates above the state average. Gadsden County, with the highest rate of spoiled ballots, also had the highest percentage of African American voters. The data further showed that eighty-three of the one hundred precincts with the highest numbers of spoiled ballots were Black-majority precincts.[55]

In light of all of this, despite the recent advance marked by the election of the first African American to the presidency, the United States has a long history of treating African Americans as less than equal even after the passage of the Fourteenth Amendment to the Constitution. For many, that inferior or disparate treatment is still apparent and merits, at the very least, further debate.[56]

Mexican Americans

While there are several groups that could be the focus of an inquiry as to whether they are in fact subordinate citizens, the history of the Mexican and Mexican American communities highlights the possibility that not all members within this society are equal, despite the attainment of a formal index of membership—citizenship. Undoubtedly, Mexican Americans are a group whose equal treatment under the law is suspect. Their theoretical inclusion as subordinates arose during the same period as the first use of the plenary powers doctrine and was similarly based on racist and nativist perspectives.

Hispanic urban centers in New Mexico and Florida predated the pilgrims' landing at Plymouth Rock. Yet Hispanics, according to most Americans, are the United States' most recent arrivals—and they have some basis for this assumption.[57] Many Americans know that the United States acquired land from the indigenous people consisting of approximately "two million square miles of territory by conquest and by purchase."[58] Not so well known is how the United States conquered Mexico in 1848 and took over half its then-existing territory. The states of California, Nevada, and Utah, as well as portions of Colorado, New Mexico, Arizona, and Wyoming, were created from a 529,000-square-mile cession by the Republic of Mexico.[59] The taking of the Mexican land was a result of the nation's westward expansion, as journalist John O'Sullivan noted in 1845:

> Away, away with all these cobweb tissues of rights of discovery, exploration, settlement, contiguity, etc. . . . The American claim is by the right of our manifest destiny to overspread and to possess the whole of the continent which Providence has given us for the development of the great experiment of liberty and federative self-government entrusted to us. It is a right such as that of the tree to the space of air and earth suitable for the full expansion of its principle and destiny of growth.[60]

Prompted by this spirit of "manifest destiny," the United States declared war against Mexico to acquire additional territory.[61] The result was the signing of the Treaty of Guadalupe Hidalgo, which states in part,

The United States of America, and the United Mexican States, [are] animated by a sincere desire to put an end to the calamities of the war which unhappily exists between the two Republics, and to establish upon a solid basis relations of peace and friendship, which shall confer reciprocal benefits upon the citizens of both, and assure the concord, harmony and mutual confidence, wherein the two peoples should live, as good neighbors. . . .[62]

Among other things, the treaty provided that the United States would respect private property rights of Mexican citizens in the newly created portions of the United States and would grant those individuals U.S. citizenship.[63] However, as had occurred with the indigenous peoples,[64] the United States never honored many of the treaty's provisions.[65]

Despite the treaty's pledge to "secure Mexicans their rights to property, by the turn of the century almost all Mexican-owned land was lost during the land grant adjudication process [and] . . . challenges from squatters, settlers and land speculators also promoted land alienation." Most fundamentally, "many Mexican citizens (transformed by the Treaty into United States citizens of Mexican descent) and their descendants never enjoyed full membership rights in this society, despite the Treaty's promise that they would."[66] As Professor Richard Delgado observed,

The Treaty of Guadalupe Hidalgo . . . purported to guarantee to Mexicans caught on the U.S. side of the border full citizenship and civil rights, as well as protection of their culture and language. The treaty, modeled after ones drawn up between the U.S. and various Indian tribes, was given similar treatment: The Mexicans' properties were stolen, rights were denied, language and culture suppressed, opportunities for employment, education, and political representation were thwarted.[67]

Mexican Americans were disenfranchised in numerous other ways, including by immigration. Latino and Latina immigrant workers have long experienced a revolving door of immigration in the United States—reminding them that in times of economic prosperity, legal and undocumented entrant are welcomed, but during times of economic instability or perceived political upheaval, Mexican immigrants as well as U.S. citizens of Mexican descent are unwelcome. During the times when Mexicans were unwelcome, U.S. citizens of Mexican descent often suffered from the deportation efforts aimed at Mexican immigrant workers. For instance, the deportation raids associated with Operation Wetback had the effect of also deporting Mexican

Americans as well as other Hispanic Americans. This phenomenon has left the Mexican American U.S. citizen in a constant status resembling both alien and citizen, and this paradox is far from new for the Mexican descendants residing in the United States.

In terms of immigration, people from Mexico were often invited to become part of this society when domestic economic demand called for such efforts. When circumstances changed, they were often reminded of their outsider status. The treatment of Mexican immigrants is explored here to highlight the almost schizophrenic way this society has treated this immigrant group—at times inviting them to join us only to throw them out when circumstances changed. While the treatment of an immigrant group does not fit neatly with this book's focus on residents within a society, as Linda Bosniak has observed, the treatment of immigrants highlights the flows of borders but also is inconsistent with the liberal ethos of democratic inclusiveness. Related to that point, the portrayal that follows is included to highlight a tension between the democratic ethos of inclusion coupled with cyclical economic demands against fears of foreign influx into this society.

In the mid-1800s, American society welcomed Mexicans to California in order to learn from them (among other things) Mexican mining techniques.[68] As at least one scholar has argued, once the Americans learned those techniques, they began to perceive Mexicans as undesirable foreign competition, and in 1850, the California legislature passed the Foreign Miners Tax to discourage Mexicans from gold mining.[69] As a result of this American perception of Mexican competition and inferiority, coupled with gerrymandering by Americans, Mexican Americans' influence in politics was greatly diminished by the 1800s.[70]

Although Mexicans' influence in politics decreased, their importance in the workforce increased. As David Gutierrez explains, "by the 1920s Mexican immigrant and Mexican-American workers dominated the unskilled and semiskilled sectors of the regional labor market."[71] Mexican American laborers were not limited to agricultural labor but also participated in construction, railroad construction and maintenance, and other tasks that Americans were not willing to perform.[72] During these periods of economic growth, those of Mexican descent were openly welcomed, but when the domestic economy took a turn for the worse, these vulnerable inhabitants were attacked and ousted.[73] Along with the immigrants, U.S. citizens of Mexican descent were also victims of American fickleness, and many were either made to feel unwelcome or were in fact repatriated, despite their legal status as U.S. citizens.

The domestic policy of inviting Mexican immigrant workers and then repatriating them along with U.S. citizens of Mexican descent was repeatedly carried out throughout the twentieth century. For instance, in 1917, when the U.S. government (in response to a labor crisis caused by increasingly strict immigration laws) established a guest worker program for agricultural laborers from Mexico,[74] roughly seventy-two thousand guest workers participated in the program from 1917 to 1921.[75] However, by the mid-1920s, a slowing economy led the government to discontinue the program and instead create the U.S. Border Patrol in an effort to curb illegal immigration.[76] In 1931, the government began conducting raids aimed at locating and deporting all undocumented workers.[77] As a result, during the Great Depression of the 1930s,[78] thousands of U.S. citizens of Mexican descent, residents, and undocumented aliens of Mexican descent were "repatriated" to Mexico.[79]

However, the term "repatriated" was inaccurately applied to this event because many people of Mexican descent who were forced to leave the United States and reside in Mexico had actually acquired U.S. citizenship status.[80] The vast majority of those deported to Mexico between 1929 and 1934 were U.S. citizens, including children born on U.S. soil.[81] Both local and federal authorities forced citizens and noncitizens of Mexican ancestry to leave the United States and return to Mexico[82]—failing to consider the rights of the numerous citizens whom they deported.[83] The repatriation campaign confirmed the subordinate status given to Mexican Americans. And arguably, the deportation of people of Mexican ancestry to Mexico exceeded the federal government's immigration power and violated these individuals' due process, equal protection, and Fourth Amendment rights.[84]

Nevertheless, the pattern of acceptance and eventual rejection of Mexican immigrants did not end with the Great Depression. As a result of the labor shortages created by World War II in 1942,[85] the United States established the Bracero Program, a guest worker program that allowed Mexicans to come to the United States and fill the demand for agricultural labor.[86] The United States established this program by way of the negotiation of a treaty between the United States and Mexico on April 4, 1942.[87]

In 1943, Congress endorsed the Bracero Program through Public Law 45.[88] Under this program, Mexicans could live and work in the United States for up to nine months per year. The United States government nonetheless made it very clear that these imported workers could not displace domestic workers.[89] By 1959, the Bracero Program had grown substantially, and in that year alone over 450,000 Mexican nationals were admitted into the program.[90]

When the first braceros returned to Mexico after the end of their term, they reported discrimination as well as substandard working and housing conditions.[91] The program also began to face strong opposition from both domestic civil rights groups and the labor sector over the poor treatment of these workers by their domestic agricultural employers.[92] Moreover, the Mexican government became dissatisfied with the United States upon hearing about abuses of civil and human rights.[93]

Eventually, the Mexican government temporarily banned the importation of Mexicans to Texas in 1943,[94] temporarily closing the doors on Mexicans who sought entry into Texas under the Bracero Program.[95] When the program ended in 1965, the United States had allowed a total of nearly five million Mexicans to enter and work in the United States as contracted braceros under the program.[96]

The Agricultural Bracero Program had its railroad counterpart in the 1940s, which was appropriately named the Railroad Bracero Program of World War II.[97] In January 1943, a U.S. ambassador to Mexico was ordered by the State Department to meet with Mexico's secretary of Exterior Relations (*Secretaría de Relaciones Exteriores*) to expand the Bracero Program beyond the agricultural industry.[98] In April 1943, Mexico and the United States reached an agreement with respect to allowing braceros to supply labor for the railroads.[99] Under this agreement, about six thousand nonagricultural workers were to be contracted to work on the railroads in the United States.[100] Braceros were contracted in Mexico City and transported to the Mexico–U.S. border.[101] Conditions in the railroad programs were no better than in the agricultural programs, as numerous braceros died on the railroads both on-duty due to train and rail accidents and off-duty due to natural causes, suicides, and fights.[102]

The last group of railroad braceros arrived in the United States in August of 1945.[103] On August 28, 1945, the United States issued a termination order and about fifty thousand railroad braceros were to be repatriated to Mexico.[104] The Bracero Programs (both agricultural and railroad) "were consistent with the thrust of U.S.–Mexican relations at the time."[105]

The implementation and termination of the Bracero Program directly affected the influx of illegal immigration. "By legalizing the supply of workers who otherwise would have entered illegally, the Bracero Program temporarily deflected the contradictions surrounding illegal immigration and thereby relieved the pressure on the INS. But those contradictions by no means disappeared, nor did the conflicts that they gave rise to."[106] During the years of the Bracero Program, illegal immigration increased.[107]

The United States' policy of bringing in a labor force from Mexico during times of high labor demand and sending them back to Mexico when the labor supply exceeded the demand (along with U.S. citizens of Mexican or apparent Mexican descent) demonstrates just how fickle the United States has been toward all people of Mexican, Central American, and South American ancestry. For instance, during the Cold War era and its resulting xenophobia, the United States established "Operation Wetback" to monitor the presence of Mexicans in the United States and deport any Mexican who resided unlawfully in the United States.[108] This program occurred during a period of heightened fear of noncitizens. [109]

As a result of the Bracero Program, many Mexicans moved to the northern parts of Mexico to be closer to the border between the United States and Mexico. Even though many Mexicans moved closer to the border, the United States locked its doors when it terminated the Bracero Program. Consequently, immigration issues became pressing as the United States did not want Mexicans in the country, but many Mexicans still crossed the border unlawfully. Amid the growth of these issues, "Operation Wetback" specifically targeted individuals of Mexican descent. During this massive campaign, the U.S. government deported over one million Mexican immigrants,[110] U.S. citizens of Mexican ancestry,[111] and, undoubtedly, other Hispanic U.S. citizens.[112]

Through "Operation Wetback," the United States treated individuals of Mexican ancestry similarly to the way it treated Mexican Americans during the repatriation of the 1930s. The Mexican American community was directly affected by this campaign because it was "aimed at racial groups, which meant that the burden of proving citizenship fell totally upon people of Mexican descent."[113] Accordingly, those unable to present such proof were arrested and sent to Mexico.[114] This hasty process of proving documentation infringed upon the rights of many Mexican Americans who were United States citizens or lawful permanent residents because some of them were unable to readily provide authorities with the documentation necessary to show their legal status in the United States.[115]

As in the Cold War era during the 1950s, the most recent tension between labor demands and governmental reactions to Mexican and other Latino immigrants arose during the beginning of the twenty-first century. Shortly after the terrorist attacks of September 11, 2001, an increased fear of outsiders resulted in increased attention to our borders and consequently in increased scrutiny of this country's immigration policy.[116] With the renewed fear of the foreigner highlighted by the non-American backgrounds of the perpetrators of the 9/11 attacks, more and more pundits and politicians began using emotionally charged terms and catch phrases such as the "immigration invasion."[117]

Political action soon followed these renewed fears. In response to the increasing interest in immigration and in accordance with his political beliefs, President George W. Bush, beginning in 2004, sought to reach a compromise and proposed a comprehensive immigration reform, which included a guest worker program.[118] In 2006, proposals for immigration reform caught the nation's attention, resulting in a barrage of news coverage, lobbying, and protests. The 109th Congress also took action toward comprehensive immigration reform through the Secure Fence Act (H.R. 6061), which sought to strengthen border controls[119] by funding a 700-mile fence along the U.S.–Mexico border.[120] This effort fell short of the comprehensive reform that many groups have long requested. Such comprehensive reform would not only include an enforcement component, such as is evidenced in the Secure Fence Act, but would also include efforts to resolve the status of undocumented workers through efforts such as guest worker programs or eventual citizenship. Although some have argued that the Secure Fence Act of 2006 is a necessary for step for immigration reform,[121] the main comprehensive immigration reform bill includes provisions for tightening the nation's borders and increasing the enforcement of immigration laws at several levels.[122]

The House and Senate comprehensive immigration reform bills have failed by not providing effective comprehensive reform. Though both bills went further than merely proposing the fencing of U.S. borders, the primary distinguishing factor between the H.R. 4437 and S. 2611 is that S. 2611 proposes a path to citizenship for foreign workers. The Senate's version, S. 2611's H-2C visa (also known as a blue card), permits employers to bring in foreign workers for up to six years.[123]

The 109th Congress passed and enacted into public law H.R.418 in order to strengthen border security and overall national security. This law stipulates that the expiration date of a driver's license (or identification card) issued to a temporary foreign visitor must match the expiration date of his or her visa. If there is no expiration date on the visa, the license or ID card must then expire in one year. Only United States–issued documents and valid foreign passports may be used to establish the identity of applicants. Each applicant provides proof of U.S. citizenship or lawful presence in the United States, and documents presented during the application process must be independently verified.[124]

Throughout American history, immigrant workers were only accepted when U.S. markets needed cheap disposable labor,[125] but when economic strife and/or fears for national security resulted in mass isolationist efforts, the need for labor waned and the workers were consequently deported. The implementation of bracero programs, "Operation Wetback," xenophobic sentiments, and more recent legislative efforts at immigration reform all illustrate that the recent outcry against immigration is not only not new but follows a long pattern of manipulating markets and excluding people who desire to work in the United States. Thus, the hysteria regarding the recent claims of a threat to our nation resulting from a massive wave of illegal immigrants is not only not new but has somehow left the collective psyche of the U.S. government and its people with little recollection of its prior efforts and manipulations.[126]

The recent incarnation of the inferior status of U.S. citizens of Mexican descent has similarly had a "slippery slope" impact on immigration. The recent political uproar over illegal immigration, largely led by conservative talk radio addressing the issue of immigration reform, demonstrates the ease of demonizing the Latina and Latino community in this country. This demonization is one obvious consequence of the venom that stems from anti-immigrant fervor. This hostility has a slippery slope effect on the Latina and Latino community, which invariably maintains a label of inferiority and foreignness.

At the center of this hostility are the depictions of a so-called mass invasion of our borders.[127] These depictions warn of an effort among "invaders" to take over America[128] and seek to emphasize its negative impact on the U.S. economy.[129] Another of the vitriolic calls for curbing immigration is the alleged crime wave that will inevitably result from the mass migration.[130] This call and others like it are made with little or no evidentiary support, yet captured the public imagination in a presidential election year[131] and will probably be the focus of political and public policy debates for decades to come.[132] Somewhat surprisingly, like the alleged attack by Martians of decades ago (or the more recent eerie depiction of ugly brown figures invading a domestic city in the film *Cloverfield*),[133] this "invasion" is largely accepted as an inevitable future for America.[134]

Consider the alarmed tone found in depictions of a demographic shift that will supposedly result from immigration. Media figures like Bill O'Reilly proclaim "the supporters [of immigration reform] hate America and want to flood the country with foreign nationals to change the complexion of our society."[135] Another prominent media figure, Lou Dobbs, CNN anchor and popular pundit, repeatedly warns against an "illegal alien invasion."[136] In fact, Dobbs made five references to an alien invasion during a one-hour segment of his show.[137] Some of Dobbs's choices for expert opinion on the issues even include reports from the Council of Conservative Citizens, a national White supremacist organization.[138] Dobbs is also known for blaming undocumented immigrants for a leprosy explosion of seven thousand cases over the last three years, while the actual leprosy figure is 250 cases over that period, and is not directly attributed to the immigrant population.[139]

Other media figures engage in similar forms of hyperbole to promote a solution to the inevitable population overthrow, while also stoking the flames of fear.[140] For instance, John Gibson once implored his viewers to "do your duty. Make more babies . . . half of the kids in this country under five are minorities and by far the greatest number are Hispanic. What does that mean? Twenty-five years from now, the majority of the population is Hispanic."[141]

Comments like Gibson's are often inaccurate—take for instance his mathematical miscalculation of a Hispanic majority within twenty-five years. Like prejudicial evidence in a courtroom, however, once the damning statement's impact is felt, its accuracy becomes largely irrelevant.[142] Specifically, those who heard Gibson's broadcast probably did not have the benefit of having census data before them, which would have established that by 2030, the Hispanic population in the United States will be approximately 20 percent of the overall population,[143] a far cry from the majority "takeover" Gibson depicts. In fact, contrary to Gibson's assertion, fifty years from now the majority of Americans will still be White and the Hispanic population will only be approaching 25 percent.[144]

Nevertheless, the irresponsible and hyperbolic assertions made by right-wing alarmists provoke fear with crass attacks. Talk show host Neal Boortz provides another example, as he declared while promoting a massive fence at a southern U.S. border: "I don't care if Mexicans pile up against that fence like tumble weeds. . . . Just run a couple of taco trucks up and down the line."[145] Similarly, the civil rights organization "La Raza" has been described as "the Klu Klux Klan of Hispanic People."[146]

The media's outspoken critics are not alone in their fear-mongering over the "browning" of America. For example, the *Washington Post* recently profiled the views of the so-called average American. One interviewee stated that she stopped shopping at Wal-Mart because she noticed she was the only non-Latino customer in the store.[147] She reportedly said, "I'm in the minority, and if we don't get control over this pretty soon, all of America will be outnumbered."[148] Another interviewee reportedly complained that "Latinos turn things into slums."[149]

Immigration also became a central issue in the 2008 presidential election. For many conservative and independent voters,[150] there was considerable frustration with the U.S. government's failure to produce any results with the perceived immigration crisis.[151] According to one report, "illegal immigration ranks as a top concern for many in an electorate increasingly pessimistic about the future."[152] According to *ABC News*, 55 percent of Republicans say illegal immigration hurts the country, and the issue of immigration is fifth in order of national importance to these voters.[153] *NBC Nightly News* reported that "the immigration debate has become the core of the fight for the GOP nomination."[154]

The Republican contenders responded accordingly. For instance, during their debate on November 28, 2007, presidential candidates Rudy Giuliani and Mitt Romney attempted to portray themselves as toughest on immigration. Instead of addressing the issue in an intelligent manner, they exchanged barbs, with Romney accusing former New York City mayor Giuliani of creating a "sanctuary city" and Giuliani attacking Romney for allegedly hiring illegal gardeners.[155] During the New Hampshire primary buildup, Romney ran a television ad that twice presented Senator John McCain's support of amnesty for illegal immigrants in a negative light.[156] Romney declared, "The current system puts up a concrete wall to the best and brightest, yet those without skill or education are able to walk across the border."[157] Candidate Michael Huckabee similarly took a get-tough stance, promising to send illegal immigrants home.[158] According to Huckabee, "if illegals cannot find work, they will go back where they belong. . . . I will do everything I can to hasten their trip home by denying them employment."[159]

Other anti-immigrant candidates took the rhetoric a step further. The anti-immigrant group's drum leader warns of the changing face of America and the terrorist threat to America. Republican presidential candidate Tom Tancredo, head of the Immigration Reform Caucus, often speaks to the threat of "radical multiculturalism." For instance, in his speech before the House of Representatives on halting illegal immigration, Tancredo warned,

> If we were to actually do what is necessary to prevent people from coming into this country to create havoc and to commit acts of terrorism, we would essentially end illegal immigration. . . . I do not understand how any American, any American regardless of the hyphen, what word we put before the hyphen, I do not understand how any American could say

please do not defend our borders because if you do, fewer of my country-men would be able to come in. Because if you feel that way, then that is your countrymen that we are keeping out, then you are not an American, of course.[160]

Then, of course, there are the even more dangerous aspects of this, because the people coming across the border, bringing illegal narcot-ics into the United States. They come with backpacks, 60 to 80 pounds on their back. Sometimes they come guarded by people carrying M-16s or various other automatic weapons. They come across the land in, again, droves, thousands. We have pictures of them.[161]

As the presidential election primaries neared, Tancredo said he intended to visit New Hampshire and Iowa, as part of a campaign to get a leader in the White House who "understands the threat illegal immigrants pose to the country's security."[162] According to Tancredo, we all need to be fearful because federal prisons overflow with illegal immigrants, some of whom aim to harm people.[163] In his words, "they need to be found before it is too late. They're coming here to kill you, and you, and me, and my grandchildren."[164]

More recently, Tancredo took hate mongering to new lows when in a recent television commercial he implied that illegal immigrants are terror-ists in the making.[165] The ad in question evidently asserted that radical jihad-ists have slipped into the flow of illegal immigration, and as a result, attacks are inevitable.[166] Despite being so offensive that anyone with contemporary sensibilities would find it hard to believe,[167] the outrageous ad depicts what appears to be a shopping mall being blown up as a consequence of illegal immigration.[168]

In a similar vein, conservative leaders from border states have established grass-roots vigilante organizations that work to halt immigration, often warning against a population, political, or terrorist overthrow.[169] For exam-ple, Glenn Spencer, leader of the anti-immigration American Patrol, operates a website filled with anti-Mexican rhetoric. On his website, he accuses the Mexican government of secretly plotting to take back the southwest United States.[170] Another vocal advocate warning of the "immigration invasion" is Joe McCutehen, who leads Project Arkansas Now and has also been accused of writing a series of antisemitic letters to the editors of local newspapers. McCutehen once delivered a speech that caused the Republican governor of his state to denounce the group.[171]

Another vocal anti-immigrant organizer is Jim Gilchrist, who is the founder of the Minuteman Project—an armed militia that purportedly attempts to engage in Border Patrol–like policing.[172] Gilchrist's statements and tactics "have drawn denunciations from faith leaders, human rights activists and even President George W. Bush, who called Gilchrist and his shotgun-toting posse vigilantes."[173] According to one report, Gilchrist allowed members of the National Alliance, one of the country's largest neo-Nazi organizations, to help with his 2005 campaign for the U.S. House of Representatives.[174]

Even the political leaders who seek to challenge the xenophobic tenor of the debate have nevertheless largely accepted the assertions of the nativists.[175] Consider the comments of U.S. Senator Ken Salazar, who, while disagreeing with the tone of the current debate, nevertheless accepted the assertion that America's population is changing in significant ways. In his words, "I have no doubt that some of those involved in the debate have their position based on fear and perhaps racism because of what's happening demographically in the country."[176] The senator, like many others in this society, accepted with little or no questioning that the country is enduring a major demographic shift. At least one democratic aide more accurately captured the tenor of the attacks: "A lot of the anti-immigration movement is jingoistic at best and racist at worst. There is a fear of white people being overrun by darker-skinned people."[177]

Despite these comments, even democratic presidential hopefuls have recently shown little sympathy in the immigration context. Consider the attacks on presidential hopeful Senator Hillary Clinton when she wavered in answering a question concerning issuing driver's licenses to undocumented immigrants.[178] After Clinton stated that she understood why a state might want to issue licenses to undocumented immigrants as a tool of identification,[179] Senator Chris Dodd found Clinton's words "troublesome" and doubted that anyone who flouts our nation's federal laws would be allowed to drive without a license.[180]

Despite the use of what appears to be the most simplistic form of demagoguery, the leaders of the anti-immigration agenda have impacted the national stage. For instance, the failure of the comprehensive immigration reform in Congress during 2006 is largely attributed to conservative talk show hosts calling for massive telephone campaigns directed at congressional leaders in order to kill immigration reform.[181] Nancy Pelosi, the speaker of the House of Representatives, observed, "talk radio, or in some cases hate radio . . . just go[es] on and on,[182] in a xenophobic, anti-immigrant" manner.[183]

Even Senator John McCain, the leading Republican presidential candidate during the 2008 election and one of the sponsors of the Senate's moderate comprehensive reform bill,[184] initially supported reform that would include a guest worker program and a path for undocumented workers to achieve citizenship.[185] However, succumbing to the outcry against such reform, he changed his position on the matter and eventually advocated for an enforcement-first approach towards immigration.[186]

Perhaps given the vacillating way in which political leaders respond to the issue, some supporters of reform have questioned the media's role in creating public opinion. Specifically, some have questioned whether cable news conglomerates such as MSNBC (which is co-owned by General Electric/NBC and Microsoft) are championing bigotry.[187] These claims raise legitimate questions concerning who owns the airwaves and why they select, actively market, and advertise spokespersons who openly advocate racially insensitive sentiments.[188]

Mark Potok of the Southern Poverty Law Center noted that hate groups "consistently try and exploit any public discussion that has some kind of racial angle, and immigration has worked for hate groups in America better than any issue in years."[189] The Anti-Defamation League (ADL) recently reported that "hateful and racist rhetoric" aimed at Latino immigrants has grown "to a level unprecedented in recent years."[190] In another report, the ADL recently observed that "as the national debate over immigration reached a fever pitch, some mainstream advocacy groups have 'reached for the playbook of hate groups'—resorting to hateful and dehumanizing stereotypes and outright bigotry to demonize immigrants."[191] The report concluded that a closer look at "many ostensibly mainstream anti-illegal immigration organizations— including those who testified before Congress or frequently appeared on news programs—promote virulent anti-Hispanic and anti-immigrant rhetoric."[192] Some of these organizations have even fostered links with extremist hate groups.[193]

Perhaps the most amazing aspect of the anti-immigrant movement's most irresponsible and outlandish attacks is that they do not provoke mass outrage and scorn. This lack of outrage raises several questions: Why in this day and age are such shameful attacks not only not rejected but in many respects either quietly or publicly applauded? Are the Latino and Latina citizens of the United States, along with their families, which are often from the countries where the attacks are focused, less deserving of respect?[194] Are these people less deserving of dignity? If racist statements are made against Asians or Black people, would they become acceptable if the focus of the particular attacks is not citizens?

As one national columnist observed, "While the 44 million Hispanics are the biggest minority in America, you don't see the kind of nationwide protests, legal actions or calls for boycotts on a scale you would probably see if these statements were directed against African Americans or Jewish Americans."[195] Is it not time for Latino people, other people of color, and like-minded Whites to call for an end to the intolerably racist and largely inaccurate attacks?[196] More important to point out, the tenor of the current debate confuses the masses, conflates legitimate concerns over the impact of immigration on local and state economies, and unfairly polarizes both sides of the immigration debate.

The goal of this project and related ones is to deflate the force of this bias and to pursue the goal of opening the door to legitimate dialogue and analysis. In lieu of this dialogue, what tends to occur is the ever-so-cautious suggestion that some of the current anti-Latino attacks are insensitive or touch upon race. Frustrations stemming from such cautious critiques raise several inevitable questions: Is it so difficult to call a bigot a bigot when the attacks are aimed at Spanish-speaking people? Why do so many United States citizens fail to stand up and challenge attacks filled with baseless stereotypes and false assertions? Are all accusations and insults acceptable merely because they occur in the name of protecting our borders or Anglo-American culture?[197]

Instead of outrage by an enlightened society, consider what occurs instead—the quiet question of whether race is a part of the immigration debate. For instance, a *Time* magazine article on increased interest in immigration (ever so gently) noted that race may play a part in the current debate: "The Democratic allegations of racism may sound like just another political ploy, but there certainly is a case to be made that racial fears are informing some of the debate on immigration policy."[198] The *Time* article nevertheless suggested a far more telling irony: that although national security is typically the basis for proposing the closure of our southern border, "Why is no one proposing sending additional National Guard Troops to secure the U.S.–Canada border?"[199] The question is not an unreasonable one, especially considering that Ahmed Ressam (also known as the "Millennium Bomber")[200] was caught at the Canadian border. Also, not one of the nineteen terrorists responsible for the September 11th attacks entered the United States from Mexico,[201] though some did from Canada and did so legally on airplanes.[202]

The preceding pages, while admittedly not as closely connected to the history of subordinating would-be citizens within a democracy, are related to the larger theme of the lack of coherence to this country's decisions concerning the appropriate measure for membership. The historical as present-day attacks on Latino and Latina documented and undocumented workers demonizes this group. These unfounded attacks also have the effect of subordinating U.S. citizens of Latino or Latina descent by invoking a marker or stigma of presumptive illegal immigrant. The psychological impact of such stigma is profound and must be addressed and rectified.

Other Non-Whites

Several legal scholars have addressed the outsider or foreign status of ethnic citizens in the United States other than African Americans and Mexican Americans. Several writings have turned to the treatment of Asian Americans to demonstrate their subordinate status notwithstanding their attainment of citizenship. According to these works,[203] American society has imposed a label of foreignness on several groups of American citizens.[204] This scholarship includes Latina and Latino citizens, Asian Americans, Arab Americans, and others who are included in the category of other non-White/non-Black subordinates.[205] In addition to being characterized as the "forgotten Americans" and the "invisible" members of society, they are arguably endowed with the immutable characteristic of alien or foreigner.[206] Noting that race relations in America are typically analyzed in the White-over-Black paradigm, Professor Gotanda has argued that this construct has the effect of facilitating the failure to examine the unique racism faced by the non-White/non-Black racial minorities.[207] In the White-over-Black paradigm, if a person is not White, then that person is socially regarded as something other than American.[208]

An example of the inferior status of other non-Whites is the historical use of the plenary powers doctrine to justify the deportation and exclusion of undesirable Asian immigrants who otherwise were entitled to enter or stay in the United States. In the Chinese Exclusion Cases, the Supreme Court first extended the doctrine to immigration. In *Chae Chan Ping v. United States*,[209] the plaintiff, a Chinese resident, obtained a required certificate of reentry pursuant to an 1884 law established by Congress and then left the United States to visit family in China. Prior to his return, Congress passed a new law precluding reentry of all Chinese workers, irrespective of whether they had a certificate of reentry. The Supreme Court rejected the claim that the government had violated an international treaty as well as the Fifth Amendment's Due Process Clause. Though acknowledging a technical violation of the treaty with China, the Court decided to enforce the congressional action under the "last in time rule," whereby a court would uphold a federal law that conflicts with a treaty even if it violates international law.[210] In subsequent cases, the Supreme Court iterated Congress's power to regulate the rights of immigrants, which was deemed an inherent power of the government to protect itself from foreign threats. In practice, then as now, the foreign threat was typically categorized in racial constructions as non-White.[211]

Chapter 5 illustrates how two of the three classic means of attaining citizenship—*jus soli* (acquisition of the status by birth by being in this country) and *jus sanguinis* (acquisition of the status by having a U.S. citizen for a parent)—were not sufficient for the attainment of full or equal citizenship status for a wide variety of people of color, including the indigenous people of the United States and the inhabitants of the island conquests. Thus, the pernicious and lesser-known side of the citizenship duality has perverted the long-standing tradition of birthright citizenship.

A New Vision of Citizenship?

On June 12, 2008, your country's Supreme Court ruled that a few hundred detainees held at an off-shore military base had the constitutional right to challenge their imprisonment in federal court by writ of habeas corpus, striking down the alternative military review process established by your country's congressional and executive branches for the so-called enemy combatants. Though the decision was from a divided Court (5-4 decision) and led the headlines in print and on conservative talk shows, your country's civil rights organizations, such as the Centre for Constitutional Rights, declared the decision "a historic victory for Executive accountability."

Despite this purported civil rights victory, the media and pundits alike failed to recognize that the decision unfortunately also had the consequence of confirming the denial of civil rights to millions of your country's citizens. Specifically, in reaching its decision concerning the rights of these prisoners, the Court also endorsed your country's expansionist past, which resulted in maintaining millions of your citizens in a subordinate or second-class citizenship status.

The citizens who remained disenfranchised by this decision were the inhabitants of your country's overseas island conquests acquired at the turn of the nineteenth and twentieth centuries. The inhabitants of these lands were never afforded the complement of constitutional rights their mainland counterparts enjoy. Surprisingly, there was no mention in the media or even academic circles concerning the maintenance of this subordinate status for millions of your countrymen and women. The illusion of membership and equality of citizenship remain intact.

Fact or Fiction?

Unfortunately, not unlike the fictional tale set forth in the beginning of this book, the above hypothetical is based on actual events. In *Boumediene v. Bush*,[1] the Supreme Court of the United States recognized certain constitutional rights for the detainees in Guantanamo Bay, but in doing so, further confirmed the disenfranchised status of millions of U.S. citizens living in U.S. dependent territories. The reason why the Court, in an essentially criminal case pertaining to noncitizens, dealt with the rights of overseas-island-inhabitant U.S. citizens is that the government argued that the Constitution did not fully apply abroad.[2] The Court therefore was compelled to address the Constitution's extraterritorial application. The Court specifically addressed one of the subjects of this book's grouping of subordinate citizens, stating, "Fundamental questions regarding the Constitution's geographic scope first arose at the dawn of the 20th century when the Nation acquired noncontiguous Territories: Puerto Rico, Guam, and the Philippines. . . ."[3]

Citing the Insular Cases addressed in this book, the Court somewhat astonishingly justified the failure to fully apply the Constitution to the U.S. citizens because "the former Spanish colonies operated under a civil-law system, without experience in the various aspects of the Anglo-American legal tradition," which resulted in the Court's creation of the legal fiction of the incorporation doctrine. As mentioned previously, the incorporation doctrine provided that the U.S. Constitution only applied fully to territories destined for statehood.[4] With very little analysis, the U.S. Supreme Court this past year essentially declared that even after a century under U.S. rule of most of these territories, the inhabitants of such lands were still unfit to accept Anglo-American legal concepts. In an analysis that resembles the travesty of the *Dred Scott* case of over a century ago, the highest court of this land formally endorsed the subordinate status of the U.S. citizens of this country's overseas territories. This is just the latest example of a Western democracy endorsing the gradations of membership. Ironically, such an open and bold confirmation of the notion of inferior membership has gone virtually unnoticed in academic or other public arenas.

By rejecting the government's argument that the noncitizens designated as enemy combatants and detained in a nonstate territory have no constitutional rights, the *Boumediene* Court appeared to address the century-long question of whether the U.S. Constitution applied to all U.S. territories. The Court, however, refused to go that far. By failing to do so, it maintained a status quo that subordinates the rights millions of U. S. citizens who happen to reside in lands captured, but not incorporated, by the United States. As a result, millions continue to exist in an alien-citizen paradox, whereby they are U.S. citizens by birth but do not enjoy basic constitutional rights and are not represented in the federal government. For instance, they cannot vote in national elections, i.e., presidential or congressional elections, and only certain fundamental constitutional rights apply to them.

In *Boumediene*, the Court recognized important rights of approximately three hundred foreign detainees but refused to change decisions well over a hundred years old—the Insular Cases—that maintained a less-than-equal status for the millions of U.S. citizen inhabitants of conquered lands such as Puerto Rico or Guam. The Court, somewhat astonishingly, justified these earlier decisions on the basis of the fact that the earlier Court was "reluctant to risk the uncertainty and instability that could result" from applying the U.S. legal system to those lands.

After well over a hundred years of rule, one would think that enough time has passed for these people to understand the Anglo-Saxon legal system, to use the Court's own language. Moreover, after a century of loyal relationships with the United States, the people of these lands, I suspect, are prepared to accept the full application of the U.S. Constitution, or at least to have the right to be first-class citizens of their own sovereign lands. At a time when the rights of a few hundred noncitizens were rightfully championed in *Boumediene*, and during an era when the results of the 2000 presidential election were delayed because of the potential denial of the most basic of rights—suffrage—to a few hundred citizens of Florida, how can it be that millions of U.S. citizens continue to be disenfranchised just because they happen to reside in cities with names such as Ponce, instead of Los Angeles or Hialeah?

Differences or gradations of citizenship are the little-known component of the construct of citizenship. While the term "citizen" is almost universally recognized as including a notion of equality among all those holding the title, the application, as well as a lesser-known aspect of the construct, also condones inequality among those who should or do hold the status. While historically these differences between the members of a society often manifested themselves in terms of differences in gender or economic class, the differences or stratifications in the domestic arena have more vividly demonstrated themselves when ethnic and racial minority groups sought full and equal membership. Unfortunately, the Supreme Court and Congress have repeatedly refused to grant full membership to individuals from such groups. While these denials have to some extent been ameliorated by constitutional amendments, to this day certain groups, such as the indigenous people of this land and the territorial island people, still hold a formal *de jure* inferior citizenship status. Other groups, such as African Americans, continue to challenge whether the formal grant of citizenship, through vehicles such as the Fourteenth Amendment to the Constitution, granted them full civil and political participation.

The pages of this book have illustrated that although the citizenship concept is largely viewed as inclusive, the thousands of years since the concept's development demonstrate a practice of it being an exclusive and exclusionary tool for Western democracies to define and control themselves. For instance, the classic works of influential theorists such as Aristotle asserted that all citizens were equal and equated the citizenry with the state. Yet very few within the society of Aristotle's construction could be eligible for citizenship. Though the Roman Empire also used citizenship constructs, and in fact granted citizenship in a more inclusive fashion than did the Greeks, even they followed the practice of differentiated membership, and not all Roman citizens were equal.

A basic flaw in contemporary understanding of the ancient and even contemporary writings on citizenship in Western democracy is the belief that the notion of citizen in a democracy should be equated with inhabitants of a society. Nothing could be further from the truth. And this fact is so even from the very beginning of the concept. Women, foreigners, children, and the poor have historically been groups that were inhabitants but were ineligible for citizenship. For instance, during the Dark Ages, a form of the concept of citizenship survived the fall of the Roman Empire, but that status also was exclusionary, largely limited to the all-important merchant class, and even within that class there were some merchant groups, such as the upper guilds, that had greater rights than the so-called lower guilds. The coming of the Renaissance and the Enlightenment theorists ushered in a renewed interest in the active citizenship of the classical period. These writers often based their theories on the importance of equality of citizenship in a democracy. Yet even they were prone to support marginalizing groups such as women into a lower political status. In the great democratic experiment that is the United States, this country followed the classical as well as the Enlightenment philosophies in order to develop its own citizenship theory and practice. Regrettably, this country has also followed the traditional practice of gradations of membership.

This book has thus examined a little-addressed phenomenon concerning the history of citizenship. What emerges from this examination is the fact that despite the repeated inclusive declarations dating back to the term's genesis, not all who have possessed the status, or by definition of the concept should have held the status, have had anything resembling the full complement of rights one would expect from the status. In the domestic arena, despite a constitutional amendment, the Fourteenth Amendment of the United States Constitution, that was premised on equality of membership, and specifically bestows citizenship on all born or naturalized in the United States, and was expressly written to endow African Americans with the status of citizenship, the history of U.S. citizenship reveals that disfavored groups rarely attained citizenship status easily. And when such groups, particularly ethnic and racial minorities, attained the *de jure* status, the United States repeatedly denied full membership or participation in the American body politic. During this country's crucial juridical period exploring the bounds and applicability of citizenship (from roughly 1822 to 1922), the Supreme Court defined citizenship in such a manner as to exclude each and every statistically significant racial minority group within the United States from full or equal citizenship.

This phenomenon of differentiated levels of participation occurred when, in addition to other disfavored groups, African Americans, the indigenous people of this land, and the inhabitants of the territorial islands challenged their status as citizens. Largely basing their decisions on racist and xenophobic notions, the Court and Congress disenfranchised these groups. Though some may trumpet the election of this country's first African American president in order to argue that racism has ended or that at the very least there are no valid arguments that there are stratifications in the membership of U.S. citizens, the lives lived by and accounts of millions of people of color in this land will probably suggest otherwise.

Moreover, as this book has sought to demonstrate, the subordinate rights of the millions of United States citizens who reside in this country's overseas territories unquestionably establish that there are formal gradations of membership within this land. Moreover, to this day, some within this society, who by the definition of the citizenship construct should be full and equal citizens, continue to have strong arguments that they nonetheless exist in a *de facto* inferior status. As witnessed by the Civil Rights Commission Report on the 2000 presidential election, which established the mass disenfranchisement of thousands of African Americans during the 2000 presidential election, groups such as African Americans may still have reason to doubt whether they do in fact enjoy all the rights associated with U.S. citizenship. Certainly, the election of President Barack Obama suggests that fears of *de facto* subordinates may at worst be a vestige of days gone by, but time will only tell if such optimism is warranted. Perhaps the day has arrived for a new feeling of inclusion for many people of color, and other disfavored groups, within this land. It may very well be that this is indeed the dawn of a new era for citizenship.

In any event, a global history of partial membership and subordinate rights cries out for a truly inclusive notion of citizenship and democracy. A new vision of citizenship is necessary: one in which the proclamations of equality are not just laudable declarations that merely espouse an ideal attainable only for certain groups within a society. The question that remains is, when will constitutional scholars, practitioners, jurists, political leaders, activists, and the populace insist that the stratifications of citizenship come to an end?

This conclusion seeks to be the first, if only a preliminary, step in the achievement of the laudable declarations associated with democracy and its underpinning concept of equal citizenship. It is a basic tenet of the law of remedies, among other sources, that the first step in achieving a relief is to recognize a wrong. This book has gone to great lengths to establish a multimillennia history of inferior rights experienced by those who should have been entitled to full and equal rights as the postulates of democracy seem to demand. Thus, the goal of demonstrating the wrong has perhaps been met.

The next step is for academicians, politicians, and perhaps popular culture leaders to publicly recognize this wrong. The Insular Cases, the history and status of this country's indigenous people, and the disenfranchisement of women should not be studied solely in specialty small seminar law classes. These basic American stories should be known to all students, starting in elementary school. Our country's leaders should then seek to formally recognize the disenfranchised status of the millions of territorial islands citizens. If only for the sake of reconciliation and in order to achieve reparations in the form of acknowledging a wrong, this American shame must come to an end. We must live up to our purportedly universalist ethos of inclusion and equality; otherwise, we live a lie.

The theories of rights-based membership championed by T. H. Marshall should be a starting point. An examination of the limited rights of the indigenous people, territorial people, same-sex couples, and long-term resident undocumented workers needs to be conducted, openly and honestly debated, and, ideally, resolved. Threshold inquiries concerning the justifications for inferior treatment need to be examined. Upon such inquiry, the merits for exclusionary practice will probably not be supported by anything other than bias and fear. On the opposite end of the status quo concerning the citizenship ideal, a growing group of theorists have begun to challenge the propriety and place that citizenship holds in this and other societies. Citizenship theorist Peter Spiro has noted that a growing body of postnational scholarship is challenging citizenship and the classic views of the nation-state as delimitations of human community, posing instead diasporas, social movements, and other nonstate groupings as competing locations of identity and governance.[5]

In light of these new critiques, perhaps this country will rise above the powerful warning of contemporary citizenship theorist Linda Bosniak, who forthrightly questions Western democratic commitments to equality and their sincerity on the subject: "the quest for unmitigated inclusion within the community can therefore serve as a regulative ideal, such inclusion is a fantasy. . . . However ostensibly committed we are to norms of universality, we liberal national subjects are chronically divided over the proper location of boundaries—boundaries of responsibility and boundaries of belonging."[6]

In an effort to establish what will perhaps be a new location for the boundaries of citizenship, I offer the following preliminary proposals for a new vision of citizenship. This new vision will build on the brilliant writings of citizenship theorists mentioned in this book. While not always agreeing with their conclusions or perspectives, this writer appreciates the daunting task of setting boundaries for inclusion and establishing sound justification for such lines of demarcation between the member and the outsider. This new model will seek to build on those impressive works and, ideally, continue a debate that will perhaps one day lead to a truly inclusive model of membership that the rhetoric of citizenship has long championed.

This new model essentially proposes a middle ground between traditional dichotomous constructs of citizenship situated in the locale of national boundaries and the recent innovative, but perhaps too idealistic, calls for rejections of borders. In an effort to invoke the aspirations of a global community, this model will look to international norms in order to provide a baseline or floor of basic human and civil rights. The model will initially turn away from the domestic examination because it is the arena of international norms where courts have appeared to struggle and address the notion of basic minimum rights that should be afforded to individuals irrespective of their membership label or marker. Such a universalist construct has theoretical support from some of the most articulate of liberal thinkers. For instance, Immanuel Kant, in his book *The Fundamental Principles of the Metaphysics of Morals*, addressed what he described as the categorical imperative as a basic tenet for moral or just laws.[7] The so-called imperative would largely be the measure for whether a law is truly good, and in particular whether it is good for the society and not merely an arbitrary determination that is aimed at benefiting only some within a society.[8] Central to his formulation was for society or a decision maker to "act as if the maxim of thy action were to become by thy will a universal law of nature."[9] Thus, central to Kant's thesis of moral laws was that they be universally applied. He observed,

> These are a few of the many actual duties, or at least what we regard as such, which obviously fall into two classes on the one principle that we have laid down. We must be able to will that a maxim of our action should be a universal law.[10]

Though Kant realized that at times universal application of laws could be difficult, he cautioned against deviating from his foundational premise of universalism, particularly when the matters were of significant importance. Such exceptions could lead one to merely create selective exceptions to serve one interest group over another.[11]

Building on the above theoretical foundation, the new vision of citizenship advocated here looks to certain foundational universal principles of minimum rights afforded to residents of lands irrespective of domestic determination of citizenship status. This sort of baseline is sought in large part because as this book has documented, domestic citizenship and immigration laws have often excluded disfavored group irrespective of the fact that the group had ostensibly met the standard for full political membership. In other words, citizenship and related laws have too often been applied selectively and in an exclusionary fashion for them to be an appropriate barometer of minimum basic rights and legal status.

Instead, this work looks to international law pronouncements and decisions that have provided basic minimum universal rights applicable to all within a land, irrespective of the domestic legal status of the individuals in question. For instance, in the Advisory Opinion on the Rights of Undocumented Migrants before the Inter-American Court of Human Rights requested by the United Mexican States, the court had to determine whether certain undocumented workers held basic labor rights based on principles of legal equality embodied in international instruments for the protection of human rights.[12] The decision specifically turned on "the meaning of . . . legal equality."[13] In other words, the decision turned on whether the United States of America could establish in its labor laws "a distinct treatment from that accorded legal residents or citizens that prejudices undocumented migrant workers in the enjoyment of their labor rights."[14] The court concluded that such efforts were in contradiction to basic international norms concerning equality.[15] Specifically, the court stated that "the principle of equality and non-discrimination is fundamental for the safeguard of human rights in both international and domestic law" and that each "state has the obligation to respect and guarantee the labor human rights of all workers, irrespective of their status as nationals or aliens. . . ."[16] The court effectively concluded that all human beings possess certain minimum human rights based upon the notion of equality. Specifically, the court found that

[a]ll persons have attributes inherent to their human dignity that may not be harmed; these attributes make them possessors of fundamental rights that may not be disregarded and which are, consequently, superior to the power of the State, whatever its political structure.[17]

In terms of rights, the court considered equality one such fundamental right. It stated that equality before the law and nondiscrimination "are elements of a general basic principle related to the protection of human rights."[18] In further discussing the importance of equality the court effectively traced Kant's categorical imperative as well the rhetoric of equality commonly associated with citizenship (but, as demonstrated above, often not applied). The court clearly and unconditionally championed the importance of equality before the law. Its pronouncement rings particularly forcefully in the citizenship context. The Inter-American Court forcefully rejected the notion of any validity of unequal treatment premised upon illegitimate notions such as bias. The court, quoting from an earlier inter-American court decision, stated,

The notion of equality springs directly from the oneness of the human family and is linked to the essential dignity of the individual. That principle cannot be reconciled with the notion that a given group has the right to privileged treatment of its perceived superiority. It is equally irreconcilable with that notion to characterize a group as inferior and treat it with hostility or otherwise subject it to discrimination in the enjoyment of rights that are accorded to others not so classified.[19]

The Inter-American Court's decision concerning undocumented workers is incredibly useful in the citizenship context despite the fact that it addressed an issue related to undocumented workers. Though the issue before the court unquestionably is related to that examined here, what is more important is that the court specifically questioned the validity of unequal treatment of individuals based upon membership labels. It rejected disparate treatment whose basis was only an arbitrary determination of preferred categories of inhabitants. That decision mirrors this project, as it not only follows Kant's categorical imperative of universal application of laws but also is premised on the need for equality before the law.

Because the citizenship construct is itself premised on the importance of the equality of all holding the title of citizenship, the construct of citizenship should not be selectively applied if groups that otherwise meet the prerequisites for membership seek full membership. Therefore, the history of denying groups full citizenship in the past, as was the case for African Americans and women, should be condemned and never repeated. Moreover, the contemporary legal fictions that relegate millions of territorial island people to a subordinate citizenship status should be condemned on the basis of theoretical constructs exposed by Kant in his moral imperative and of international norms as seen in the case of the undocumented workers mentioned above. Such a foundation of minimum rights based on the importance of equality and the universal application of laws provides a useful floor for a citizenship construct. This baseline of minimum rights, which is based on international minimum human rights, would have the effect of ensuring that all who are otherwise eligible for full and equal membership actually can attain it.

Additional aspects of the construct of citizenship are needed to ensure that the rights associated with citizenship can actually be achieved. In other words, it is not enough to merely be able to attain the status of citizen, as W. E. B. Du Bois warned well over a century ago in his book *Black Reconstruction*. It is not enough for emancipated people to hold the title of citizen; they must enjoy all of the rights associated with the title.[20] In an effort to continue to look at citizenship as a legal marker that entitles those holding the status to full membership, the works of T. H. Marshall offer guidance. Marshall's tripartite framework of the political, civil, and social rights associated with citizenship remains useful in examining those challenging their status as equals. Marshall noted that the political component of citizenship ensures the rights of participation as seen through suffrage. The social component of citizenship effectively ensures one's access to the rights associated with being a member of the welfare state. The civil component is premised on the notion of equality before the law. These three aspects of the construct continue to provide a sound basis for continuing to examine the rights to and claims for equal and full membership by all claiming to be less than full members of the body politic.

The above vision of citizenship, which looks to both international minimum norms and well-recognized existing domestic frameworks, is one that can ensure that citizenship labels be applied both evenly and universally.

Moreover, said framework is fluid enough to address claims of unequal or unfair treatment based on motivations that are less than legitimate. This last section of this project, while not the longest by any measure, was certainly the most challenging. With some good fortune, this framework will hopefully prompt further discussion and eventually lead to a truly inclusive model for membership. As this book has demonstrated, if current constructs continue to be deployed, uneven and unfair application of an allegedly universalist principal will continue, and millions will remain less than equal.

Notes

CHAPTER 1

1. Ellen S. Podgor, Jose Padilla, and Martha Stewart, *Who Shall Be Charged with Criminal Conduct?*, 109 Penn. St. L. Rev. 1059 (2005); Leti Volpp, *Impossible Subjects: Illegal Aliens and Alien Citizens*, 103 Mich. L. Rev. 1595 (2005).

2. *Hamdi v. Rumsfeld*, 316 F.3d 450 (4th Cir. 2002).

3. *Padilla ex rel. Newman v. Bush*, 233 F.Supp.2d 564 (S.D.N.Y. 2002), rev'd, *Padilla ex rel. Newman v. Rumsfeld*, 352 F.3d 695 (2d Cir. 2003), rev'd, *Rumsfeld v. Padilla*, 542 U.S. 426 (2004).

4. *See, e.g.,* David Cole, *Enemy Aliens*, 54 Stan. L. Rev. 953 (2002); Thomas W. Joo, *Presumed Disloyal: Executive Power, Judicial Deference, and the Construction of Race before and after September 11*, 34 Colum. Hum. Rts. L. Rev. 1 (2002). *See also* "Rights and the New Reality: Self-Inflicted Wounds; Secret Deportation Hearings, U.S. Citizens Denied Due Process While in Custody. These Evoke Memories of Dictatorships and Undermine the Health of Our Democracy," L.A. Times, Sept. 10, 2002, at B12 (mentioning that disparate treatment of Hamdi, Lindh, and Padilla drew questions from Senator McCain and other leaders, including at least one federal judge).

5. Natsu Taylor Saito, *Interning the "Non-Alien" Other: The Illusory Protections of Citizenship*, 68 L. & Contemp. Probs. 173, 208-10 (2005) (arguing Padilla is both an internal Other by virtue of his race and ethnicity, and perceived as an external Other as a result of his conversion to Islam and the political associations attributed to him); Joanna Woolman, *The Legal Origins of the Term"Enemy Combatant" Do Not Support Its Present-Day Use*, 7 J. L. & Soc. Challenges 145, 159-60 (2005); Eric K. Yamamoto, *White (House) Lies: Why the Public Must Compel the Courts to Hold the President Accountable for National Security Abuses*, 68 Law & Contemp. Probs. 285, 313-14 (2005) (explaining that Lindh, a White American from a middle-class family in California, fit the description for enemy combatant, but the government declined to label him as such; Hamdi, a U.S. citizen of Arab descent, and Padilla, a Puerto Rican, did not fit the description but were labeled enemy combatants).

6. While not the focus of this project, a brief discussion of pertinent law relating to the treatment of citizens suspected of disloyalty would be helpful. The leading case on the subject is *Ex parte Milligan*, 71 U.S. 2 (1866), in which the Court addressed the propriety of a military court's jurisdiction over a citizen who was not a member of a military force. The Court held that the military court had no jurisdiction over such a person and rejected the government's argument that the Bill of Rights did not apply during times of war. *Id.* at 118-30. The Court concluded that the military trial violated Milligan's Sixth Amendment right to a trial before an impartial jury and his Fifth Amendment right to a grand jury. *Id.* The second leading case on the subject is *Ex parte Quirin*, 317 U.S. 1 (1942). In that case, departing from *Milligan*, the Court refused to find that either the Fifth or Sixth amendments prevented a naturalized U.S. citizen accused of conspiring with a foreign wartime enemy from being tried by a military

tribunal. The Court found no distinction between citizen and foreign belligerents. *Id.* at 37-38. The Court distinguished *Quirin* from *Milligan* by noting that "Milligan, not being a part of or associated with the armed forces of the enemy, was a non-belligerent, not subject to the law of war. . . ." *Id.* at 45.

7. *See, e.g.,* Juliet Stumpt, *Citizens of an Enemy Land: Enemy Combatants, Aliens, and the Constitutional Rights of the Pseudo-Citizen,* 38 U.C. Davis L. Rev. 79 (2004).

8. At least one other person has recently argued that the "enemy combatant" cases of Hamdi and Padilla have blurred citizenship constructions. *See* Stumpt, *supra* note 7.

9. Akhil Reed Amar, *The Bill of Rights and the Fourteenth Amendment,* 101 Yale L.J. 1193, 1262-84 (1992).

10. Jonathan C. Drimmer, *The Nephews of Uncle Sam: The History, Evolution, and Application of Birthright Citizenship in the United States,* 9 Geo. Immigr. L.J. 667, 667 (1995).

11. Alexander M. Bickel, *The Morality of Consent* 33 (Yale Univ. Press 1975).

12. *Id.*

13. Derek Heater, *Citizenship: The Civic Ideal in World History, Politics, and Education* 291 (Manchester Univ. Press 1990).

14. *The Basic Works of Aristotle* 1176 (Richard McKeon ed., 1941). The Aristotelian construction recognizes that "he who has the power to take part in the deliberative or judicial administration of any state is said by us to be a citizen of that state." *Id.* at 1177.

15. Johnny Parker, *When Johnny Came Marching Home Again: A Critical Review of Contemporary Equal Protection Interpretation,* 37 How. L. J. 393, 396 (1994). Justice Harlan, in *Afroyim v. Rusk,* 387 U.S. 253 (1967), observed, "[the] citizenry is the country and the country is its citizenry." *Id.* at 268 (Harlan, J., dissenting). Chief Justice Waite once declared that citizenship "conveys the idea of membership of a nation." *Minor v. Happersett,* 88 U.S. (21 Wall.) 162, 166 (1875). In other words, citizenship is a broad concept that not only signifies the rights afforded in the Constitution but is also supposed to guarantee an "individual's membership in a political community and the resulting relationship of allegiance and protection that binds the citizen and the state." Note, *Membership Has Its Privileges and Immunities: Congressional Power to Define and Enforce the Rights of National Citizenship,* 102 Harv. L. Rev. 1925, 1932 n.42 (1989). It includes "the sense of permanent inclusion in the American political community in a non-subordinate condition." Jose A. Cabranes, *Citizenship and the American Empire: Notes on the Legislative History of the United States Citizenship of Puerto Ricans,* 127 U. Pa. L. Rev. 391, n.12 (1978). Thus, citizenship signifies an individual's "full membership" in a political community where the ideal of equal membership is theoretically to prevail. Kenneth L. Karst, *Citizenship, Race, and Marginality,* 30 Wm. & Mary L. Rev. 1, 3-4 (1988). Citizenship thus refers not only to delineated rights but to a broad concept of full membership or incorporation into the body politic. A correlative of this concept is a sense of belonging and participation in the community that is the nation. His last component, which contains both legal and conceptual aspects, demonstrates a psychological component of the term. This construction of the term suggests the anointment of citizenship as recognizing an important title that goes to the heart of the individual's feeling of inclusion as well as the collective citizenry's sense of the virtue of this democracy. *See* Cabranes, *supra,* at 5 n.12.

16. Drimmer, *supra* note 10 at 667-68. The scholars can find considerable support in the founding fathers' interpretation of this construct prior to the drafting of the Constitution. For instance, the authors of the Federalist Papers addressed a form of national citizenship in which citizens were to be endowed with equal rights. John Jay, in Federalist No. 2, observed that "to all general purposes we have uniformly been one people—each individual citizen every where [sic] enjoying the same national rights, privileges and protection." The Federalist No. 2, at 10 (John Jay). Madison, in Federalist No. 57, observed, "Who are to be the electors of the Federal Representatives [in Congress]? Not the rich more than the poor; not the learned more than the ignorant; not the haughty

heirs of distinguished names, more than the humble sons of obscure and unpropitious fortune. The electors are to be the great body of the people of the United States. . . . No qualification of wealth, of birth, of religious faith, or of civil profession is permitted to fetter the judgment or disappoint the inclination of the people." The Federalist No. 57 (James Madison).

17. *Ng Fung Ho v. White*, 259 U.S. 276, 284 (1922).

18. *Sugarman v. Dougall*, 413 U.S. 634, 652 (1973) (Rehnquist, J., dissenting).

19. *Perez v. Brownell*, 356 U.S. 44, 78 (1958) (Warren, C.J., dissenting).

20. *Afroyim v. Rusk*, 387 U.S. 253 (1967) (Harlan, J., dissenting),

21. *Minor v. Happersett*, 88 U.S. (21 Wall.) 162, 166 (1875).

22. Hannah Arendt, *The Origins of Totalitarianism* 296 (Harcourt Brace 1979). Arendt was one of the first to recognize that Nazi Germany and the Soviet Union were two sides of the same coin rather than opposing philosophies of Right and Left.

23. Johnny Parker, *When Johnny Came Home Again: A Critical Review of Contemporary Equal Protection Interpretation*, 37 How. L.J. 393, 396 (1994). Here, Parker writes that "[t]he concept of citizenship is fundamental to constitutional interpretation." *Id.*

24. Yaffa Zilbershats, *Reconsidering the Concept of Citizenship*, 36 Tex. Int'l L.J. 689, 690 (2001). Zilbershats, in noting that nationality is the manifestation between an individual and the state, writes that there are no clear criteria for defining this connection. *Id.* at 691. In his words, "There is no clear international law stating in which circumstances a State must confer nationality upon a person and when a person has the right to become a citizen. The uncertainty and lack of definition in international law ensue from the fact that international law has sanctified the principle of State sovereignty and non-intervention on the part of one State in the affairs of another." *Id.* Accordingly, he says that "State sovereignty has primarily been reflected in the power of the State to determine who will be its permanent and preferred members, i.e.,

who will be its citizens. Indeed, every State has established its own rules regarding when, how, and upon whom nationality will be conferred." *Id.*

25. Jose A. Cabranes, *Citizenship and the American Empire: Notes on the Legislative History of the United States Citizenship of Puerto Ricans*, 127 U. Pa. L. Rev. 391, n.12 (1978).

26. Kenneth L. Karst, *Citizenship, Race, and Marginality*, 30 Wm. & Mary L. Rev. 1, 3-4 (1988).

27. Scholars have also agreed that the concept of citizenship is associated with notions of equality. Professor Ackerman observed that "in claiming citizenship, an individual is—first and foremost—asserting the existence of a social relationship between himself and others. More specifically, a citizen is (by definition) someone who can properly claim the right to be treated as a fellow member of the political community." Bruce A. Ackerman, *Social Justice in the Liberal State* 74 (1980). Professor Fox, who recently examined the history of the term, observed that "Madison and the other authors of The Federalist Papers may have had little to say about the substance of . . . citizenship, but they did believe that such a thing existed, that it defined a sphere of equality." James W. Fox, Jr., *Citizenship, Poverty, and Federalism: 1787-1882*, 60 U. Pitt. L. Rev. 421, 439 (1999). James Kettner similarly noted, "revolution created the Status of 'America citizen' and produced an expression of the general principles that ought to govern membership in a free society . . . and it ought to confer equal rights." James H. Kettner, *The Development of American Citizenship, 1608-1870* 10 (1978).

28. This last component, which contains both legal and conceptual aspects, demonstrates a psychological component of the term. This construction of the term suggests the anointment of citizenship as recognizing an important title that goes to the heart of the individual's feeling of inclusion as well as the collective citizenry's sense of the virtue of this democracy. *See* Cabranes, *supra* note 25 at 5 n.12.

29. For an interesting debate on civil rights versus national security post-9/11, read

Thomas E. Baker & John F. Stack, *At War with Civil Rights and Civil Liberties* (Rowan & Littlefield 2005).

30. A well-known example is the ongoing struggle with the caste system of India, a phenomenon acknowledged even in election laws that prevent inciting hatred between the classes of citizens. Brenda Cossman & Ratna Kapur, *Secularism's Last Sigh: The Hindu Right, the Courts, and India's Struggle for Democracy*, 38 Harv. Int'l L.J. 113, 120. Another obvious example is the treatment of Jews in Europe, who have a long history of being accorded less than full citizenship rights. This treatment, dating to early in the Common Era, was memorialized by the Romans in the Theodosian Code of 425 C.E. and Justinian Code of 570 C.E., prohibiting participation in government and restricting life, livelihood, and property ownership. Norman F. Cantor, *The Sacred Chain: The History of the Jews* 110 (HarperCollins 1994). Indeed, the Justinian Code prescribed death for those who broke provisions requiring particular religious affiliations for all citizens. Thomas M. Franck, *Is Personal Freedom a Western Value?*, 91 Am. J. Int'l L. 593, 609 n.100 (1997).

31. While a host of reasons for these forms will be suggested, the fact remains that despite the rhetoric of equality and egalitarianism, American citizens live under differing models of incorporation and participation. *See* Ediberto Román, *Members and Outsiders:An Examination of the Models of United States Citizenship as Well as Questions concerning European Union Citizenship*, 9 U. Miami Int'l & Comp. L. Rev. 81, 88 (2000).

32. Engin F. Isin, *Being Political: Genealogies of Citizenship* 1 (Univ. Minn. Press 2002).

33. Derek Heater, *A Brief History of Citizenship* 3 (NYU Press 2004).

34. *See, e. g.*, Margaret R Somers, *Rights, Relationality, Membership: Rethinking the Making and Meaning of Citizenship*, 19 Law & Social Inquiry 63 (1994); Nancy Fraser and Linda Gordon, Civil Citizenship against Social Citizenship?, in *The Condition of Citizenship* (Bart van Steenbergen, ed., Sage 1994).

35. *Id.* at 4.

36. Peter Riesenberg, *Citizenship in the Western Tradition* xv (N.C. Univ. Press 1992).

37. *Id.*

38. Linda Bosniak, *The Citizen and the Alien* (Princeton Univ. Press 2006).

39. *Id.* at 124.

40. *Id.* at 136-39.

41. When reading Professor Bosniak's forward-looking approach, I was reminded of the construction of membership I witnessed during my youth in the series *Star Trek*. I was a fan of the rational-thinking Spock, and perhaps my cynicism will subside in favor of a coherent framework.

42. *See, e.g.*, Sedition Act of 1798, ch. 73, 1 Stat. 596 (expired 1891) (making it a federal offense to make false criticisms of the government or its officials, or to excite hatred of the people of the United States); *Ex parte Milligan*, 71 U.S. 2 (1866) (invalidating President Lincoln's suspension of the writ of habeas corpus); *Schenck v. United States*, 249 U.S. 47 (1919) (the World War I–era prosecution of war critics); *Korematsu v. United States*, 323 U.S. 214 (1944) (upholding Japanese internment); *Dennis v. United States*, 341 U.S. 494 (1951) (upholding the McCarthy-era twenty-year imprisonment of individuals for teaching the works of Marx and Lenin).

43. *See, e.g.*, Arvin Lugay, *"In Defense of Internment": Why Some Americans Are More "Equal" Than Others*, 12 Asian L.J. 209 (2005) (reviewing Michelle Malkin, *In Defense of Internment: The Case for Racial Profiling in World War Two and the War on Terror* (2004)). *See* also Jack Utter, "The Discovery Doctrine, the Tribes, and the Truth," Indian Country Today, June 7, 2000, available at http://www.indiancountry.com/content. cfm?id=2541.

44. Lugay, *supra* note 43 at 209.

45. Raj Bhala, *Hegelian Reflections on Unilateral Action in the World Trading System*, 15 Berkeley J. Int'l L. 159, 187-90 (1997) (describing Hegelian dialectic); Michel Rosenfeld, *Comment: Spinoza's Dialectic and the Paradoxes of Tolerance: A Foundation for Pluralism?*, 25 Cardozo L. Rev. 759, 767-70 (2003) (contrasting approaches to dialectic of Benedict de Spinoza and G. W. F. Hegel).

46. Etienne Balibar, *We, the People of Europe? Reflections on Transnational Citizenship* 50 (Princeton Univ. Press 2004) (describing citizenship as a "dialectic of conflicts and solidarities"); Will Kymlicka, *Politics in the Vernacular: Nationalism, Multiculturalism, and Citizenship* 1 (Oxford Univ. Press 2001) (describing citizenship and naturalization laws as playing out a "dialectic of nation-building and minority rights").

47. *See Ex parte Milligan*, 71 U.S. at 2; *Ex parte Quirin*, 317 U.S. at 1. For a brief review of each, see *supra* note 6.

48. The central thesis here is to expose the fact that the gradations of membership have not merely arisen during the exigencies of war or political crises, but they have always been part of the obstacles faced by disfavored groups seeking full membership.

49. *See, e.g.*, Aya Gruber, *Raising the Red Flag: The Continued Relevance of the Japanese Internment in the Post-Hamdi World*, 54 U. Kan. L. Rev. 307 (2006); Jerry Kang, *Thinking through Internment: 12/7 and 9/11*, 9 Asian L.J. 195 (2002); Natsu Taylor Saito, Symbolism under Siege: Japanese American Redress and the "Racing" of Arab Americans as "Terrorists," 8 Asian L.J. 1 (2001); Leti Volpp, *The Citizen and the Terrorist*, 49 UCLA L. Rev. 1575 (2002); see also Erwin Chermerinsky, *Civil Liberties and the War on Terrorism*, 45 Washburn L.J. 1 (2005); Thomas Healy, *The Rise of Unnecessary Constitutional Rulings*, 83 N.C. L. Rev. 847 (2005); Lee Epstein, Daniel E. Ho, Gary Fing, Jeffrey A. Segal, *The Supreme Court during Crises: How War Affects Only Non-War Cases*, 80 N.Y.U. L. Rev. 1 (2005); Earl M. Maltz, *The Exigencies of War*, 36 Rutgers L.J. 861 (2005).

50. Recent scholarship on the war on terror has raised the questions of whether the concept of citizenship is itself a limit on executive power. *See, e.g.*, Jerome A. Barron, *Citizenship Matters: The Enemy Combatant Cases*, 19 Notre Dame J. L. Ethics & Pub. Pol'y 33 (2005). *See also* Utter, *supra* note 43 (tracing the role of the state as "institutionalized superiority of one people over another, found in the Discovery Doctrine" back to Aristotle).

51. Will Kymlicka & Wayne Norman, *Return of the Citizen: A Survey of Recent Work on Citizenship Theory*, 104 Ethics 352, 352 (1994) (further noting that the concept of citizenship had been out of fashion since the late 1970s).

52. *Id.* The authors suggest that the academic debate is seen as a "natural evolution in the political discourse because the concept of citizenship seems to integrate the demands of justice and community membership—the central concepts of political philosophy in the 1970s and 1980s, respectively. Citizenship is intimately linked to the ideas of individual entitlement on the one hand and of attachment to a particular community on the other. Thus it may help clarify what is really at stake in the debate between liberals and communitarians." *Id.*

53. Aristotle, *Politics* Book III, ch. 5.

54. Benedict R. Anderson, *Imagined Communities: Reflections on the Origin and Spread of Nationalism* (1991); see also Cathrine Powell, *Lifting Our Veil of Ignorance: Culture, Constitutionalism, and Women's Human Rights in Post–September 11 America*, 57 Hastings L.J. 331, 343 (2005) ("We know also from Benedict Anderson's work that culture and community are imagined, often in response to, in solidarity with, or in opposition to colonialism, trade, immigration, and other transnational projects.").

55. Eric Foner, *Who Owns History* 150-56 (2002) (referencing U.S. Const. pmbl).

56. Michael Walzer, *Spheres of Justice: A Defense of Pluralism and Equality* 32 (1983).

57. The focus of this book is on the construction of citizenship in Western societies. Asian, African, and other constructions of the term are beyond the scope of this project.

58. *See* Barron, *supra* note 50 at 34.

59. The once *de jure* and arguably still *de facto* subordinate citizenship status of women may be further explored in several other works. *See, e.g.*, Gretchen Ritter, *Women's Citizenship and the Problem of Legal Parenthood in the United States in the 1960s and 1970s*, 13 Tex. J. Women & L. 1 (2003); Catherine L. Fisk, *In Pursuit of Equity: Women, Men, and the Quest for Economic Citizenship in 20th- Century America*,

51 Buff. L. Rev. 409 (2003); Christine Chinkin & Kate Paradine, *Vision and Reality: Democracy and Citizenship of Women in the Dayton Peace Accords*, 26 Yale J. Int'l L. 103 (2001).

CHAPTER 2

1. Engin F. Isin, *Being Political: Genealogies of Citizenship* 1 (Univ. Minn. Press 2002).

2. Ulrich K. Preuss, *The Ambiguous Meaning of Citizenship* (Dec. 1, 2003) (unpublished paper, presented at the University of Chicago Law School, Center for Comparative Constitutionalism), available at http:// ccc.uchicago. edu/docs/preuss.pdf.

3. J. G. A. Pocock, *The Ideal of Citizenship since Classical Times*, 99 Queens Quarterly 1 (1992)

4. *The Oxford History of the Classical World* 19 (Oxford Univ. Press 1986).

5. *Id.*

6. *Id.* at 207.

7. *Id.*

8. Peter Riesenberg, *Citizenship in the Western Tradition* 3 (N.C. Univ. Press 1992).

9. *Id.*

10. Derek Heater, *A Brief History of Citizenship* 15 (NYU Press 2004).

11. *Id.*

12. *Id.* at 14.

13. Plato, *The Republic* 1 (translated ed. 1963).

14. *Id.*

15. *Id.* at 16.

16. *Id.*

17. *Id.* at 15-16.

18. *Id.*

19. Aristotle, *Politics* Book III ch. 1.

20. Aristotle, *Politics*, 1283b.

21. Aristotle, *Politics*, 1275b.

22. *See* Heater, *supra* note 10 at 17.

23. Pocock, *supra* note 3 at 36.

24. Gary J. Nederman, *Mechanics and Citizens: The Reception of the Aristotelian Idea of Citizenship in Late Medieval Europe*, 40 Vivarium 75 (2002).

25. *Id.* at 76.

26. For an interesting analysis regarding gender fluidity and the blending of the citizenship construct this fluidity caused, *see*

review of David Halperin, *One Hundred Years of Homosexuality*, Diacritics (1986).

27. *Id.* at 76.

28. *Id.* at 78.

29. *Id.*

30. Aristotle, *Politics* 1275a3-20.

31. Nederman, *supra* note 24 at 78.

32. Aristotle, *Politics* 1278a2-12.

33. Nederman, *supra* note 24 at 79.

34. Aristotle, *Politics* 1328b32-41.

35. Pocock, *supra* note 3 at 36.

36. *Id.*

37. *See* Isin, *supra* note 1 at 79.

38. *Id.*

39. *Id.*

40. Michael Grant & Rachel Kitzinger, eds. *Civilization of the Ancient Mediterranean* 457 (Oxford Univ. Press 1988).

41. *See* Isin, *supra* note 1 at 79.

42. William James Booth, *Foreigners: Insiders, Outsiders, and the Ethics of Membership*, 59 Rev. of Politics 259, 259-60 (1999).

43. Philip Brook Manville, *The Origins of Citizenship in Ancient Athens* 11 (Princeton Univ. Press 1990).

44. *Id.*

45. *Id.*

46. *Id.*

47. *Id.*

48. *Id.*

49. *Id.*

50. *See* Booth, *supra* note 42 at 260.

51. *Id.*

52. Even early criticisms of democracy, such as Socrates' questioning of *metics* (resident aliens) being on an equal level with a townsman and a townsman with a *xenos* (foreigner), seem to implicitly acknowledge the virtue and logic of gradations within Greek society. *See* Booth, *supra* note 42 at 261 (quoting Plato's *Republic* at 562e).

53. Isin, *supra* note 1 at 80.

54. *Id.*

55. *Id.* at 78.

56. Erwin Chemerinsky, *Articles and Commentary on Equality: In Defense of Equality; A Reply to Professor Western, 81 Mich. L. Rev. 575 (1983)* (arguing that "no value is more thoroughly entrenched in Western culture than is the notion of equality").

57. Kenneth L. Karst, *Why Equality Matters*, 17 Ga. L. Rev. 245 (1983) (arguing that "implicit in the values of citizenship . . . is the notion of equal membership in the community").

58. Aristotle, *Politics, supra* note 19, ch. 4.

59. *See* Heater, *supra* note 10 at 78 (quoting the *Politics*).

60. *Id.* at 78 (quoting the *Politics*, 1261a10).

61. J. G. A. Pocock, *supra* note 3 at 1 (discussing the Greek origin of "classical" liberalism).

62. Natsu Taylor Saito, *Interning the "Non-Alien" Other: The Illusory Protections of Citizenship*, 68 L. & Contemp. Probs. 173 (2005) (arguing that the World War II Japanese internment was not aberrational, and that the United States is presently repeating the same mistake by "racing" Arab Americans as "terrorists"); Volpp, *Impossible Subjects: Illegal Aliens and Alien Citizens*, 103 Mich. Law. Rev. 1595 (2005) (arguing that post-9/11, United States culture treats individuals of Middle Eastern, Arab, or Muslim descent as racial minorities and accords them reduced respect and protection).

63. Aristotle, *supra* note 19.

64. *Id.*

65. Aristotle, *supra* note 19. Aristotle concedes that this ideal—i.e., that every member of society be a virtuous person—is not possible and that the state is therefore imperfect, in that not every member can be a citizen. He writes, "if the state cannot be entirely composed of good men, and yet each citizen is expected to do his own business well, and must therefore have virtue, still inasmuch as all the citizens cannot be alike, the virtue of the citizen and of the good man cannot coincide. All must have the virtue of the good citizen—thus, and thus only, can the state be perfect; but they will not have the virtue of a good man, unless we assume that in the good state all the citizens must be good." *Id.*

66. *See* Heater, *supra* note 10 at 21.

67. *Id.*

68. *Id.*

69. Isin, *supra* note 1 at 80.

70. *Id.*

71. *Id.*

72. Peter Riesenberg, *Citizenship in the Western Tradition: Plato to Rousseau* 15 (N. C. Univ. Press 1992); *see also* James W. Fox, Jr., *Citizenship, Poverty, and Federalism: 1787-1882*, 60 U. Pitt. L. Rev. 421, 429 (1999) (noting that Greeks developed a construction of citizenship that combined political participation in the *polis* with membership in the *polity*). The first three classes of the society—requiring five hundred, three hundred, and two hundred measures of produce from their land—were eligible to hold offices proportionate to their wealth. Those with less than this wealth were members of the assembly and could serve as jurors. Joseph A. Almeida, *Justice as an Aspect of the Polis Idea in Solon's Political Poems* 10-11 (Boston: Brill 2003).

73. Riesenberg, *supra* note 72 at 6.

74. *Id.* at 45.

75. *Id.*

76. C. Nicolet, *The World of the Citizen in Republican Rome* 17 (P. S. Falls trans., Univ. California Press 1980).

77. Isin, *supra* note 1 at 94.

78. *Id.*

79. Grant & Kitzinger, *supra* note 40 at 564.

80. *Id.* at 565.

81. A. N. Sherwin-White, *The Roman Citizenship* 384 (Oxford Univ. Press 1988).

82. Grant & Kitzinger, *supra* note 40 at 565.

83. *Id.*

84. *Id.* at 568-69.

85. *Id.* at 569.

86. *Id.*

87. David Noy, *Foreigners at Rome* 11 (David Brown 2000).

88. Heater, *supra* note 10 at 30.

89. *Id.* at 30-31.

90. *Id.* at 53. *But see Dred Scott v. Sandford*, 60 U.S. 393, 478 (1856) (Daniel, J., concurring). Justice Daniel argued that the emancipation of a former slave, under Roman law, did not confer citizenship status on the slave. He assumed the status of the "lower grades of domestic residents," which were called "freedmen" in Rome. Justice Daniel further noted that it was the decline of the Roman Empire when citizenship rights were extended; this

resulted in the "proud distinctions of the republic being gradually abolished[.]" *Id.* (quoting Edward Gibbon, *The History of the Decline and Fall of the Roman Empire* vol. 3, chap. 44, at 183 (London 1825).

91. *Scott*, 60 U.S. at 478.

92. *Id.*

93. J. Rufus Fears, *Antiquity: The Example of Rome, in an Uncertain Legacy: Essays on the Pursuit of Liberty* 7 (Edward B. McLean ed., Intercollegiate Studies Institute 1997).

94. E. T. Salmon, *Roman Colonization under the Republic* 117 (Cornell Univ. Press 1970). Some of these gradations were designated by community, its location, and relationship with Rome. *Id.* at 40, 70. In other instances, gradations affected individual non-Romans living within Italy. *Id.* at 102, 117-18. For example, citizenship was withheld from those who could not speak Latin, *id.* at 149, while xenophobia and an "innate conviction of their own superiority" were demonstrated by the continuing expulsion of even enfranchised immigrants. *Id.* at 102.

95. Isin, *supra* note 1 at 101.

96. *Id.*

97. *Id.*

98. Isin, *supra* note 1 at 94.

99. John Wacher, *The Roman World* 685 (Routledge 2002).

100. *Id.*

101. Wacher, *supra* note 99 at 687.

102. *See* Heater, *supra* note 10 at 33.

103. Heater, *supra* note 10 at 33.

104. Nicolet, *supra* note 76 at 26.

105. *Id.*

106. *Id.*

107. *Id.*; *see also* Riesenberg, *supra* note 72 at 58.

108. *Id.*

109. Nicolet, *supra* note 76 at 26 (also describing the limited grants of citizenship as a form of "punishment").

110. For a brief and interesting collection of works discussing how nation-states recognized the concept of citizenship with gradations of membership, read *Privileges and Rights of Citizenship: Law and the Juridical Construction of Civil Society* (Julius Kirshner & Laurent Mayali, eds. 2002).

111. Eventually, as the Athenian empire expanded, Solon and other Greek leaders also admitted new citizens. *See* Donald Kagan, *The Fall of the Athenian Empire* 10 (1999).

CHAPTER 3

1. Dirk Hoerder, Christiana Harzig, & Adrian Shubert, *The Historical Practice of Diversity: Transcultural Interactions from the Early Modern Mediterranean to the Postcolonial World* 203 (Berghahn Books 2003).

2. Derek Heater, *Citizenship: The Civic Ideal in World History, Politics, and Education* 23 (Manchester Univ. Press 2004).

3. Feliks Gross, *Citizenship and Ethnicity: The Growth and Development of a Democratic Multiethnic Institution* 11 (Greenwood Press 1999).

4. *Id.*

5. *Id.* at 53.

6. *Id.*

7. Max Weber, *Economy and Society*, Guenther Roth & Claiu Wittich (eds.), vol 3 (Bedminster Press 1968).

8. *Id.* at 222.

9. *Id.*

10. *Id.*

11. Max Weber, *The City* 55 (Free Press 1958).

12. *Id.*

13. Peter Riesenberg, *Citizenship in the Western Tradition: Plato to Rousseau* 15 (N.C. Univ. Press, 1992).

14. *See* Weber, *supra* note 7 at 55.

15. Keith Faulks, *Citzenship* 21 (Routledge 2000).

16. Heater, *supra* note 2 at 51.

17. *Id.* at 123.

18. *See supra* note 3 at 56-57 (Gross describes the setting of medieval Europe as a sea, with the cities acting as "islands of urban and civic freedom." The city was a community where the individual could find freedom and "relative legal equality," luxuries that were not offered to the serfs or peasants of the countryside.).

19. This gave *de facto* independence to imperial towns in central and northern Italy. *See supra* note 3 at 170.

20. *Id.*

21. *Id.* at 116.

22. *Id.* at 107.

23. *Id.* at 108.

24. *Id.* at 110.

25. *Id.* at 109.

26. Peter Riesenberg, *Citizenship in the Western Tradition: Plato to Rousseau* 95 (N.C. Univ. Press 1992).

27. *Supra* note 3 at 10.

28. *Supra* note 5.

29. Max Weber, *The City* 55 (Free Press 1958).

30. *See* Keith Faulks, *Citizenship* 21 (Routledge 2000) (citing Weber).

31. *Id.*

32. *Id.* at 21.

33. *Id.* (quoting Riesenberg, *supra* note 26 at 187).

34. Elaine Andrews Lialas, *John Dewey's Theory of Citizenship and Community in the Developing American Democracy as Seen through the Philosophy of Pragmatism as a Public Administration Model for the Citizen's Role in Public Governance*. Dissertation, available at http://scholar.lib.ut.edu/theses/available/etd-031599-17395/unrestricted/front/pdf.

35. Derek Heater, *A Brief History of Citizenship* 53 (NYU Press 2004).

36. *Id.* at 54.

37. *Id.* at 55.

38. *Id.* at 56.

39. *Id.* at 57.

40. *Id.*

41. *Id.* at 50.

42. *Id.* at 106.

43. *Id.*

44. Henri Pirenne, *Medieval Cities and the Revival of Trade* 52 (1974).

45. *Id.* at 53.

46. Riesenberg, *supra* note 26 at 106.

47. *Id.*

48. *Id.* at 142.

49. *See* Weber, *Historical Emergence of Citizenship* 228 (1954).

50. *Id.* at 237-40.

51. Riesenberg, *supra* note 26 at 109.

52. *Id.* at 142.

53. *See supra* note 3 at 58-59. Gross explains that although city communities were tightly knit, cultural identity was still very strong. Cities were not inhabited by surrounding peoples indigenous to the land but by people from many lands, and with them came their language and culture. The desire to hold onto one's culture and continue to be a part of one's native land brought the necessity of dual citizenship. And as I have explained in this book, the city offering a form of citizenship to certain citizens not residing within the city was still beneficial in the sense that the citizen probably was still paying taxes to his native city.

54. *See supra* note 26 at 143. Riesenberg goes further and lists such benefits and powers as "legal competence against a foreigner, economic power in a boycott, political power through the legitimate acquisition of a political office, occupancy of which meant security for one's self, family, dependents."

55. *Id.*

56. *See supra* note 3 at 57. Gross mentions the incolae, habitatores, and subjects not as a hierarchy of citizenship but as classes of noncitizens. However, he concedes that as the "laws . . . varied [from city to city, so did] the concept and meaning of citizenship."

57. *See supra* note 26 at 144. Riesenberg discusses these four types of citizenship by looking to the views of such jurists as Barolus, Azo, Jacobus Rebuffi, Baldus, and Riminaldus. He cites the following works: Bartolus, *Opera D.* 50.1.1 (1585); Azo, *Summa C.* 10.38 (1610); Petrus Antiboli, *De muneribus*; Baldus, *Consilia* 4:cons. 445; and Johannes Riminaldi, *Consilia* 3:cons. 479.

58. Riesenberg, *supra* note 26 at 109.

59. *Id.*

60. *Id.* at 60.

61. *Id.*

62. *Id.*

63. *Id.*

64. *Id.*

65. *Id.*

66. *Id.* at 145.

67. Heater, *supra* note 2 at 23.

68. Heater, *supra* note 35 at 51.

69. Riesenberg, *supra* note 26 at 113.

70. *Id.* at 111.

71. *Id.*

72. *Id.*

73. *Id.* at 108.

74. Henri Pirenne, *Economic and Social History of Medieval Europe* 47 (Harvest Books 1956).

75. *Id.*

76. *Id.* at 50.

77. *Id.*

78. *Id.* at 109.

79. *Id.*

80. *Id.*

81. *See* Henri Pirenne, *Mohammed and Charlemagne* (Jacques Pirenne ed., Barnes & Noble Books 1980) (1939) (attributing the rise of Islam and the Arab positioning on the Mediterranean to the rise of the Dark Ages).

82. *See* Edward Gibbon, *The Decline and Fall of the Roman Empire* (J. B. Bury ed., Heritage Press 1946) (1737-1794). (In his book, Edward Gibbon describes Christianity as a cause for the Dark Ages.)

83. *See* Ken Wohletz, *Were the Dark Ages Triggered by Volcano-Related Climate Changes in the 6th Century?*, EOS Trans. Amer. Geophysics Union 48(81), F1305 (2000), available at http://www.ees1.lanl.gov/Wohletz/Krakatau.htm (discussing the possibility of Krakatau being the triggering effect of the Dark Ages).

84. *Id.*

85. *Id.*

86. *Supra* note 5 at 53.

87. *Supra* note 3 at 97.

88. *Id.* at 98.

89. The reference to the term "G_d, " instead of spelling out the word here and below is done purposefully in order to avoid using his name in vain.

90. *Id.*

91. *Id.* at 104.

92. *Id.* at 98.

93. Gross, *supra* note 3 at 55-56.

94. *Id.* at 55.

95. The church's inheritance was not exactly started by the church; it was started with the king of the Franks being crowned Caesar by the Pope.

96. Elaine Andrews Lialas, *John Dewey's Theory of Citizenship and Community in the Developing American Democracy as Seen through the Philosophy of Pragmatism as a Pub-lic Administration Model for the Citizen's Role in Public Governance.* Dissertation, available at http://scholar.lib.ut.edu/theses/available/etd-031599-17395/unrestricted/front/pdf.

97. *Id.*

98. *See* Riesenberg, *supra* note 26 at 88.

99. *Id.*

100. Ernst Curtius, *Curtius' The History of Greece.* Translated by Adolphus William Ward 4:9-10 (Scribner, Armstrong n.d.)

101. *Id.*

102. Lialas, *supra* note 96.

103. *Id.*

104. Curtius, *supra* note 100 at 92.

105. *Id.*

106. Lialas, *supra* note 96.

107. *Id.* at 96.

108. Derek Heater, *Citizenship: The Civic Ideal in World History, Politics, and Education* 23 (Manchester Univ. Press 1990).

109. *Id.* at 44.

110. *Id.* at 23.

111. *Id.* at 24.

112. *Id.* at 46.

113. Quentin Skinner & Bo Strath, *States and Citizens: History, Theory, Prospects* 54 (Cambridge Univ. Press 2003).

114. Riesenberg, *supra* note 26 at 87.

115. *Id.* at 97.

116. *Id.* at 99.

117. Lialas, *supra* note 96.

118. *Id.*

119. *Id.* at 54.

120. *Id.* at 55.

121. *Id.*

122. *Id.* at 106.

123. *Id.*

124. Pirenne, *supra* note 76 at 48.

125. *Id.*

126. *Id.* at 49.

127. *Id.*

128. Riesenberg, *supra* note 26 at 105.

129. Henri Pirenne, *Medieval Cities: Their Origins and the Revival of Trade* 138 (Princeton Univ. Press 1923).

130. Id. at 139.

131. Heater, *supra* note 35 at 54.

132. *Id.*

133. Max Weber, *The City* 55 (Free Press 1958).

134. *Id.*
135. Riesenberg, *supra* note 26 at 55.
136. *Id.* at 124.
137. *Id.* at 46.
138. Riesenberg, *supra* note 26 at 112.
139. *Id.* at 113.
140. *Id.* at 114.
141. *Id.* at 117.
142. Quentin Skinner & Bo Strath, *States and Citizens: History, Theory, Prospects* 66 (Cambridge Univ. Press 2003).
143. *Id.* at 68.
144. *Id.* at 57.
145. Riesenberg, *supra* note 26 at 115.
146. *Id.* at 116.
147. *Id.*
148. *Id.* at 117.
149. Heater, *supra* note 35 at 48.
150. *Id.* at 50.
151. Skinner & Strath, *supra* note 142 at 53.

CHAPTER 4

1. Peter Riesenberg, *Citizenship in the Western Tradition: Plato to Rousseau* 15 (N.C. Univ. Press 1992).
2. *Id.*
3. Derek Heater, *A Brief History of Citizenship* 45 (NYU Press 2004).
4. *Id.* at 44.
5. *Id.*
6. *Id.* at 45.
7. Derek Heater, *Citizenship: The Civic Ideal in World History, Politics, and Education* 25 (Manchester Univ. Press 2004).
8. *Id.*
9. Riesenberg, *supra* note 1 at 188.
10. Heater, *supra* note 3 at 24.
11. *Id.*
12. *Id.* at 46.
13. Bruni, *Funeral Oration*, quoted in H. Baron, *The Crises of the Early Italian Renaissance* 419 (Princeton Univ. Press 1966).
14. Heater, *supra* note 3 at 25.
15. *Id.*
16. *Id.*
17. *Id.* at 24.
18. Riesenberg, *supra* note 1 at 189.
19. *Id.*
20. *Id.*

21. Heater, *supra* note 3 at 53-54.
22. Note that among other things, Italy deviated from classical thinking during the 1930s when it became a fascist state.
23. *Id.*

CHAPTER 5

1. *Id.* at 56.
2. Peter Riesenberg, *Citizenship in the Western Tradition: Plato to Rousseau* 35 (N.C. Univ. Press 1992).
3. *Citizenship in the History of Political Philosophy*, available at http://science.jrank.org/pages/8629/Citizenship-Overview-Citizenship-in-History-Political-Philosophy.html.
4. Riesenberg, *supra* note 2 at 194.
5. *Id.* at 195.
6. *Citizenship in the History of Political Philosophy*, available at http://science.jrank.org/pages/8629/Citizenship-Overview-Citizenship-in-History-Political-Philosophy.html.
7. *Id.*
8. Riesenberg, *supra* note 2 at 194.
9. *Id.*
10. *Id.*
11. *Id.* at 196.
12. *Id.*
13. *Id.*
14. *Hobbes, Locke, Montesquieu, and Rousseau on Government*, available at www.gardenoflearning.com/4philosophersarticle.
15. *Id.*
16. *Id.*
17. Stephen G. Daniel, *Civility and Sociability: Hobbes on Man and Citizen*, available at cat.inist.fr/?aModele=afficheN&cpsidt=12465357.
18. *Id.*
19. *Id.*
20. David L. Wardle, *The Influence of John Locke's Religious Beliefs on the Creation and Adoption of the United States Constitution*, 26 Seattle U. L. Rev. 291, 297 (2002).
21. *Id.* at 297.
22. George M. Stephens, *Locke, Jefferson, and the Justices* 2 (Algora Publishing 2002). *See also* http://www.utm.edu/research/iep/l/locke.htm.
23. Notably, early Americans supplemented Locke with various English philo-

sophical radicals as well as with French bourgeois revolutionaries. *See* David Abraham,
*Liberty without Equality: The Property-Rights
Connection in a "Negative Citizenship" Regime*,
21 Law & Soc. Inquiry 1, 5 (Winter 1996).

24. Http://www.utm.edu/research/iep/l/
locke.htm. The site provides a synopsis of
Locke's *Two Treatises on Government*.

25. John Locke, *The Second Treatise of Government* (J. W. Gough ed., MacMillan 1946)
(1690).

26. *Id.* at §95.

27. *Id.*

28. *Id.* at §88.

29. Annette Nay, *Could the American
Revolution Have Happened without the Age of
Enlightenment?*, available at http://www.three-
peaks.net/annette/Enlightenment.htm.

30. *The Political Philosophy of John Locke
and Thomas Jefferson*, available at Thom-
asHurley.com.

31. Locke, *supra* note 25.

32. *Id.*

33. *The Political Philosophy of John Locke
and Thomas Jefferson*, available at Thom-
asHurley.com.

34. *Id.*

35. Locke, *supra* note 25 at §95.

36. *See Citizenship in the History of Political
Philosophy*, *supra* note 3.

37. *The Political Philosophy of John Locke
and Thomas Jefferson*, available at Thom-
asHurley.com.

38. Locke, *supra* note 25.

39. *The Political Philosophy of John Locke
and Thomas Jefferson*, available at Thom-
asHurley.com.

40. *Id.*

41. E. A. Lailas, *Historical Development of
Citizenship and Community* (1998), available
at http://scholar.lib.vt.edu/theses/available/
etd-031599-173954/unrestricted/etd4.pdf.

42. *Id.*

43. *Id.*

44. *Dred Scott v. Sanford*, 60 U.S. 323
(1857). In *Dred Scott*, the Court had found
that freed slaves could never become members of such a community, and as such, they
were not entitled to its protections. *See also*
Rebecca E. Zietlow, *Belonging, Protection, and*

*Equality: The Neglected Citizenship Clause and
the Limits of Federalism*, 62 U. Pitt. L. Rev. 281,
312, 313 (Winter 2000).

45. "The Lockean-Jeffersonian-Madi-
sonian idea that liberty and the capacity to
participate in public governance alike require
the possession of property clearly prevailed
among the Founders and their successors. To
be sure, what they understood by 'property'
could be expansive: more than 'estate,' it
could include liberties and security, the very
rights on whose basis property could be
accumulated. Thus, there is property in rights
as well as a right to property." *See* Abraham,
supra note 23 at 1.

46. *Id.* at 4, 5.

47. Newt Gingrich, *Preface to* Stephens,
supra note 22 at 3.

48. *Id.*

49. *See generally*, Theodore P. Rebard, *A
Few Words on John Locke*, 40 Am. J. Juris. 199
(1995). The author notes, "for this doctrine
has its own life, and like the work of the
sorcerer's apprentice, has its own, as it were,
vitality." *Id.* at 200.

50. A "positivist" being an adherent to the
doctrine that all true knowledge is derived
from observable phenomena, rather than
speculation or reasoning.

51. *Id* at 200-201.

52. *Id* at 202. In note 10, Rebard refers to
John Searle's *How to Derive "Ought" from "Is,"*
73 Philosophical Review (1964), reprinted
in Filippa Foot's *Theories of Ethics* 101-14
(Oxford Univ. Press, 1967): (1) Jones uttered
the words, "I here promise to pay you, Smith,
five dollars." (2) Jones promised to pay Smith
five dollars. (3) Jones placed himself under
(undertook) an obligation to pay Smith five
dollars. (4) Jones is under an obligation to
pay Smith five dollars. (5) Jones ought to
pay Smith five dollars. It is important to
note, though, that this "obligation" is purely
artificial, and artificial as contingent upon
the ARBITRARY decision to submit to the
rules (themselves arbitrary) of what he calls
"the promising game," which is precisely
analogous to any game, in that while, *e.g.*,
HAVING AGREED TO PLAY BASEBALL
one OUGHT then also abandon one's "at

bat" after three strikes, there is no obligation to undertake to play baseball at all, nor to keep playing baseball. To make himself even clearer, Searle points out that the facts in question here are "institutional facts" and differ from the facts of nature; such facts as are relevant in the "promising game" are connected by merely conventional "constitutive rules." In net effect, then, Searle would have to agree that there is no naturally binding character to a mere contract, and that one is in no way obligated to fulfill or continue a contract.

53. Donna Dickenson, *Property, Women, and Politics* 65 (Rutgers Univ. Press 1997).

54. *Id.*

55. *Id.* at 72.

56. Nancy J. Hirschman & Kristie M. McClure, eds., *Feminist Interpretations of John Locke* 132 (Penn State Univ. Press 2007).

57. *Id.*

58. Barbara Arneil, *Women as Wives, Servants, and Slaves: Rethinking the Public/Private Divide* 1 (Univ. British Columbia Press 1999).

59. *Id.*

60. Carole Pateman, *The Disorder of Women: Democracy, Feminism, and Political Theory* 1 (Stanford Univ. Press 1989).

61. Mary Lyndon Shanley & Carole Pateman, *Feminist Interpretations of Political Theory* 81 (Penn State Univ. Press 1991) (chapter authored by Melissa A. Butler).

62. Dickenson, *supra* note 53 at 75.

63. Susan Okin, *Women in Western Political Thought* 3-4 (Princeton Univ. Press 1979).

64. *Id.*

65. *Id.*

66. Andrea Nye, *Philosophy and Feminism* 4-5 (Twayne 1995).

67. *Id.* at 4.

68. *Id.* at 8 (quoting Nancy Holland, *Is Women's Philosophy Possible?* (Rowman & Littlefield 1990)).

69. *Id.*

70. *Id.* at 8.

71. Citizenship and Immigration Seminar Handout (copies available from the author).

72. *Id.*

73. *Id.*

74. *Id.*

75. *Id.*

76. *Id.*

77. *Id.*

78. Madeleine Dobie, *Foreign Bodies: Gender, Language, and Culture in French Orientalism* 39 (Stanford Univ. Press 2001).

79. *Id.* (explaining that climate was thought to be a factor in justifying slavery). *See also* Chris Nyland, Biology and Environment: Montesquieu's Relativist Analysis of Gender Behaviour in *The Status of Women in Classical Economic Thought* 63, 68 (Robert Dimand & Chris Nyland eds., Edward Elgar Publishing 2003).

80. *Supra* note 2.

81. Bhikhu Parekh, Vico and Montesquieu: Limits of Pluralist Imagination, in *Civilization and Oppression* 55, 66 (Catherine Wilson ed., Univ. Calgary Press 1999).

82. *Supra* note 6.

83. *Id.*

84. Parekh, *supra* note 81 at 64.

85. Madeleine Dobie, *Foreign Bodies: Gender, Language, and Culture in French Orientalism* 55 (Stanford Univ. Press 2001).

86. *Id.* at 41.

87. *Id.* at 40.

88. Nyland, *supra* note 79 at 63, 64.

89. *Id.*

90. *Id.*

91. *Id.*

92. Montesquieu, *Essai Sur Les Causes Qui Peuvent Affecter les Espirits et les Caracteres'*, in Roger Caillois, *Oeuvres Completes de Montesquieu* 45 (Roger Caillois ed., vol. 2. 1951).

93. Nyland, *supra* note 79 at 63, 68.

94. *Id. See* Parekh, *supra* note 81 at 55, 65.

95. *Id.*

96. *Id.*

97. *Id.*

98. *Id.*

99. *See supra* note 86.

100. *Id.* at 74.

101. *Id.*

102. *Id.* at 75.

103. *Id.*

104. *See supra* note 93.

105. Dobie, *supra* note 85 at 52.

106. Nyland, *supra* note 79 at 63, 72.

107. *Id.* at 73.

108. *Id.* at 70.

109. *Id.*

110. Judith N. Shklar, *Political Thought and Political Thinkers* 246 (Stanley Hoffmann ed., Univ. Chicago Press 1998).

111. *Supra* note 93.

112. Montesquieu, *Lettres persanes*, in *Oeuvres completes* 102-3 (Roger Caillois ed., vol. 1. 1951) (1721).

113. *Id.*

114. Nyland, *supra* note 79 at 63, 71.

115. Montesquieu, *supra* note 112.

116. Nyland, *supra* note 79 at 63, 73.

117. *Id.*

118. Montesquieu, *De l'Esprit des lois*, in *Oeuvres Completes* (Roger Caillois ed., vol. 2. 1951) (1748).

119. Nyland, *supra* note 79 at 63.

120. Dobie, *supra* note 85 at 45.

121. Henry Vyverberg, *Historical Pessimism in the French Enlightenment* 166-67 (Harvard Univ. Press 1958).

122. I would like to thank my former research assistant, Stewart Hartstone, for his diligent research efforts with respect to this section.

123. Vyverberg, *supra* note 121 at 167.

124. Jean Jacques Rousseau, *Discourse on the Origin of Inequality* (1992 ed.).

125. *Id.* at 78.

126. *See id.* at 81-82. Like other animals, natural man's primary concern is self-preservation, an instinct Rousseau refers to as *amour de soi*, or self-love, and as such, all of his actions are generally to serve this purpose. The savage man is deprived of any sort of enlightenment if his desires do not go beyond his physical needs. "The only good things he knows in the universe are food, a female and repose, and the only evils he fears are pain and hunger." *Id.* He understands not the concept of moral obligation, as this is said to be a product of social interaction, which, as there is not even a true form of communication at this point, does not exist. Indeed, "males and females united fortuitously according to encounters, opportunities and desires . . . and they separated with the same ease." *Id.*

127. *Id.* at 81.

128. *See id.* at 97. According to Rousseau, man in the state of nature is less strong and agile than some of the other animals in the forest but is "most advantageously organized of all." Whereas most animals have but their own instincts to rely upon, man is able to watch the actions of other animals and assimilate those instincts, allowing man to obtain sustenance from many various sources, and hence, much more easily. More important than man's ability to adopt the instincts of others, however, is his ability to ignore his own. It is in this way that the natural man experiences pure free will. "Nature commands all animals, and the beast obeys. Man receives the same impulsion, but he recognizes himself as being free to acquiesce or resist; and it is above all in this consciousness of his freedom that the spirituality of his soul reveals itself. . . ."

129. *See id.* at 98-99.

130. *See* Zev M. Trachtenberg, *Making Citizens: Rousseau's Political Theory of Culture* 82 (Routledge 1993).

131. *See id.* at 83. Rousseau provides further support for his argument by pointing out that Hobbes's depiction of the natural man could not be accurate because it ignores what Rousseau saw as a universal virtue instilled in all animals: compassion. Citing the aversion of horses against trampling a living body and the distress any creature experiences upon passing a corpse of its own species, Rousseau addressed how compassion, and more specifically pity, takes the place of laws in the state of nature, generally preventing one man from harming another. Thus, Rousseau argued that *amour de soi* prevents man from forming social relationships, while pity subdues any aggression that may come from that instinct. Rousseau concluded part 1 with the "savage man, wandering in the forests without work, without speech, without a home, without war, and without relationships, [as] equally without any need of his fellow men and without any desire to hurt them." Man is independent, man is free, man is happy, and as he is unenlightened to the vanity that society will bring, man is equal. But "[t]he first man who, after fencing off a piece of land, took it upon

himself to say 'This belongs to me' and found people simple-minded enough to believe him, was the true founder of civil society." In part 2 of *The Second Discourse*, Rousseau's account describes how, for some reason unbeknownst to him, historical in context (perhaps food shortages or other hardships), humans began to associate with one another, forming small social groups. It is these unnatural associations that Rousseau considers to be the foundation of societies rife with inequality.

Rousseau acknowledges two different types of inequality: natural or physical inequality and moral or political inequality. Natural inequality consists of the varying physical attributes among men such as "age, health, strength of the body and qualities of the mind or soul." Moral and political inequality "consists of the different privileges which some enjoy to the prejudice of others—such as their being richer, more honored, more powerful than others, and even getting themselves obeyed by others." Rousseau did not attempt to explain the source of natural inequality or if there is some kind of "essential connection between the two types of inequality." In a series of rhetorical questions, he simply argued that natural inequality could not have been a primary cause of the transition to instituted inequality since there were no socially dependent relationships within which to exploit such differences among men. Assuredly, it is the latter of the two—moral or political inequality—that is the main focus of Rousseau's analysis as it is the type that "is established, or at least authorized, by the consent of men." As "the human race spread, men's difficulties multiplied with their numbers." Various climates and locations gave way to regional ways of life, requiring men to become industrious in the name of survival. Those living along the shores created fishing poles while those in the forest invented bows and arrows, and these new resources demonstrated to man his increased superiority over animals. It is this acknowledgment that develops the foundation for one of the main ingredients of inequality: "Thus the first look he directed into himself provoked his first stirring of pride; and while hardly as yet knowing how to distinguish between ranks, he asserted the priority of his species, and so prepared himself from afar to claim priority for himself as an individual."

People regularly gathered outside their huts to socialize, singing and dancing, and people would compare one to another, but more importantly, in doing so, wanted to be looked at themselves. Public esteem was becoming a desired commodity; those who could dance or sing the best became the most highly regarded, and Rousseau declares this to be the first step towards inequality and vice. "From those first preferences there arose, on the one side, vanity and scorn, on the other, shame and envy, and the fermentation produced by these new leavens finally produced compounds fatal to happiness and innocence." Rousseau terms vanity, the new form of self-love, "*amour propre*," representing a drastic change in man's mentality, judging self-worth only through the eyes of others.

132. *Second Discourse, supra* note 124 at 115.

133. *See* Trachtenberg, *supra* note 130 at 88.

134. *Id.* at 122. It is in nascent society that man first develops a sense of morality as well. As people are looking to others to judge their own self-worth, the idea of consideration towards others forms and becomes something of a societal rule; one who intentionally violates it would be punished, often severely. *Amour propre*, or a man's pride, took such a violation as a direct insult, demanding a violent reaction of vengeance. *Id.* This was a time before laws and civil authority, and it was due to fear of harsh punishment and condemnation—the "first duties of civility"—that people would abide by the morals of nascent society.

135. *Id.* at 118.

136. *Id.* at 117.

137. *See id.*

138. *See id.* at 118. (Rousseau posits that natural inequality actually does play a role here: "the stronger did more productive work, the more adroit did better work, the more ingenious devised ways of abridging his labour. . . .").

139. *Id.*

140. *Id.* at 119. Property estates multiplied and eventually reached the point where every estate bordered another, and there was no free land remaining. Those who were previously unable to claim an estate and did not exemplify the qualities necessary to excel became the poor—not because they lost anything, but because they remained the same as others changed around them. However, the poor still needed subsistence, and thus they faced a harsh choice. Some chose to work for it, developing (and rapidly expanding) the dominion-servitude relationship. Others fell into a life of violence and robbery, stealing from the rich—at first motivated by their basic needs, stealing to survive. However, across all man, unbridled passions stifled natural pity, "making men greedy, ambitious and bad."

141. *See id.* at 122.

142. *Id.*

143. *Id.*

144. *Id.* at 124.

145. *Id.*

146. *Id.* at 124-25. Besides, since the right to property is only conventional and of human institution, everyone may dispose at will of what he possesses; but this is not the case with the essential gifts of nature, such as life and liberty, which everyone is allowed to enjoy and of which it is at least doubtful whether anyone has the right to divest himself.

147. *Id.*

148. *Id.* at 129.

149. *Id.*

150. Jean Jacques Rousseau, *The Social Contract* introduction 27 (trans. Maurice Cranston (Penguin, 1968). But see Ben Franklin: "Those who would sacrifice liberty for security deserve neither and will lose both."

151. *See id.* at 137.

152. *Social Contract, supra* note 150 at 61 (emphasis added).

153. The general will is an incredibly important concept. It is further important to note that there is a difference between the will of all and the general will, the former being a simple majority, the latter being the best interests of the whole. Each member of the sovereign commits himself to overcome his own personal will and dedicate himself to the general will instead, even if this means injuring his own private interests. This is what it means in Rousseau's mind to be a moral and virtuous citizen. In the *Second Discourse*, Rousseau argued that the advent of property and civil society destroyed the equality men enjoyed only in the natural state, sending them into a society of misery and inequality. In the *Social Contract*, Rousseau seems to completely change his mind. "[A]lthough in civil society man surrenders some of the advantages that belong to the state of nature, he gains in return far greater ones . . . he should constantly bless the happy hour that lifted him forever from the state of nature and from a stupid, limited animal made a creature of intelligence and a man." He also seemed to suggest that when men formed government and positive law, they agreed to relinquish their liberty in order to achieve the goal of a stable and secure society via a revocable contract. However, Rousseau then argued that the social contract not only prevents this, but improves upon natural equality in that it eliminates natural inequality. "[T]he social pact, far from destroying natural equality, substitutes, on the contrary, a moral and lawful equality for whatever physical inequality that nature may have imposed on mankind; so that however unequal in strength and intelligence, men become equal by covenant and by right." "Whichever way we look at it, we always return to the same conclusion: namely that the social pact establishes equality among citizens in that they all pledge themselves under the same conditions and must all enjoy the same rights."

154. *Id.* at 49. Rousseau discussed slavery within the context of social order, quickly concluding that nobody has a "right" to slavery, and it is rather a condition that while it may be created by force can only be perpetuated by the slave's own cowardice. As Rousseau asserts, men are born "free and equal" and will "surrender their freedom only when they see advantage in doing so." After

dismissing the "Right of the Strongest" as the *sine qua non* for slavery, Rousseau concludes that the duty of obedience can only be created by and owed to a legitimate power, and since no man has a natural authority over another, such legitimate power must be based on covenants. But what kind of covenant would (or could) a man enter into that would oblige him to alienate his freedom? The answer, as Rousseau explains, is none, for there can be no valid covenant between two people where one can say "I hereby make a covenant with you which is wholly at your expense and wholly to my advantage."

Thus, however we look at the question, the "right" of slavery is seen to be void; void, not only because it cannot be justified, but also because it is nonsensical, because it has no meaning. The words "slavery" and "right" are contradictory, they cancel each other out. Whether as between one man and another, or between one man and a whole people, it would always be absurd to say: "I hereby make a covenant with you which is wholly at your expense and wholly to my advantage; I will respect it so long as I please and you shall respect it so long as I wish." (Book I, Chapter 4, p. 58)

"Without expanding uselessly on these details, anyone must see that since the bonds of servitude are formed only through the mutual dependence of men and the reciprocal needs that unite them, it is impossible to enslave a man without first putting him in a situation where he cannot do without another man, and since such a situation does not exist in the state of nature, each man there is free of the yoke, and the law of the strongest is rendered vain." *Id.*

155. *Id.* at 51.

156. Jean-Jacques Rousseau, *Émile* 322 (Barbara Foxley, trans., Aldine Press 1974) (1911) [hereinafter *Émile*].

157. Paul Thomas, *Jean-Jacques Rousseau, Sexist?*, 17 Constructing Feminist Studies: The French 195 (1991).

158. Wollstonecraft's comments in *A Vindication of the Rights of Woman*.

159. *See Second Discourse, supra* note 124 at 112.

160. *See* Thomas, *supra* note 157.

161. *See* Thomas, *supra* note 157 at 202-4.

162. *See Émile.*

163. *See Émile* at 321.

164. *See Émile* at 321.

165. Jean-Jacques Rousseau, *La Nouvelle Héloise* (Judith H. McDowell, trans. Pennsylvania State Univ. Press 1968) [hereinafter *La Nouvelle Héloise*].

166. *La Nouvelle Héloise* at 32.

167. Thomas, *supra* note 158.

168. *Id.* at 202-3, 214. To support this point, Thomas points to the *Second Discourse*'s dedication to the Republic of Geneva, in which Rousseau writes, "Could I forget that precious half of the commonwealth which assures happiness of the other. . . . Lovable and virtuous women of Geneva—the destiny of your sex will always be to govern ours." *Id.* Even confined to the household, women nonetheless have power. "Their power is considerable. It is, however, power that is alternately erotic and maternal." *Id.* Thomas argues that woman's role then is to use her erotic power within the private sphere to help prepare man for his duties in the public sphere. "The exercise of political power, according to Rousseau, is and ought to be the province of men, fortified by the solace, comfort and distraction that women, hearth, and home might provide." *Id.* By exercising her erotic powers and satisfying man's passionate desires, she is able to help man overcome his inner divisions of passion and *amour propre*, enabling him to more clearly abide by the general will. Thus, while women are confined to the household, they are so powerful that they still can and do influence the general will through the exercise of their erotic powers, albeit indirectly. However, Thomas also argues that this power over men creates a double standard: if women exercise such influence to help man, their power can also serve to corrupt man. As man must ignore his vanity in order to serve the general will, and women have the power and responsibility to help subdue that vanity, it only follows that when man is overcome by it during the

exercise of his political powers, it is woman's fault for not exercising her powers to properly control it. Thus, Thomas makes the argument that Rousseau believes, through this logic, that "a large share of the blame for what has gone wrong in humanity's successive wrong turnings can be laid at the door of women." *Id.*

169. *See* Lori J. Marso, *The Stories of Citizens: Rousseau, Montesquieu, and de Stael Challenge Enlightenment Reason*, 30 Polity 435 (1998).

170. *See id.* at 437.

171. *See id.* at 446.

172. *See id.* at 446. Marso also discusses the notion that women might make better "citizens" than men because their established gender role allows them better opportunity to understand the problems of other people, thereby rendering them more equipped to act on behalf of the general will. With this in mind, Marso looks to Julie's character development throughout the story, focusing on how she was loved by all and "listens and speaks to her friends and family in a language that recognizes individual needs and desires." This is something that Rousseau's male citizens generally struggle with, as they are "taught to embody exaggerated traits of masculinity—self-containment, autonomy, impartiality, objectivity, rationality, and detachment." *Id.* Combining Julie's traits with Wolmar's lack thereof, Marso argues that this indicates that Julie may be the better citizen, as because she is able to identify the needs of others, she must have better judgment than Wolmar (Rousseau's man) when it comes to making decisions and acting in the name of the general will. *Id.*

173. Penny Weiss examines Émile and addresses the most common criticism surrounding the book: that the differences between Émile and Sophie's education and training is that Émile's leads to freedom and equality while Sophie's leads to domestic enslavement. *See* Penny A. Weiss, *Sex, Freedom, and Equality in Rousseau's* Émile, 22 Polity 603 (1990). Indeed, Weiss even lists several other commentators' opinions speaking to the same conclusion. Weiss responds that the differences in education given to Émile and Sophie are not predicated on Rousseau's sexism, and further can actually be reconciled. Weiss argues that Rousseau's differential treatment is not based on his belief that there are natural sex differences, but rather that sex roles are created for the social and political ends they stand to serve. She further asserts that the sexes "are educated to become different, but the training of both generally appeals to an identical understanding of the human condition and of what problems political arrangements must address." *Id.*

Weiss goes on to examine and reconcile specific examples from Émile's and Sophie's educational experiences. The physical fitness aspects of their programs are, at face value, in stark contrast. Émile's education focuses on strengthening his body and accustoming him to physical hardships. "No activities are forbidden . . . nothing is too taxing, too dangerous, or too adventurous," and while he was frequently injured, Rousseau asserts that freedom makes up for the wounds. Sophie, on the other hand, is only subjected to "agreeable, moderate, and salutary exercise," and participates in "no games which bruise or injure the skin." *Id.* The common interpretation is that the respective exercises speak to Émile's self-sufficiency and Sophie's dependency: "the weak need assistance and protection, the strong do not and thus can be free." Weiss points out that this interpretation fails to examine the similarities, "pays insufficient attention to the ends of the physical education, and fails to place it in the broader context of Rousseau's politics." *Id.* For example, one of Rousseau's philosophies was to exercise and develop the body before the mind, and both programs, while different in rigor, align with this philosophy. Also, while rejecting education that is only guided by the needs of the future adult, Rousseau does believe that if there is reasonable certainty that a child will encounter a certain situation as an adult, and preparation during youth will reduce the suffering involved, that preparation is justifiable. Émile and Sophie will experience different things as adults, and hence their preparation should vary. Still, the principle forming the education is the same, and not necessarily motivated by pure sexism. Thus, looking to Émile's physical exercise, Weiss notes that as a citizen of a republic, Émile will someday be in the army. Exposing Émile to "hardship in order to create a person . . . who is able to remain healthy in various environments and situations . . . and be free from certain dependencies" is perfectly in tune with Rousseau's principle of future utility, as is Sophie's lack of such preparation. *Id.*

174. *The Parallels between the Enlightenment and the Constitution,* available at jjmonkey1@usa.net.

175. *Id.*
176. *Id.*
177. *Id.*
178. *Id.*
179. *Id.*
180. *Id.*
181. *Id.*
182. *Id.*
183. *Id.*
184. *Id.*
185. *Id.*
186. *Id.*
187. *Id.*
188. *Id.*
189. *Id.*

CHAPTER 6

1. *See Dred Scott v. Sandford,* 60 U.S. 393, 481-82 (1856) (holding that African Americans are not citizens as contemplated by the federal or state constitutions).

2. *See Goodell v. Jackson,* 20 Johns. Rep. 693, 712 (1822) (holding that Indians are not citizens, but are distinct tribes or nations).

3. Natsu Taylor Saito, *Asserting Plenary Power over the "Other": Indians, Immigrants, Colonial Subjects, and Why U.S. Jurisprudence Needs to Incorporate International Law,* 20 Yale L. Pol'y Rev. 427 (2002).

4. *See* Abel A. Bartley, *The Fourteenth Amendment: The Great Equalizer of the American People,* 36 Akron L. Rev. 473,481 (2003) ("Despite adoption of the Thirteenth Amendment, most former slaves found their status

little changed. While the amendment ensured that humans would no longer be considered property, it did not grant equality." Institution of "Black Codes" in many states "returned the belief in sub humans and restored the idea of human chattel. . . . Collectively, the 'Black codes' were intended to reduce the status of African Americans to a level just above slavery and to demolish thoughts of racial equality.").

5. As Justice Ginsburg noted in her dissent in *Adarand Constructors, Inc. v. Pena,* 515 U.S. 200 (1995),

> numerous instances of unequal treatment . . . reflective of a system of racial caste only recently ended, are evident in our workplaces, markets and neighborhoods. Job applicants with identical resumes, qualifications, and interview styles still experience different receptions, depending on their race. White and African-American consumers still encounter different deals. People of color looking for housing still face discriminatory treatment by landlords, real estate agents, and mortgage lenders. Minority entrepreneurs sometimes fail to gain contracts though they are the low bidders, and they are sometimes refused work even after winning contracts. Bias both conscious and unconscious, reflecting traditional and unexamined habits of thought, keeps up barriers that must come down if equal opportunity and nondiscrimination are ever genuinely to become this country's law and practice. *Id.* at 273-74 (references omitted)

6. *See Dred Scott v. Sandford,* 60 U.S. 393, 481-82 (1856) (holding that African Americans are not citizens as contemplated by the federal or state constitutions); *Goodell v. Jackson,* 20 Johns. Rep. 693,712 (1822) (holding that Indians are not citizens, but are distinct tribes or nations); Saito, *supra* note 3. Since the adoption of the Constitution is the clause giving Congress ". . . Power to dispose of and make all needful Rules and Regulations respecting the Territory or other Property belonging to the United States. . . .

" U.S. Const. Art IV § 3. American Indians have long been subject to plenary powers of the United States, variously attributed to the Constitution's war powers (Art. I § 8), treaty powers (Art. II § 2), and commerce clauses (Art. I § 8). *See* Lawrence Baca, "The Legal Status of American Indians," in Volume 4, *Handbook of American Citizens* 230, 231 (Smithsonian 1988). Finally, while the Thirteenth Amendment superseded the U.S. Const. Art. IV § 2 requirement that slaves be returned to their owners, as noted earlier, it did not grant equality to persons of color, hence facilitating adoption of Jim Crow laws in several states, which were ratified by the famous doctrine of "separate but equal" in *Plessy v. Ferguson*, 163 U.S. 537 (1896).

7. Saito, *supra* note 3.

8. *Id.* at 37-47. Despite the likely assumption that the English doctrine of *jus soli* (one who is born within a nation's jurisdiction is a citizen of the country) would govern citizenship rights in America, the United States did not apply this doctrine to racial minorities. Any doubts about these exclusions were clarified in the *Dred Scott* decision, which held that Blacks could not be citizens, even if free persons—a rule until the Civil Rights Act of 1866 and the adoption of the Fourteenth Amendment.

9. *See id.* at 49-77. Even though after 1870 naturalization was open also to Blacks, in only one case did a petitioner for citizenship even attempt to assert a claim other than on the basis of being "White." *See, e.g.,* Ian Haney Lopez, *White by Law* (NYU Press 1996).

10. *See, e.g., United States v. Kagama,* 118 U.S. 375 (1886) (upholding a law that subjected Native Americans to federal law as valid and constitutional; being within the limits of the United States, they are subject to acts of Congress).

11. Saito, *supra* note 3 at 428.

12. 60 U.S. 393 (1856).

13. 163 U.S. 537 (1896) (holding that a statute requiring railroads carrying passengers to provide equal but separate accommodations for White or colored races was constitutional).

14. 112 U.S. 94 (1884) (holding that an Indian born a member of one of the Indian tribes within the United States, which still exists and is recognized as a tribe by the government of the United States, who has voluntarily separated himself from his tribe and taken up his residence among the White citizens of a state, but who has not been naturalized or taxed or recognized as a citizen, either by the United States or by the state, is not a citizen of the United States, within the Fourteenth Amendment).

15. 118 U.S. 375 (1886).

16. 187 U.S. 553, 565 (1903) (holding that Congress may pass laws that are in conflict with treaties made with the Native Americans).

17. These cases grew out of the Chinese Exclusion Act of 1882, which prevented immigration of Chinese laborers. *See* Chinese Exclusion Act of 1882, 47 Cong. Ch. 126, 22 Stat. 58 (May 6, 1882). Upon its original sunset, the law was expanded ten years later to tighten all immigration and travel from China. *See* Act to Prohibit the Coming of Chinese Persons into the United States, 52 Cong. Ch. 60, 27 Stat. 25 (May 5, 1892). For more on the immigration of Chinese into the United States, *see* Waverly B. Lowell ed., National Archives and Records Administration, Paper 99, *Chinese Immigration and Chinese in the United States* (1996), available at http://www.archives.gov/locations/finding-aids/chinese-immigration.html.

18. The Insular Cases were several separate opinions during the first two decades of the twentieth century that determined the status and applicability of the United States Constitution to territories, facilitating U.S. imperialism without granting full citizenship rights to territorial residents. For a revisionist view of the doctrine established by the cases, *see* Christina Duffy Burnett, *United States: American Expansion and Territorial Annexation*, 72 U. Chi. L. Rev. 797 (2005).

19. 118 U.S. 375 (1886).

20. 130 U.S. 581 (1889) (holding that Congress has power, even in times of peace, to exclude aliens from, or prevent their return

to, the United States, for any reason it may deem sufficient).

21. 137 U.S. 202 (1890) (holding that Congress can pass legislation concerning Guano Islands discovered by citizens of the United States, and extending the criminal jurisdiction of the U.S. courts to such islands).

22. 142 U.S. 651 (1892) (declaring constitutional an act by Congress that provides for the exclusion from admission into the United States of certain classes of aliens).

23. 149 U.S. 698 (1893) (reaffirming that the power to exclude or to expel aliens is vested in the political departments of the government).

24. 174 U.S. 445 (1899) (stating that the lands of the Cherokee Nation are not held in individual ownership but are public lands, held for the equal benefit of all the members).

25. 187 U.S. 294 (1902) (holding that full administrative power was possessed by Congress over Indian tribal property).

26. 187 U.S. 553 (1903).

27. 182 U.S. 1 (1901) (holding that upon the ratification of the treaty with Spain, Porto [sic] Rico ceased to be a foreign country and became a territory of the United States, and that duties were no longer collectible upon merchandise brought from that island).

28. 182 U.S. 244 (1901) (holding that because Porto [sic] Rico was not a part of the United States for purposes of Article 1, section 8 of the U.S. Constitution, Congress can impose a duty on goods shipped from Porto [sic] Rico to the United States).

29. 182 U.S. 221 (1901) (holding that Hawaii and Porto [sic] Rico were not foreign countries for purposes of the tariff laws of the United States).

30. 183 U.S. 151 (1901) (holding that on the cession of Puerto Rico to the United States, the United States could no longer levy duties on goods shipped from the United States into Puerto Rico).

31. 183 U.S. 176 (1901) (holding that the Philippines, after their cession to the United States by Spain, was not a foreign country for purposes of the tariff laws of the United States).

32. 190 U.S. 197 (1903) (accepting the cession made by the Republic of Hawaii, and continuing the municipal legislation of the islands, not contrary to the U.S. Constitution, until Congress should otherwise determine).

33. 195 U.S. 100 (1904) (holding that because Congress had enacted a statutory Bill of Rights for the Philippines that prohibited double jeopardy, such provision barred an appellate court from finding a criminal defendant guilty after acquittal by trial court).

34. 195 U.S. 138 (1904) (stating that the right of trial by jury was not extended by the federal Constitution, without legislation and of its own force, to the Philippine Islands).

35. 182 U.S. 392 (1901) (holding that ports in Puerto Rico were ports within the United States for purposes of the U.S. coastwise laws).

36. 258 U.S. 298 (1922) (the Sixth Amendment right to trial by jury does not apply to territories belonging to the United States that have not been incorporated into the union).

37. 130 U.S. 582.

38. 142 U.S. 651.

39. *Id.* at 659.

40. 299 U.S. 304, 318 (1936) (declaring that "the powers to declare and wage war, to conclude peace, to make treaties, to maintain diplomatic relations with other sovereignties, if they had never been mentioned in the Constitution, would have vested in the federal government as necessary concomitants of nationality").

41. *Id.*

42. For a brief history and analysis of this doctrine and its application to American Indians, see Vine Deloria, Jr. & David Wilkins, *Tribes, Treaties, and Constitutional Tribulations* 21-31 (Univ. of Texas Press 1999) (offering a full historical analysis of the relationship between the Constitution and Indians).

43. Saito, *supra* note 3 at 436 (discussing how the plenary powers doctrine has been asserted over Indians and other immigrants).

44. *See United States v. Ritchie*, 58 U.S. 525 (1854) (stating, "From their degraded condition . . . and ignorance generally, the privi-

leges extended to them in the administration of the government must have been limited; and they still, doubtless, required its fostering care and protection").

45. 58 U.S. 525 (1854).

46. *See* David E. Wilkins, *American Indian Sovereignty and the U.S. Supreme Court: The Masking of Justice* 25-27, 45 (Univ. Texas Press 1997) (discussing fifteen landmark cases in which the Supreme Court truncated Indian human rights). *See also* Deloria and Wilkins, *supra* note 42 at 29.

47. *See generally*, Dee Brown, *Bury My Heart at Wounded Knee* (Holt Rinehart 1972) (giving eyewitness accounts of the U.S. government's attempts to acquire Native Americans' land by using threats, deception, and murder); Vine Deloria Jr., *Behind the Trail of Broken Treaties* (Dell 1974) (raising questions about the status of Native Americans within the political landscapes); Gloria Jahoda, *The Trail of Tears* (Random House 1975) (describing how White settlers forced Indian tribes off the Plains).

48. Wilkins, *supra* note 46 at 64.

49. *See* Robert A. Williams, Jr., *The American Indian in Western Legal Thought* (Oxford Univ. Press 1990).

50. *Johnson v. M'Intosh*, 21 U.S. 543, 573 (1823) (stating "the exclusion of all other Europeans, necessarily gave to the nation making the discovery the sole right of acquiring the soil from the natives, and establishing settlements upon it. It was a right with which no European could interfere. It was a right which all asserted for themselves, and to the assertion of which, by others, all asserted").

51. Dan Braveman, *Tribal Sovereignty: Them and Us* 82 Or. L. Rev. 75, 101 (Spring 2003).

52. *M'Intosh*, 21 U.S. at 543.

53. *See* Jack Utter, "The Discovery Doctrine, the Tribes, and the Truth," Indian Country Today, June 7, 2000, available at http://www.indiancountry.com/content.cfm?id=2541. *See also*, Vine Deloria, Jr. & Clifford M Lytle, *American Indians, American Justice* 2-6 (Univ. Texas Press 1983); Deloria and Wilkins, *supra* note 42 at 4-5; Wilkins, *supra* note 46 at 31-32.

54. *Id. See also* Vine Deloria, Jr., *Of Utmost Good Faith* 6-37 (Straight Arrow Books 1971); Utter, *supra* note 53.

55. *See* David H. Getches & Charles F. Wilkinson, *Federal Indian Law: Cases and Materials* 43 (1986). The *M'Intosh* case dealt with a dispute over who had title over a tract of land in Illinois that had previously been inhabited by the indigenous people, specifically, the Piankeshaw Indians. Interestingly, none of the parties in this civil action was an indigenous person. On May 23, 1609, King James I of England established a body politic for the establishment of the first colony of Virginia and granted it powers of government, including the rights to the territory in North America known as Virginia. Great Britain's power over the land known as the colony of Virginia in North America, including the land conveyed by the Piankeshaw, terminated shortly after the deeds were executed. On May 6, 1776, the colony of Virginia became independent of Great Britain. As a result, the exclusive right to the land arguably transferred from Great Britain to Virginia, and Virginia shortly thereafter passed legislation that stated that no person has or ever had the right to buy land from the indigenous without authorization for the benefit of the colony of Virginia. Even though the Piankeshaw Indians occupied and ceded the land, Virginia subsequently claimed it and ceded it to the United States. William M'Intosh, a citizen of Illinois, subsequently bought the same tract of land previously conveyed by the Piankeshaw to Thomas Johnson from the United States. A suit to determine ownership of the land ensued. The district court entered a judgment in favor of the defendant and held the grant by the United States as valid. The Supreme Court agreed, holding that the title of the government was valid and superior to the Indian title. The Court based its decision on the discovery doctrine and the rights of a discoverer to have title to land. In delivering the Court's opinion, Chief Justice Marshall noted that they were admitted to be the rightful occupants of the soil, with a legal as well as just claim to retain possession of it, and to use it according to their own discretion,

but their rights to complete sovereignty, as independent nations, were necessarily diminished, and their power to dispose of the soil at their own will, to whomsoever they pleased, was denied by the original fundamental principle that discovery gave exclusive title to those who made it.

56. *M'Intosh*, 21 U.S. at 594.

57. *Worcester v. Georgia*, 31 U.S. 515 (1832) (holding that the state of Georgia did not have the right to redraw boundary lines negotiated by treaty between the Indian tribes and Congress).

58. Getches & Wilkinson, *supra* note 55 at 43. One provision of Georgia law made it unlawful for a White person to reside within the Cherokee Nation as of the first day of March of 1831 without a license or permit from the governor. It stipulated that a White person without a license residing within the Cherokee Nation and without having taken an oath was guilty of a high misdemeanor. The plaintiff in error, Samuel A. Worcester, was a non-Cherokee missionary who resided on a Cherokee reservation located within the state of Georgia. The president of the United States had given Worcester permission to execute his religious mission on the reservation to teach and preach to the Cherokees. Notwithstanding this authorization, Worcester did not carry a license or permit from the governor of Georgia and had not taken an oath to support the laws of Georgia. On July 15, 1831, authorities arrested Worcester while he was preaching within the boundaries of the Cherokee Nation, but also within the state of Georgia. Worcester was a resident of the Cherokee Nation, which he claimed was out of the state court's jurisdiction. The trial court sentenced Worcester to four years of hard labor. Worcester then sought a writ of error from the Supreme Court of the United States.

59. *Id.* at 557.

60. *Id.* at 561-62.

61. This decision regarding a nonindigenous person's right to become an indigenous citizen without pledging allegiance to a state of the United States might be limited to the facts of this case, where the president of the United States authorized a White person to carry on a religious mission consistent with the American value of teaching the indigenous people. The conflict between the congressional act and the president's granting permission to Worcester played a major role in the Court's decision to recognize indigenous sovereignty and limit the power of the state of Georgia with regard to the right of a nonindigenous person to become a resident of an indigenous nation located within the state of Georgia. It is unclear whether the Supreme Court would have made the same decision if the president of the United States had not authorized the individual to carry on a religious mission in an indigenous nation. As a result of this ambiguity, the Worcester decision regarding the Cherokee Nation's sovereignty may be undermined by the facts, and the indigenous nation's power to allow a nonindigenous person to reside within the indigenous nation without permission from a state of the United States and without having taken an oath to that state might be subject to authorization of the United States.

62. *United States v. Rogers*, 45 U.S. 567 (1846) (holding that Congress may, by law, punish any offense committed in a territory occupied by the Indians and not within the limits of any state). According to the defendant, who was challenging the federal court's jurisdiction, the congressional act authorizing jurisdiction over a crime committed within the Indian land located within United States territory when the crime is committed by a White person or against a White person contained an exception when the crime was committed by an Indian against the property or person of another Indian. According to the Supreme Court, a mature adult could not become a Cherokee Indian voluntarily without the authorization of the United States government. The Court noted that a "white man" can choose to belong to an indigenous tribe, but he is not of the "Indian race" and, therefore, remains under the laws of the United States. As a result, the Court suppressed its prior recognition of indigenous sovereignty and replaced it with the notion of inferiority and foreignness. The indigenous nation's power to recognize a person as an

indigenous citizen diminished while the United States' power to disregard such status when it deems it beneficial for the United States' interests increased. The Cherokees' acceptance of Rogers as one of them was immaterial because the United States was the arbiter over whether one was a member of an indigenous nation. The Court was unwilling to recognize the voluntary expatriation of a United States citizen residing within a territory of the United States. Because of the Court's reluctance to accept the power of the Cherokee Nation to confer citizenship upon a person not born Cherokee, the Court to some extent banned the naturalization process for non-Cherokee United States citizens who desired to become Cherokee citizens. Thus, less than a decade and a half after Worcester's recognition of indigenous sovereignty, the Court had a different vision of indigenous sovereignty—one with limited rights.

63. Id.

64. See Cherokee Nation v. Georgia, 30 U.S. 1 (1831).

65. Id.

66. See Sarah H. Cleveland, Powers Inherent in Sovereignty: Indians, Aliens, Territories, and the Nineteenth-Century Origins of Plenary Power over Foreign Affairs, 81 Tex. L. Rev. 1, 57 (2002).

67. 112 U. S. 94 (1886) (holding that if Native Americans born within the United States had not been naturalized and had not become citizens through any treaty or statute, these Native Americans were not citizens within the meaning of the Fourteenth Amendment).

68. Id.

69. Id. at 95. He had lived in the state of Nebraska for more than six months prior to April 6, 1880, the date of election for city council and other officers; had been a resident of Doublas County for more than forty days; and had resided in the district for more than ten days.

70. Id.

71. Id. at 97.

72. Id.

73. Id.

74. Id. at 100.

75. See Cleveland, supra note 66 at 57 (quoting Elk v. Wilkins).

76. Id.

77. Scott, 60 U .S.393 (1856).

78. Elk, 112 U.S. at 101.

79. Id.

80. See Robert B. Porter, The Demise of the Ongweghoweh and the Rise of the Native Americans: Redressing the Genocidal Act of Forcing American Citizenship upon Indigenous Peoples, 15 Harv. Black Letter L.J. 107 (1999).

81. Jackson v. Goodell, 20 Johns. Rep. 693, 712 ("Though born within our territorial limits, the Indians are considered as born under the jurisdiction of their tribes. They are not our subjects, born within the purview of the law, because they are not born in obedience to us.").

82. Id.

83. United States v. Celestine, 215 U.S. 278 (1909). Van Devanter was clearly speaking of a radically different standard of citizenship for Indians: a diminished citizenship modified by whatever conditions Congress decided to impose. Congress, in bestowing citizenship upon allotted individuals, often against their will, empowered itself with the right to set and, if necessary, to reset the conditions upon which that citizenship was received and which rights or privileges could thereafter be exercised.

84. Id.

85. See United States v. Sandoval, 231 U.S. 28 (1913).

86. Id.

87. See United States v. Nice, 241 U.S. 591 (1916).

88. 187 U.S. 553, 565 (1903) (holding that Congress may pass laws that are in conflict with treaties made with the Native Americans).

89. Id.

90. Id. at 565.

91. Id.

92. Scott, 60 U.S. 393.

93. Shortly after the United States government considered indigenous people to be something other than citizens, the government entered into treaties with tribes in order to maintain a relationship that would

purportedly afford each side a sense of sovereignty. Not long after the United States created the euphemism of sovereignty and entered into treaties with the indigenous people, the United States government ceased to use treaties and simply "told the indigenous peoples what they could and could not do, and where they could do it." As a result of the perception of the indigenous people that they were part of their own sovereign tribes and subject to tribal law, the United States took the position that the federal government could dismiss them as a separate people living in certain sections of America who could be controlled and had no recourse.

Although the United States government had entered into treaties with the indigenous nations, it subsequently passed legislation that disregarded the terms and procedures stipulated in such treaties. For instance, in 1867, the Kiowa and Comanche tribes entered the Medicine Lodge Treaty Act of 1867 with the United States. Article XII of the treaty established a procedure for the cession of a tract of land of an Indian reservation to anyone, including the United States. The procedure required three-fourths of all adult male Indians of the reservation to sign to cede the land. In an October 6, 1892, agreement, the tribes surrendered to the United States the rights to reservation land. The agreement provided for the allotment of land to the indigenous people and the conveyance of a fee simple title to them and their heirs after twenty-five years. In the 1903 case of *Lone Wolf v. Hitchcock*, Lone Wolf and other tribal members challenged an agreement between the United States and 456 male Indians that allowed for the allotment of tribal land and compensation. The basis of the challenge was that the agreement and a congressional act that carried it into effect violated the Medicine Lodge Treaty of 1867 because the indigenous' assent was obtained by fraud and less than three-fourths of the males on the reservation signed the agreement. On June 6, 1901, Lone Wolf filed a complaint that sought an injunction against the secretary of the Interior, the commissioner of Indian Affairs, and the commissioner of the

General Land Office. The complaint was filed in the equity side of the Supreme Court of the District of Columbia for Wolf himself and the tribal members of the Kiowa, Comanche, and Apache Indians in Oklahoma. On June 21, 1901, the Supreme Court of the District of Columbia denied Wolf's application for an injunction and a demurrer was sustained. A few weeks later, the president of the United States proclaimed that the land ceded by the Indians was to be opened for entry and settlement in August of 1901. Wolf appealed the lower court's judgment for the defendant. The court of appeals affirmed that judgment. He appealed again and the Supreme Court accepted the case.

Wolf claimed that the United States engaged in an unlawful taking under the Fifth Amendment of the Constitution. However, the Court found that the tribes did not have a fee simple title and Congress could divest the land without following the procedure required by a prior treaty. Not unlike its conclusion in *M'Intosh,* the Court used the plenary powers doctrine as a tool to justify the naked taking of land from the indigenous. The Court noted, "Congress possessed full power in the matter; the judiciary cannot question or inquire into the motives which prompted the enactment of this legislation."

The Court used a landmark immigration case to justify Congress's power to deal with the so-called foreigners within the United States. Consequently, the Court analogized the status of the indigenous people in the United States to the status of the Chinese immigrants seeking entry into the United States. The Court cited the Chinese Exclusion Cases as primary authority in order to support the congressional agreement that conflicted with a prior treaty. Hence, the Court emphasized the foreign status of the indigenous people and stated that the tribes could only seek relief by appealing to the Congress, not the Supreme Court. In doing so, the Court reaffirmed the dependent status of the tribes by stating that the indigenous people were wards of the federal government.

Many scholars have referred to the impact of *Lone Wolf* for the indigenous as a decision of similar caliber or impact as *Dred Scott* for African Americans. The ultimate impact of *Lone Wolf* is the diminution of indigenous rights regarding treaties and land, and the affirmation of Congress's absolute power over Indian affairs, including the abrogation of treaties. During this era, the Court used similar tortured logic in its decisions subordinating other racial and ethnic minorities, such as *Dred Scott* for African American and the Chinese Exclusion Cases for immigrants, to justify the subordination of indigenous people.

94. Porter, *supra* note 80 at 153.

95. *Id.*

96. Saito, *supra* note 3 at 441.

97. Eventually, the complete disregard for indigenous people's rights gave way to compromises of subordinate citizenship. The eventual process of granting United States citizenship to indigenous people occurred over a considerable period of time. The first step was the grant of citizenship as an "incentive" to remove these people to the West. Thus, some early treaties between the Indian nations and the United States provided for the attainment of citizenship. Congress then began to grant citizenship to certain tribes through legislation. Other efforts were made via treaty with Mexico in the Treaty of Guadalupe Hidalgo, in which the Pueblo Indians were deemed United States citizens by their failure to "choose" Mexican citizenship. Yet another step was through the Allotment Act, where indigenous peoples were granted citizenship upon issuance of an allotment. Under the Allotment Act, tribal lands were extinguished and the Indians who chose to receive allotments were obligated to accept United States citizenship. With the passage of the 1924 Indian American Citizenship Act, the United States government imposed a form of citizenship on all indigenous people and declared them to have concurrent citizenship with their respective tribes. By 1924, indigenous people could become United States citizens through legislation, treaty, allotment, and a patent in fee simple by adopting the habits of civilized life. Even at the time of granting citizenship to the indig-

enous people, the United States expressed the need for assimilation and Americanization.

98. The Supreme Court's treatment of indigenous people for analogizing or distinguishing purposes in dicta has varied. For instance, in *Scott v. Sandford*, the Supreme Court characterized the indigenous tribe in a positive manner. However, this positive treatment appeared merely in dicta and was only used as a tool to differentiate the status of the indigenous from the status of the African Americans with regard to access to citizenship. Professor Wilkins notes that this language "seems to be merely a rhetorical ploy used to diminish the human and civil rights of African Americans." In reality, the Supreme Court has used various tactics to diminish the rights of both African Americans and the indigenous people. Although United States citizens, the indigenous people's status differs from that of the majority of United States citizens with regard to civil, social, and human rights.

99. David E. Wilkins, *African Americans and Aboriginal Peoples: Similarities and Differences in Historical Experiences*, 90 Cornell L. Rev. 515, 522 (January 2005).

100. *See* Willard Hughes Rollings, *Citizenship and Suffrage: The Native American Struggle for Civil Rights in the American West, 1830-1965*, 5 Nev. L. J. 126, 134 (Fall 2004).

101. Peter Spiro, *Beyond Citizenship: American Identity after Globalization* (Oxford Univ. Press 2008) (American identity has always been capacious as a concept but narrowed in its application); *see also* Ediberto Román, *The Alien Citizen Paradox and Other Consequences of U.S. Colonialism*, 26 Fla. St. U. L. Rev. 1 (1998) (examining the anomalous second-class citizenship of the inhabitants of Puerto Rico, who hold a status with attributes of both citizen and foreigner).

102. *See e.g.*, Ediberto Román, *The Other American Colonies: An International and Constitutional Law Examination of This Country's Nineteenth- and Twentieth-Century Island Conquests* (Carolina Academic Press 2006).

103. *Id.*

104. *Downes v. Bidwell*, 182 U.S. 244 (1901).

105. *See* Saito, *supra* note 3.

106. *See e.g.*, Ediberto Román, *The Alien-Citizen Paradox and Other Consequences of United States Colonialism*, 26 Fl. St. L. Rev. 1 (1998) (coining the phrase "alien-citizen paradox" in part because of the legal U.S. citizenship status of this group but also because of the concomitant inferior rights held by this group, such as the inability to vote in national elections).

107. *Id.*

108. *See, e.g., id., supra* note 106 at 1-47 (observing that the residents of Puerto Rico retain an alien attribute despite being United States citizens as they cannot vote for president and vice-president and do not have representation in Congress).

109. *See* Congressional Research Service Memorandum: Discretion of Congress Respecting Citizenship Status of Puerto Rico (Mar. 9, 1989), in 2 *Puerto Rico: Political Status Referendum,1989-1991* 81-85 (Puerto Rico Fed. Affairs Admin. ed., 1992).

110. *See* United States Const. art. IV, §3, cl. 2 (declaring that Congress has the "[p]ower to dispose of and make all needful Rules and Regulations respecting the Territory or other Property belonging to the United States").

111. *See* Treaty of Paris, Dec. 10, 1898, United States–Spain, 30 Stat. 1754.

112. *See id.* at IX, 30 Stat. at 1759.

113. *See* Jose Julian Alvarez Gonzalez, *The Empire Strikes Out: Congressional Ruminations on the Citizenship Status of Puerto Ricans*, 27 Harv. J. on Legis. 309, 318-30 (1990).

114. Official website for U.S. Office of Insular Affairs, available at http://www.doi.gov/oia/firstpginfo/islandfactsheet.htm.

115. *See* Saito, *supra* note 3. Following the Second World War, the United States acquired Japan's effective control over the islands in the Pacific known as Micronesia from the United Nations. It did so by agreeing to become the administrating authority of the Trust Territory pursuant to the Trusteeship Agreement with the United Nations in 1947 (61 Stat. 3301, T.I.A.S. No. 1665,8 U.N.T.S. 189). Pursuant to its agreement with the United Nations, the United States agreed to assist these nations to achieve self-government and independence. After decades under U.S. control, these territories changed their international status to denote autonomy, including the creation of the Commonwealth of the Northern Mariana Islands (90 Stat. 263 (1976) (reprinted in Pub. L. No. 94-241)), the Federated States of Micronesia (90 Stat. 263 (1976) (reprinted in Pub. L. No. 94-241)), the Republic of the Marshall Islands (100 Stat. 3672, 3675, 3676 (1786)), and the Republic of Palau (100 Stat. 3672 (1986) (reprinted in Pub. L. No. 99-658)).Though individually negotiated and purportedly resulting in sovereign states, each entity created or is creating a close, *sui generis* political relationship with the United States.

Despite the attainment of this *sui generis* political relationship, the United States still largely controls these lands. For instance, although Palau sought to be a "freely associated state," when Palau attempted to pass a "nuclear free" constitution, the United States asserted its control over Palau and invalidated the results of the constitutional endeavor. Although the United States acquired the territory pursuant to the United Nations' trust agreement and not pursuant to the Territorial Clause, the United States once again asserted that Congress enjoyed plenary power over the territory. In response to United States pressure, the Palau District Legislature nullified the draft constitution and canceled the scheduled plebiscite. Nonetheless, as a result of a lawsuit filed by supporters of the constitution, the July plebiscite went ahead and 92 percent of the electorate voted in favor of the constitution. The High Court of the Trust Territories, however, refused to certify the results because of the nullifying legislation.

Another example of the compromised sovereignty within these territories includes the Covenant with the Northern Marianas, where the United States maintained limited sovereignty in order to protect its strategic interests. That Covenant also gave the United States authority to conduct the territory's foreign affairs. The United States has used this power to dictate issues beyond foreign affairs. When challenged (as it was with the post–Spanish-American War acquisitions), the United States asserted its authority pursuant to its Territorial Clause powers. Again, this occurred notwithstanding this territory being acquired through the creation of a trust pursuant to the United Nations' trusteeship system, and not through the Territorial Clause. With respect to the Republic of Palau, the United States refused negotiations on the nuclear-free constitution, demanding that it have the right to transport nuclear-powered ships as well as ships and aircraft armed with nuclear weapons in order to carry out its defense obligation. In addition, the compact allowed the United States to use its eminent domain powers over lands for military purposes, but the Palauan government was ordered to pay private citizens for the United States' takings.

116. *See* Treaty of Paris, Dec. 10, 1898, United States–Spain Art. II, T.S. No. 343.

117. *Id.* Art. IX; see also U.S. Const. art. IV, § 3, cl. 2 ("The Congress shall have power to dispose of and make all needful rules and regulations respecting the territory or other property belonging to the United States").

118. Jose Cabranes, *Citizenship and the American Empire* 1 (Yale Univ. Press 1979).

119. *Id. See also* Treaty of Peace, Friendship, Limits, and Settlement between the United States of America and the Mexican Republic, Feb. 2, 1848.

120. Julius w. Pratt, *America's Colonial Experiment* 68 (Prentice Hall 1950).

121. *See* Román, *supra* note 102.

122. *De Lima v. Bidwell*, 182 U.S. 1 (1901).

123. *Id.* at 3. The plaintiff in *De Lima*, D. A. De Lima & Co., paid duties under protest for the importation of sugar from San Juan, Puerto Rico, to the port of New York in 1889. He brought a cause of action in the Supreme Court of New York for back pay of those duties, alleging that they were illegally taken by the collector of the port of New York. The case was removed to the circuit court of the United States after the collector of the port of New York requested the case be removed. The collector demurred and the circuit court sustained the demurrer on the grounds that the complaint failed to state a cause of action and the court lacked jurisdiction. The Supreme Court heard the case on writ of error. At the heart of *De Lima* were the questions of whether Puerto Rico was a foreign country or a domestic part of the United States and whether the transportation of goods, such as sugar, from Puerto Rico to New York constituted importation of goods in the United States.

The *De Lima* Court used the plenary powers doctrine to establish the status of Puerto Rico and subject the island to the will of Congress. The Court noted that section 2 of the Foraker Act, the territories' first organic act, "makes a distinction between foreign countries and Puerto Rico, by enacting that the same duties shall be paid upon 'all articles imported into Porto [sic] Rico from ports other than those of the United States, which are required by law to be collected upon articles imported to the United States from foreign countries. '" The Court analyzed precedent that indicated that a territory in the possession of the United States is not a foreign country.

The *De Lima* Court recognized that Chief Justice Taney held in *Scott v. Sandford* that the Territorial Clause of the Constitution does not apply to territories acquired by the United States after the treaty with Great Britain. However, the Court countered that holding with regard to its application to Puerto Rico by Justice Marshall's extension of the Territorial Clause to Florida while it was a territory in *American Ins. Co. v. Bales of Cotton*. As a result, the Court found that Puerto Rico's status as a territory was supported by precedent. The Court reasoned that Puerto Rico could not be both a domestic and foreign country. Consequently, the Court held that Puerto Rico was a territory of the United States, and the import taxes taken from De Lima for the transportation of sugar from Puerto Rico to New York should not have been exacted. As a result, Congress's power over Puerto Rico includes "the right to acquire territory [and] involves the right to govern and dispose of it." Puerto Rico and its inhabitants have since been subject to the will of Congress in numerous ways.

124. U.S. Const. art. IV, 3, cl. 2.

125. *See e.g., Balzac v. Porto Rico,* 258 U.S. 298 (1922); *Dorr v. United States,* 195 U.S. 138 (1904); *De Lima v. Bidwell,* 182 U.S. 1 (1901); *Goetze v. United States,* 182 U.S. 221 (1901); *Crossman v. United States,* 182 U.S. 221 (1901); *Dooley v. United States,* 182 U.S. 222 (1901); *Huus v. N.Y. & Porto Rico S.S. Co.,* 182 U.S. 392 (1901); *Fourteen Diamond Rings v. United States,* 183 U.S. 176 (1901); Juan R. Torruella, *The Supreme Court and Puerto Rico: The Doctrine of Separate and Unequal* 40 (1985).

126. In this view, "according to the spirit of the Constitution, the subjection of annexed territory to exclusive federal control is an abnormal and temporary stage necessarily preceding the normal and permanent condition of statehood." *Constitutional Aspects of Annexation,* 12 Harv. L. Rev. 291, 292 (1898). This view permitted United States expansion but would accord the newly acquired off-shore territories the same treatment as the continental territorial acquisitions.

127. Ediberto Román, *Empire Forgotten: The United States' Colonization of Puerto Rico,* 42 Vill. L. Rev. 1119, 1120-23 (1997); Román, *supra* note 106 at 3-4.

128. 182 U.S. 244 (1901).

129. 182 U.S. at 247.

130. Arnold H. Leibowitz, *Defining Status: A Comprehensive Analysis of United States Territorial Relations* 3, 7 (1989).

131. *Downes,* 182 U.S. at 247.

132. *Id.*

133. *Id.* at 249.

134. *Id.* at 287.

135. *See id.* at 267-68.

136. *Downes v. Bidwell,* 182 U.S. 244 (1901).

137. *Id.*

138. Efren Rivera Ramos, *The Legal Construction of American Colonialism: The Insular Cases (1901-1922),* 65 Rev. Jur. U.P.R. 225, 246-47 (1996).

139. U.S. Const. art. 1, 8, cl. 1.

140. *See* Leibowitz, *supra* note 130 at 21.

141. *Id.* at 22.

142. *Id.*

143. Román, *supra* note 127 at 1120.

144. *Downes v. Bidwell,* 182 U.S. 244, 287 (1901).

145. *Id.* at 279.

146. *Id.* at 282.

147. *Id.* at 287.

148. *Id.* at 250-51.

149. *See id.* at 251.

150. *Id.* at 287. The Court, nonetheless, acknowledged that Congress's power was subject to the Constitution's "fundamental limitations in favor of personal rights." *Id.* at 268.

151. *See id.* at 302-3 (White, J., concurring).

152. *Id.* at 303 (quoting *American Ins. Co. v. Canter,* 26 U.S. (1 Pet.) 511, 542 (1828)).

153. *Id.* at 302 (emphasis added).

154. *Id.* at 293.

155. *See* Gerald L. Neuman, *Whose Constitution?,* 100 Yale L.J. 909, 961 (1991).

156. *See* Deborah D. Herrera, *Unincorporated and Exploited: Differential Treatment for Trust Territory Claimants—Why Doesn't the Constitution Follow the Flag?,* 2 Seton Hall Const. L.J. 593, 613 (1992) (discussing Justice White's conclusion in *Downes* that "incorporation could not occur merely by the exercise of the treaty-making power; it required congressional legislation"); see also *Downes,* 182 U.S. at 339 (White, J., concurring).

157. *See* Neuman, *supra* note 155 at 961.

158. *See id.*

159. *Downes,* 182 U.S. at 313 (White, J., concurring).

160. *Id.*

161. *See* Ramos, *supra* note 138 at 247-49 (1996). In this impressive work, the author addresses the notion of the conquerer's inherent "'right'" to expand, which is, at least in part, a result of a "perceived 'tradition of expansion,' developed through a century of an almost continuous practice of territorial enlargement throughout the continent." *Id.*

162. *See id.* at 245-50.

163. *Downes,* 182 U.S. at 306 (White, J., concurring). In an eloquent dissent in *Downes,* Justice Harlan courageously objected to the logic and morality of the incorporation doctrine: "The Constitution speaks not simply to the States in their organized capacities, but to all peoples, whether of States or territories." *Id.* at 378 (Harlan, J., dissenting).

164. *Id.* at 306.

165. The label of "alien-citizen" can also theoretically apply equally to the other non-White citizens addressed in the previous section.

166. *De Lima v. Bidwell*, 182 U.S. 1 (1901); *Downes v. Bidwell*, 182 U.S. 244 (1901).

167. *Id.*

168. The question at the heart of the case before the Supreme Court in *Downes* was whether the territory known as Puerto Rico became part of the United States within Article I Section 8 of the Constitution of the United States, which declares that duties shall be uniform throughout the nation. The Court answered this question in the negative: "the island of Porto [sic] Rico is a territory appurtenant and belonging to the United States, but not a part of the United States within the revenue clauses of the Constitution." As a result, the Court found that the Foraker Act constitutionally imposes duties on imports from Puerto Rico. The Court upheld Congress's plenary power over the territory.

169. Gerald L. Neuman, *Strangers to the Constitution: Immigrants, Borders, and Fundamental Law* 100 (Princeton Univ. Press 1996).

170. *See, e.g., Dorr v. United States*, 195 U.S. 138, 139 (1904); *Balzac v. Porto Rico*, 258 U.S. 298, 305 (1922).

171. 195 U.S. 138 (1904).

172. *See Dorr*, 195 U.S. at 142-43.

173. 258 U.S. 298 (1922).

174. *See id.* at 307-9.

175. *See id.* at 309.

176. *Id.* at 310. The *Balzac* Court, somewhat surprisingly, made completely inconsistent statements concerning the citizenship status of the people of Puerto Rico. Despite holding that such citizens did not have a constitutional right to trial by jury under the Sixth Amendment, the Court announced that the grant of United States citizenship to the people of Puerto Rico was "to put them as individuals on an exact equality with citizens from the American homeland." *Id.* at 311.

177. *Id.* at 283.

178. In the remaining Insular Cases, the Supreme Court continued to affirm Congress's plenary power over the territorial people. Aside from *De Lima* and *Downes,* the Supreme Court decided the issue of the applicability of the tariff laws of the United States to Puerto Rico. In *Goetze* v. *United States,* the Court held that Hawaii and Puerto Rico were not foreign countries for purposes of the tariff laws of the United States. The Court extended the notion of Puerto Rico's domestic status in *Dooley v. United States,* where the Court held that on the cession of Puerto Rico to the United States, the United States could no longer levy duties on goods shipped from the United States to Puerto Rico. The Court in *Huus v. Porto* [sic] *Rico* held that ports in Puerto Rico were ports within the United States for purposes of the United States coastwise laws. Although the Insular Cases to some extent reveal an acceptance of Puerto Rico as a domestic territory, the Court emphasized the distinct status of the island and with time acquiesced to differential treatment of the island's inhabitants.

Though several of the Court's decisions recognized certain constitutionally guaranteed rights, such as due process and equal protection, several Supreme Court decisions highlighted a difference in the constitutional safeguards available to the people of an unincorporated territory of the United States, such as Puerto Rico. The Court, in *Balzac v. Porto [sic] Rico,* held that the Sixth Amendment guarantee of a "speedy and public trial, by an impartial jury" in criminal prosecution does not apply to the residents of Puerto Rico, unless such rights are made applicable by the local legislature. In *Ocampo v. United States,* the Court held that the Fifth Amendment right to presentment or indictment by a grand jury is inapplicable to the inhabitants of unincorporated territories. In *Dowdell v. United States,* the Court denied a criminal defendant in an unincorporated territory the Sixth Amendment right to confront witnesses. In *Dorr,* the Court held that the Sixth Amendment right to a jury trial was not a fundamental right as applied to the unincorporated territories. Finally, in *Balzac,* the Court reasoned that these rights were not fundamental rights, but procedural rights established by those societies of more sophisticated Anglo-Saxon origin.

179. *See., e.g., United States v. Verdugo-Urguidez*, 494 U.S. 259, 267-68 (1990); *Rosario*, 446 U.S. 651, 653-54 (1980); *Reid v. Covert*, 354 U.S. 1, 13 (1957).

180. 354 U.S. 1 (1957).

181. *See id.* at 13 (stating that the Supreme Court had previously refused to apply certain constitutional safeguards to the territories).

182. *Id.*

183. *Bellei*, 401 U.S. 815 (1971).

184. *See id.* at 386 (holding valid a federal statute that removes citizenship upon failure to comply with a residential requirement).

185. *See id.* at 831.

186. *See* S. REP. NO.1 01-481, at 10-11 (1990) ("Under present law, federal social welfare programs under the Social Security Act such as AFDC, Medicaid, Aid to the Aged, Blind and Disabled, Foster Care and Adoption Assistance, and Social Services block grant operate differently in Puerto Rico than they do in the states. Under statehood, both the amount of the welfare benefits and percentage of the population receiving them would increase."); *see also* T. Alexander Aleinikoff, *Puerto Rico and the Constitution: Conundrums and Prospects*, 11 Const. Commentary 15, 15 (1994).

187. *See Califano v. Torres*, 435 U.S. 1, 2 (1978) (holding that government benefits of a state citizen do not transfer when that citizen moves to Puerto Rico).

188. *See* Social Security Amendments of 1972, Pub. L. No. 92-603, § 303(b), 86 Stat. 1329, 1494 (repealing Titles I, X, and XIV of the Social Security Act with the exception that these titles would still apply to Puerto Rico, Guam, and the Virgin Islands); *see also* 42 U.S.C. § 1308(a)91 (Supp. 1997) (specifying the amount of Social Security payments to Puerto Rico, Guam, the Virgin Islands, and American Samoa); *see also* 41 U.S.C. § 1396(b) (1994).

189. *See* 42 U.S.C. § 1396(b) 91994).

190. Lizabeth A. McKibben, *The Political Relationship between the United States and Pacific Island Entities: The Path to Self-Government in the Northern Mariana Islands, Palau, and Guam*, 31 Harv. Int'l L.J. 257, 258 (1990).

191. *Id.* at 287-89.

192. *See* 48 U.S.C. 1711-1715 (1994 & Supp. V 2000).

193. *Territory of Guam v. Olsen*, 431 U.S. 195, 202 (1977).

194. *Nat'l Bank v. County of Yankton*, 101 U.S. 129, 133 (1879).

195. Neil S. Solomon, *The Guam Constitutional Convention of 1977*, 19 Va. J. Int'l L. 725, 744 (1979).

196. *Id.*

197. *See* Román, *supra* note 102 at 255.

198. Jon M. Van Dyke, *The Evolving Legal Relationships between the United States and Its Affiliated U.S.-Flag Islands*, 14 Univ. Haw. L. Rev. 445, 494-95 (1992).

199. *Id.*

200. *Id.*

201. *Id.* at 496.

202. *Id.* at 498.

203. *Id.*

204. *Id.*

205. Haunani-Kay Trask, *Politics in the Pacific Islands: Imperialism and Native Self-Determination*, 16 Amerasia J. 1, 2 (1990).

206. *Id.*

207. Commonwealth–Covenant to Establish–Northern Mariana Islands, Pub. L. 94-241, 90 Stat. 263 (1976).

208. *Id.*

209. *Id.*

210. *Id.*

211. Haunani-Kay Trask, *Politics in the Pacific Islands: Imperialism and Native Self-Determination*, 16 Amerasia J. 1, 2 (1990).

212. Samoanet, *About American Somoa*, at http://www.samoanet.com/amsamoa/ (last modified Aug. 2, 1997).

213. James R. Thornbury, *A Time for a Change in the South Pacific?*, 67 Rev. Jur. U.P.R. 1099, 1102 (1998) n.284.

214. *Id.* at 1102.

215. *See generally* John Wesley Coulter, *The Pacific Dependencies of the United States* 101 (Macmillan 1957).

216. *Corporation of the Presiding Bishop of the Church of Jesus Christ of Latter-day Saints v. Holdel*, 230 F 2nd 374 (D.C. Circ. 1987).

217. *Id.*

218. *Id.*

219. *Id.* at 1101 (emphasis added).

220. *Id.*

221. *Id.*

222. *Id.*

223. *Id.*

224. *See* Thornbury, *supra* note 213 at 1102.

225. *Id.* at 156.

226. Puerto Rican citizens, with the exception of federal employees, are exempt from federal income taxes on income earned in Puerto Rico. *See* IRC United States § 936 (1994).

227. *See id.; see also Califano*, 435 U.S. at 4-5.

228. 83 U.S. 130 (1872).

229. 208 U.S. 412 (1908).

230. 83 U.S. at 141.

231. Efren Rivera Ramos, *supra* note 138 at 235 (reviewing the role of the United States Supreme Court in justifying United State imperialism). Ironically, the United States, as the colonial sovereign, exercises jurisdiction over the most basic aspect of life in the territory as it does in the states, including communications, currency, labor relations, postal service, environment, foreign affairs, and military defense.

232. *See, e.g.*, Ruth Schwartz Cohen, *More Work for Mother: The Ironies of Household Technology from the Open Hearth to the Microwave* 16-17 (American History Review 1985).

233. *Id.*

234. Lee Ann Banaszak, *Why Movements Succeed or Fail* 3 (Princeton Univ. Press 1996).

235. *Id.*

236. *Id.*

237. *Id.* at 6.

238. *Id.* at 8.

239. *Id.*

240. *Id.* at 8.

241. *Id.*

242. *Id.*

243. Holly J. McCammon, Karen E. Campbell, Ellen M. Granberg, & Christine Mowery, *How Movements Win: Gendered Opportunity Structures and U.S. Women's Suffrage Movements, 1866 to 1919*, 66 Am. Soc. Rev. 49 (Feb. 2001) (providing a full chart delineating the year in which each state granted suffrage to women).

244. *Id.*

245. Cohen, *supra* note 228 at 16-17.

246. *Id.*

247. Rosalyn Terborg-Penn, *African-American Women in the Struggle for the Vote, 1850-1920* 5 (Indiana Univ. Press 1998).

248. *See* Dorothy Roberts, *Killing the Black Body: Race, Reproduction, and the Meaning of Liberty* (Knopf Doubleday 1998).

249. *See* Kate Snow & Dana Bash, CNN Washington Bureau, *Republicans Want Hearings into Vieques Decision* (June 14, 2001), available at http://www.cnn.com/2001/ALL-POlitics/06/14/congress.vieques.02/index.html.

250. *Id.*

CHAPTER 7

1. The historic 1954 *Brown I* decision, which declared the *Plessey* "separate but equal" doctrine unconstitutional, was not followed for quite some time. This in part could be due to the fact that in the *Brown II* decision, where the Court had to declare a remedy, it failed to demand an immediate eradication of segregation in public schools.

2. Malcolm X, *Wisdom of Malcolm X* (Black Label 1991) (Compact Disc Number BLCD3-001).

3. U.S. Const. art. I, §2.

4. 60 U.S. 393 (1856).

5. Natsu Taylor Saito, *Asserting Plenary Power over the "Other": Indians, Immigrants, Colonial Subjects, and Why U.S. Jurisprudence Needs to Incorporate International Law*, 20 Yale L. Pol'y Rev. 427(2002). Despite the likely assumption that the English doctrine of *jus soli* (one who is born within a nation's jurisdiction is a citizen of the country) would govern citizenship rights in America, the United States did not apply this doctrine to racial minorities. Any doubts about these exclusions were clarified in the *Dred Scott* decision, which held that Blacks could not be citizens, even if free persons—a rule until the Civil Rights Act of 1866 and the adoption of the Fourteenth Amendment.

6. *See Id.* at 449-77. Even though after 1870 naturalization was open also to Blacks, in only one case did a petitioner for citizenship

even attempt to assert a claim other than on the basis of being "White." *See, e.g.,* Ian Haney-Lopez, *White by Law* (NYU Press 1996).

7. 60 U.S. 393 (1856).

8. 163 U.S. 537 (1896) (holding that a statute requiring railroads carrying passengers to provide equal but a separate accommodation for White or colored races was constitutional).

9. 112 U.S. 94 (1884) (holding that an Indian-born member of an Indian tribe (that still exists and is recognized as a tribe by the government of the United States) who has voluntarily separated himself from his tribe and taken up his residence among the White citizens of a state, but who has not been naturalized or taxed or recognized as a citizen, either by the United States or by the state, is not a citizen of the United States, within the Fourteenth Amendment).

10. 118 U.S. 375 (1886).

11. 187 U.S. 553, 565 (1903) (holding that Congress may pass laws that are in conflict with treaties made with the Native Americans).

12. These cases grew out of the Chinese Exclusion Act of 1882, which prevented immigration of Chinese laborers. *See* Chinese Exclusion Act of 1882, 47 Cong. Ch. 126, 22 Stat. 58 (May 6, 1882). Upon its original sunset, the law was expanded ten years later to tighten all immigration and travel from China. *See* Act to Prohibit the Coming of Chinese Persons into the United States, 52 Cong. Ch. 60, 27 Stat. 25 (May 5, 1892). For more on the immigration of Chinese into the United States, *see* Waverly B. Lowell ed., National Archives and Records Administration, Paper 99, *Chinese Immigration and Chinese in the United States*, (1996), available at http://www.archives.gov/locations/finding-aids/chinese-immigration.html.

13. The Insular Cases determined the status and applicability of the United States Constitution to territories, facilitating U.S. imperialism without granting full citizenship rights to territorial residents. For a revisionist view of the doctrine established by the cases, *see* Christina Duffy Burnett, *United States:*

American Expansion and Territorial Annexation, 72 U. Chi. L. Rev. 797 (2005).

14. Samuel Delany has written on how gay rights and the civil rights movement worked hand in hand at one point in the 1960s. *See Dangerous Liasions* (New Press 2003). Citizenship gradations based on sexuality certainly call for a contemporary (and. perhaps unexpectedly, a not-so-contemporary) analysis.

15. Jonathan C. Drimmer, *The Nephews of Uncle Sam: The History, Evolution, and Application of Birthright Citizenship in the United States,* 9 Geo. Immigr. L.J. 667, 691-94 (1995).

16. *Scott v. Sandford,* 60 U.S. 393 (1856).

17. *Id.* at 404-5.

18. *Id.* at 404. Here, the Court's decision comports with a decades-old opinion of United States Attorney General William Wirt. When asked by President Monroe whether free Negroes in Virginia were citizens, Wirt responded, "I am of the opinion that the Constitution, by the description of 'citizens of the United States,' intended those only who enjoyed the full and equal privileges of white citizens in the State of their residence. . . . Then, free people of color in Virginia are not citizens of the United States." 1 U.S. Op. Atty. Gen. 507, quoted in John Pearson Roche, *The Quest for the Dream: The Development of Civil Rights and Human Relations* 18 (1968).

19. *Scott,* 60 U.S. at 407.

20. *Id.* Accepting differing models of membership, the Court refused to recognize African Americans, even those born free, as citizens because "[i]t is not a power to raise to the rank of citizen any one born in the United States, who, from birth or parentage, by the laws of the country, belongs to an inferior and subordinate class." *Id.* at 417.

21. *Scott,* 60 U.S. at 404-5.

22. *Id.* at 481-82.

23. *Id.* at 477-78 (for discussion at length of the Roman construction of citizenship, which the Court cited in *Scott* as indicative of the intent of the Founders and, hence, as fundamental to its rationale (as quoted) and ultimate decision).

24. *See* Eric Foner, *Reconstruction, 1863-1877* 25-26 (Harper & Row 1988). Even northern states did not grant equality and full

citizenship to the free Black population prior to the Civil War.

25. *Id.* (citing Leon F. Litwach, *North of Slavery: The Negro in the Free States, 1790-1860* (Chicago, 1961)).

26. Robert J. Kaczorowski, *The Politics of Judicial Interpretation: The Federal Courts, Department of Justice, and Civil Rights, 1866-1876* 5 (Oceana, 1986).

27. W. E. B. Du Bois, *Black Reconstruction in America: An Essay toward a History of the Part Which Black Folk Played in the Attempt to Reconstruct Democracy in America, 1860-1880* 289 (Free Press 1963).

28. *Id.* at 132.

29. *Id.* at 136.

30. *Id.* at 289-90. Reconstruction evoked great fear of political equality in the South, which had already begun passing Black Codes in many of its states. The northern states also did not present a unified front in the protection of the rights of the newly freed slaves. "In the fall elections of 1867 . . . Ohio rejected a Negro suffrage amendment. . . . New Jersey refused to delete 'White' from its suffrage requirements, and Maryland adopted a new law that gave the vote to whites only." John Hope Franklin, *Reconstruction: After the Civil War* 74 (Univ. Chicago Press 1961).

31. *See generally* Stetson Kennedy, *Jim Crow Guide to the U.S.A.: The Laws, Customs, and Etiquette Governing the Conduct of Nonwhites and Other Minorities as Second-Class Citizens* (Greenwood Press 1974).

32. *United States v. Stanley* (Civil Rights Cases), 109 U.S. 3, 11 (1883) (Striking down a statute that would have ensured African Americans equal access to public accommodations, the Court essentially endorsed the subordinate form of membership then held by African Americans.).

33. *Id.*

34. Christopher A. Bracey, *Dignity in Race Jurisprudence*, 7 Journal of Constitutional Law 667 (2005).

35. *Id.; see also* Kennedy, *supra* note 31.

36. Drimmer, *supra* note 15.

37. *Plessy*, 163 U.S. at 551 (rejecting petitioner's argument that the separation of the two races stamped one race with a badge of inferiority).

38. *Id.* at 544. The Court reiterated that notwithstanding the amendment's declarations that "all persons born or naturalized" would be citizens, African Americans were only citizens in name but not citizens in practice. The concepts of "equality of rights" and "equality of opportunity" were inapplicable to them. Drimmer, *supra* note 15 at 396. Even after the constitutional amendment that was enacted to acknowledge their freedom and equality, the Supreme Court reiterated that they were not true citizens, but second-class citizens, or in Malcolm X's words, perhaps still slaves.

39. *Plessy*, 163 U.S. at 544.

40. *Id.* at 544.

41. *Brown v. Bd. of Educ.*, 347 U.S. 483 (1954) (overturning *Plessy v. Ferguson* and the "separate but equal" doctrine, holding that the doctrine had no place in public education and that segregation constituted a denial of the equal protection óf the laws under the Fourteenth Amendment, and holding that separate educational facilities were inherently unequal).

42. I am often reminded of this subordinated status when I recall when a dear friend, who happens to be African American and named Rodney King, oddly enough, wanted to leave my house after a long debate about racial politics at around 2:00 a.m. I told him to stay because the bus station, the New York/New Jersey Port Authority, wasn't very safe. He simply reminded me, "Ed, remember I'm Black, everyone sees me as a criminal, so they are scared—I've got more problems with cops." This saddened me, and still does because my friend, who happens to be the most honest and honorable man I have ever met, could never take off the chains of stigma and subordination. It reminded me that despite my pride and willingness to fight for racial justice, I can hide. Because of racial constructions based on skin color, I can put on a suit or sweats and be the proverbial boy next door. My best friend can rarely, if ever, do that, and I hope I never forget that fact.

43. For a detailed exposé of the too-often-substantiated perception that Blacks often face greater scrutiny at the hands of police officers than Whites, *see* David A. Harris, *The Stories, the Statistics, and the Law: Why "Driving While Black" Matters*, 84 Minn. L. Rev. 265 (1999).

44. Ellis Cose, *The Rage of a Privileged Class* 4-10 (HarperPerennial 1993) ("You feel the rage of people, [of] your group . . . just being the dogs of society."). Note on micro-aggression: often nonminority speakers and actors are oblivious to the repetitive, debasing innuendoes, even unintended disrespectful comments that comprise micro-aggression. *See* Peggy C. Davis, *Symposium: Popular Legal Culture, Law as Micro-aggression*, 98 Yale L.J. 1559 (1989). Prof. Ayres explains micro-aggression as "one of those many sudden, stunning, or dispiriting transactions that . . . can be thought of as small acts of racism, consciously or unconsciously perpetrated, welling up from the assumptions about racial matters most of us absorb from the cultural heritage in which we come of age in the United States." Ian Ayres, *Fair Driving*, 104 Harv. L. Rev. 817 (1991) *quoted in* Richard Delgado & Jean Stefancic, *Critical Race Theory: An Introduction* (NYU Press 2001).

45. U.S. Census Bureau, Data Set, Profile of General Demographic Characteristics: 2000, in *Census 2000 Summary File 1 (SF 1) 100*-Percent Data, at DP-1 (Sept. 2002), available at http://factfinder.census.gov/servlet/QTTable?_bm=n&_lang=en&qr_name=DEC_2000_SF1_U_DP1&ds_name=DEC_2000_SF1_U&geo_id=04000US11.

46. Jasmin B. Raskin, *Is This America? The District of Columbia and the Right to Vote*, 34 Harv. C.R.-C.L.L. Rev. 39, 40 (1999). *See also* Aaron E. Price, *A Representative Democracy: An Unfulfilled Ideal for Citizens of the District of Columbia*, 7 U. D.C. L. Rev. 77 (2003).

47. U.S. Const. amend. XXIII.

48. Amber L. Cottle, *Silent Citizens: United States Territorial Residents and the Right to Vote in Presidential Elections*, 1995 U. Chi. Legal F. 315, 325 (1995).

49. Currently, Congresswoman Eleanor Holmes Norton represents the District of Columbia in this capacity. She is in her tenth term as a congresswoman from D.C.

50. As of this writing, shadow senator Paul Strauss and shadow senator Florence Pendleton serve the District of Columbia.

51. As of this writing, shadow representative Ray Browne serves the District of Columbia.

52. Raskin, *supra* note 46 at 43-44.

53. U.S. Comm'n on C.R., Report, *Executive Summary*, Report on Voting Irregularities in Florida during the 2000 Presidential Election (June 2001), available at http://www.usccr.gov/pubs/vote2000/report/exesum.htm.

54. *Id.*

55. *Id.*

56. The very question of whether the passage of the Fourteenth Amendment and *Brown* ended the vestiges of inferiority reminds me of a sad exchange with a nonminority law professor who was going to teach a Race and the Law seminar after I decided to teach at another school. After he asked to visit my class in order to assist him in teaching the course, he was surprised that one of my assigned books was on the subject of Critical Race Theory. Moreover, he mentioned that he intended to end his Race and the Law course with *Brown I*. Upon hearing him say these things, I almost shed a tear for his future students and nonetheless suggested he read the book concerning Critical Race Theory that I had assigned to my students.

57. Harry Pachon, *Special Report: What Color Is the Constitution? Crossing the Border of Discrimination: Has the Civil Rights Movement Ignored Generations of Hispanics?*, 15 Hum. Rts. Q. 32, 33 (1988).

58. Christine A. Klein, *Treaties of Conquest: Property Rights, Indian Treaties, and the Treaty of Guadalupe Hidalgo*, 26 N.M.L. Rev. 201, 201 (1996).

59. *Id.*

60. *Id.* at 208 (*citing* Richard White, *It's Your Misfortune and None of My Own: A History of the American West* 73 (Univ. Oklahoma Press 1991)).

61. *Id.*

62. Guadalupe T. Luna, *En El Nombre De Dios Todo-Poderoso: The Treaty of Guadalupe Hidalgo and Narrativos Legales*, 5 Sw. J. L. & Trade Am. 45 (1998) (citing to Treaty of Peace, Friendship, Limits, and Settlement with the Republic of Mexico, United States–Mex., 9 Stat. 922 (Feb. 2, 1848)).

63. Klein, *supra* note 58 at 215.

64. Richard Delgado, *Derrick Bell and the Ideology of Racial Reform: Will We Ever Be Saved? And We Are Not Saved: The Elusive Quest for Racial Justice, by Derrick Bell*, 97 Yale L.J. 923, 940 (1988).

65. Luna, *supra* note 62 at 71.

66. Kevin R. Johnson, *An Essay on Immigration, Citizenship, and U.S./Mexico Relations: The Tale of Two Treaties*, 5 Sw. J. L. & Trade Am. 121, 123 (1998).

67. Delgado, *supra* note 64 at 940.

68. David G. Gutierrez, *Walls and Mirrors: Mexican Americans, Mexican Immigrants, and the Politics of Ethnicity* 19 (Univ. California Press 1995).

69. *Id.*

70. *Id.*

71. *Id.* at 45.

72. *Id.*

73. *Id.*

74. *Id.* at 180.

75. *Id.*

76. *See* Kiera Lobreglio, *The Border Security and Immigration Improvement Act; A Modern Solution to a Historic Problem*, 78 St. John's L. Rev. 933, 936-39 (2004).

77. Lauren Gilbert, *Fields of Hope, Fields of Despair: Legisprudential and Historic Perspectives on the Agjobs Bill of 2003*, 42 Harv. J. On. Legis. 417, 427 (2005) ("By 1931, in the midst of the Great Depression, the United States determined that it was time for the Mexicans to depart." The Bureau of Immigration, "which was then under the authority of the Department of Labor, [located and removed] all non-citizens illegally in the United States, targeting particular immigrants involved in labor disputes.").

78. *See* Francisco E. Balderrama & Raymond Rodriguez, *Decade of Betrayal: Mexican Repatriation in the 1930s* 98-99 (Univ. New Mexico Press 1995) (exploring the history of "repatriation" during the Great Depression).

79. *Id.*

80. Kevin R. Johnson, *The Huddled Masses Myth: Immigration and Civil Rights* (NYU Press 2004).

81. *Id.* at 6.

82. *Id.*

83. *Id.*

84. *Id.* at 10.

85. *See generally* Lorenzo A. Alvarado, *A Lesson from My Grandfather, the Bracero*, 22 Chicano-Latino L. Rev. 55 (2001) (providing a vivid and well-documented history of the Bracero Program).

86. *See, e.g.*, Francisco E. Balderrama and Raymond Rodriquez, *Decade of Betrayal: Mexican Repatriation in the 1930s* (Univ. New Mexico Press 1995).

87. Kitty Calavita, *Inside the State: The Bracero Program, Immigration, and the I.N.S.* 19 (Routledge 1992).

88. *See* 57 Stat. 70-73. Extensions, modifications, and additional appropriations were enacted in December 1943 (57 Stat. 643); February 1944 (58 Stat. 11); December 1944 (58 Stat. 853); July 1945 (59 Stat. 645); and April 1947 (61 Stat. 55).

89. *See* Alvarado, *supra* note 85 at 57 (noting how the lack of U.S. government control led to many abuses by domestic employers against immigrant workers).

90. Lobreglio, *supra* note 76 at 937.

91. Barbara A. Driscoll, *The Tracks North: The Railroad Bracero Program of World War II* 56 (Univ. Texas Press 1999).

92. Lobreglio, *supra* note 76 at 937.

93. Driscoll, *supra* note 91 at 56.

94. Gutierrez, *supra* note 68 at 40.

95. Such abuses are prohibited in the International Convention on the Protection of the Rights of All Migrant Workers and Members of Their Families. *See* G.A. res. 45/158 annex, 45 U.N. GAOR Supp. (No. 49A) at 262, Doc. A/45/49 (1990).

96. Calavita, *supra* note 87 at 1.

97. Gutierrez, *supra* note 68 at 40.

98. *Id.* at 67.

99. *Id.* at 71.

100. *Id.*

101. *Id.* at 77.

102. *Id.* at 10.

103. *Id.*

104. *Id.* at 152.

105. *Id.* at 39.

106. Calavita, *supra* note 87 at 108.

107. *Id.* at 32.

108. Juan Ramon Garcia, *Operation Wetback: The Mass Deportation of Mexican American Undocumented Workers in 1954* 229-31 (Greenwood Press 1980); *see also* Julian Samora, *Los Mojados: The Wetback Story* 52 (Univ. Notre Dame Press 1971).

109. *Id.*

110. *Id.* at 227.

111. *Id.*

112. *See* Ronald T. Takaki, *A Different Mirror* (Little, Brown 1993).

113. *Id.*

114. *Id.*

115. *Id.*

116. *But see* The Illegal Immigration Reform and Immigrant Responsibility Act of 1996, and the Antiterrorism and Effective Death Penalty Act of 1996, which doubled the numbers of immigrants in detention within two years. *See* Analysis of Immigration Detention Policies, American Civil Liberties Union, Aug. 8, 1999, available at http://www.aclu.org/iigrant/detention/11771leg19990818.html (last visited Jan. 20, 2008).

117. *See supra* notes 57-111 and accompanying text. *See also* sources identified at http://www.google.com/search?q=aliens+arabs+site:cnn.com/transcripts&hl=en&start=10&sa=N (last visited Jan. 20, 2008).

118. *Id.*

119. *See* Secure Fence Act, H.R. 6061, 109th Cong. (2006).

120. *Id.*

121. *See* Rachel L. Swarms, "Split over Immigration Reflects Nation's Struggle," N.Y. Times, Mar. 29, 2006, available at 2006 WLNR 5217845 (discussing both the House of Representatives and more lenient Senate bills on immigration reform).

122. *Id.*

123. Another major point of difference between the Senate and House bills for comprehensive immigration reform is that S.2611 proposes a 370-mile fence along highly populated areas near the border, while H.R. 4437 proposes a 700-mile fence. Also, S.2611 does not mention any expanded role for local law enforcement for border enforcement tasks, but H.R. 4437 does. The Senate bill includes an English-only proposal that makes English the "national language" of the United States, thereby taking aim at discouraging services in any other language than English. Notwithstanding the bill's focus on heightened border security and making English the nation's sole official national language, some analysts have compared it to the Immigration Reform and Control Act of 1986.

124. Several resolutions, such as H.R. 610 and 621, supporting H.R.4437 (comprehensive immigration reform bill known as "Border Protection, Antiterrorism, and Illegal Immigration Control Act of 2005"), were proposed in the House, but ultimately went nowhere. This bill is the comprehensive immigration reform proposed in December 2005 and referred to the Senate in January 2006. The purpose is to strengthen the enforcement of immigration laws (codified in the INA) and enhance border security. The major focus points of the act include changing some of the terminology in the Immigration and Nationality Act (INA), securing U.S. borders (Title I), fencing and other border security improvements (Title X), employment eligibility verification (Title VII), judicial review of visa revocation (Title VIII Sec. 802). Another comprehensive immigration bill introduced in the 109th Congress and passed by the Senate in May 2006, S.2611, known as the "Comprehensive Immigration Reform Act of 2006," has not been enacted.

125. *See e.g.,* John Bowe, *Nobodies: Modern American Slave Labor and the Dark Side of the New Global Economy* (Random House 2007) (studying locations in Florida, Oklahoma, and the U.S.–owned Pacific island of Saipan, where slavery cases have been brought to light as recently as 2006).

126. *See generally,* Alvarado, *supra* note 85 at 65 (concluding that current proposals for a guest worker program should be rejected

because "there is no need for a temporary worker program, and the risks associated with its implementation necessitate its rejection. This is the lesson that should be learned from my grandfather's life as a Bracero").

127. *See, e.g.*, Michelle Malkin, *Invasion: How America Still Welcomes Terrorists, Criminals, and Other Menaces to Our Shores* (Regnery 2002) (asserting that "Congress, pressured by ethnicity lobbyists, corporations, the travel industry, and open border activists, aided the September 11 terrorists").

128. *Id.*

129. William H. Calhoun, "Illegal Immigration: The Invasion Continues," The NewsBlaze, available at http://newsblaze.com/story/20061024213611nnn.nb/topstory.html (last visited 10/28/09) ("Our once great and noble land will be just another third-world wasteland, not unlike Mexico City or New Delhi.").

130. *Id.* (The United States will become "an unrecognizable amalgamation of third-world crime. . . .").

131. *See* Iowa-Republicans-Exit Polls, available at www.msnbc.msn.com/id/21228177 (last visited Jan. 20, 2008).

132. *See* www.washingtonpost.com/wp-dyn/content/artcle/2008/01/12/AR2008011200329.html (last visited Feb. 15, 2008).

133. *Cloverfield* (Universal Films, 2008).

134. The popularity of the anti-immigrant attacks is not only limited to isolationists and nativists; it is also based on the misguided belief that immigration can be stopped, despite the fact that history suggests otherwise.

135. Think Progress-Pelosi,*"Hate Radio" Hijacked Political Discourse*, available at http://thinkprogress.org/2007/06/28/pelosi-talkradio/ (last visited Jan. 20, 2008).

136. *Id.*

137. *See Lou Dobbs Tonight*, Examination of Issues Arising from Illegal Aliens in the U.S., CNN, Mar. 21, 2005, available at http://transcripts.cnn.com/TRANSCRIPTS/0503/21/ldt.01.html (last visited Jan. 20, 2008) (Dobbs's alien invasion references continued even to the program's end, where he

concluded the evening's episode by saying, "Please join us tomorrow—the invasion of illegal aliens into this country, our special reports continue. We'll be reporting on the government's failure to enforce our immigration laws, and how that led to a state of emergency in one county.").

138. *See* Campaign for a United America, *Voices of Intolerance—Lou Dobbs*, available at http://campaignforaunitedamerica.org/index.php/voices/lou_dobbs/ (last visited Jan. 20, 2008) (among Dobbs's sentiments on American cultural homogeny is his statement, "I don't think there should be a St. Patrick's Day . . . we ought to be celebrating what is common about this country, what we enjoy as similarities as people.").

139. *Id.*

140. *See* Andrew Dobbs, *Bill O'Reilly Is a Racist*, Burnt Orange Report, Mar. 30, 2004, available at http://www.burntorangereport.com/archives/001301.html (last visited Jan. 20, 2008).

141. Massimo Calabresi, "Is Racism Fueling the Immigration Debate?" Time, May 17, 2006, available at http://www.time.com/time/nation/article/0,8599,1195250,00.html (last visited Jan. 20, 2008).

142. *Gibson Responded to Criticism of "Make More Babies" Remarks—By Invoking Europe's Rising Muslim Population*, Media Matters, May 18, 2006, available at http://mediamatters.org/items/200605180001 (last visited Jan. 20, 2008). Shortly after making his mathematically challenged comments concerning the demographic shift in this country, Gibson responded to criticism of his "make more babies" comments in a subsequent "My Word" segment. He stated that there are "[s]ome misunderstandings" regarding his earlier comments, adding that although he was accused of being a racist by some, "my concern was simply that I didn't want America to become Europe, where the birth rate is so low the continent is fast being populated by immigrants, mainly from Muslim countries. . . ."

143. *Id.*

144. *Id.*

145. *See* Think Progress, *supra* note 135.

146. *Id.*

147. *The Carpetbagger Report,* Jun. 30, 2007, available at http://www.thecarpetbaggerreport.com/archives/11298.html (last visited Jan. 20, 2008).

148. *Id.*

149. *Congressional Record on Destruction of U.S. Border Forests and Border Deserts, U.S. House Testimony by Rep. Tom Tancredo,* Mar. 4, 2003, available at http://www.desertinvasion.us/pol/congr_record_2003mar04.html (last visited Jan. 20, 2008).

150. *See* Noelle Phillips, "Immigration Dominates GOP Issues in South Carolina," The State, Jan 7, 2008, available at http://www.thestate.com/politics/story/277053.html (last visited Jan. 20, 2008).

151. Michelle Mittelstadt, "Dems Straddle Border, GOP Field Hawkish," Houston Chronicle, Nov. 11, 2007.

152. *Id.*

153. "GOP Debate's Focus on Immigration Drives Coverage," The Frontrunner, Nov. 30, 2007.

154. *Id.*

155. *Id.*

156. *See* Interview with John McCain, *Meet the Press,* Jan. 6, 2008.

157. *Id.*

158. David Olinger, "Border Wars Personal out West," Denver Post, Jan. 28, 2008, available at http://www.denverpost.com/lacrosse/ci_8088009 (last visited Feb. 15, 2008) (noting a difference by some between "the good Mexicans and the Latinos").

159. *Id.*

160. *Id.*

161. *Id.*

162. United States Border Control—In the News, Jun. 12, 2005, available at http://www.usbc.org/info/2005/jun/trancredo.htm (last visited Jan. 20, 2008).

163. *Id.*

164. *Id.*

165. Ruben Navarrette, Jr., "Honesty in Immigration Debate," San Diego Union-Tribune, Nov. 21, 2007, B-7 (noting that "too many Americans keep falling into old habits and repeating a historically familiar depiction of immigrants—legal or illegal—as inferior

to natives, defective in their culture, slow to assimilate, prone to criminal activity and devoid of any positive values.").

166. Brian Tumulty, "N.Y. Driver's License Controversy Spills Over to 2008 Election," Gannett News Service, Nov. 15, 2007, Pg. ARC. *See also* "Democrats Plot Electoral Strategy on Immigration," Technology Daily, Nov. 16, 2007.

167. The ad, which originally aired in Iowa, never fully reached a wide national viewing audience.

168. *Id.*

169. *See, e.g.,* Richard D. Lamm & Gary Imhoff, *The Immigration Time Bomb: The Fragmenting and Destruction of America by Immigration* (Dutton 1985); Lawrence Auster, *The Path to National Suicide: An Essay on Immigration and Multiculturalism* (American Immigration Control Foundation 1991).

170. SPLCenter.org, *Broken Record,* available at http://www.splcenter.org/intelreport/article.jsp?aid=589&printable=1 (last visited Oct. 18, 2007).

171. *Id.*

172. Campaign for a United America, *Voices of Intolerance—Jim Gilchrist,* available at http://campaignforaunitedamerica.org/index.php?/voices/jim_gilchrist/ (last visited Jan. 20, 2008).

173. *Id.*

174. *See Voices of Intolerance—Jim Gilchrist, supra* note 172.

175. As alluded to above, conservatives are not alone in their fear of the Mexican border. *See, e.g.,* Glenn F. Bunting, "Boxer's Bid to Put National Guard at Border Is Stymied: Immigration: Pentagon Refuses to Implement Senator's Plan, Which It Says Lacks Legal Authority," L.A. Times, Aug. 6, 1994, at A1.

176. *See Broken Record, supra* note 170.

177. *Id.*

178. Jonathan Gurwitz, "Democrats Suffer Dukakis Moment," San Antonio Express-News, Nov. 18, 2007, 3H.

179. This article labels the subject of recent immigration debates as undocumented workers, in part due to that classification closely resembling their status in this land. In addition, as scholars have previously observed,

the logic behind the label "illegal immigrant" is circular and conclusory. *See* Gerald P. Lopez, *Undocumented Mexican Migration: In Search of a Just Immigration Law and Policy*, 28 UCLA L. Rev. 615 (1981); Linda S. Bosniak, *Exclusion and Membership: The Dual Identity of the Undocumented Worker under United States Law*, 1988 Wis. L. Rev. 955 (1988).

180. *Id.*

181. *See* Ediberto Román, *Coalitions and Collective Memories: A Search for Common Ground*, 58 Mercer L. Rev. 637 (2007) (documenting the immigration reform efforts of 2006 and the opposition raised by talk radio).

182. For additional examples of talk radio's attacks, *see, e.g., Savage's Trifecta: Smears of Hispanics, Gays, and Jews*, Media Matters for America, May 12, 2006, available at http:// mediamatters.org/items/200605120017 (last visited Jan. 20, 2008) ("our brown brethren" may "erase" the "European-American, or white person" who is more "benevolent" and "enlightened"). *Republican Rush Limbaugh on Illegal Immigration, Hispanics against Republicans*, Jul. 6, 2007, available at http://hispanicsagainstrepublicans.blogsot.com/2007/07/republican-rush-limbaugh-on-illegal-immigration (last visited Jan. 20, 2008) (video).

183. Pelosi, *supra* note 135.

184. The latest iteration of the comprehensive reform bill, the Comprehensive Immigration Reform Act of 2007, S. 1348, failed a cloture motion in June 2007.

185. *Id.*

186. Ruben Navarette Jr., *What? Latinos Should Support McCain on Immigration*, Immigrationporfblog, January 29, 2008, available at http://lawprofessors.typepad.com/immigration/2008/01/navarette-latin.html.

187. *See Action Alert: GE, Microsoft Bring Bigotry to Life*, Fairness & Accuracy in Reporting, Feb. 12, 2003, available at http://www.fair.org/index.php?page=1632 (last visited Jan. 20, 2008) (questioning MSNBC's hiring of Michael Savage, who regularly refers to non-White nations as "turd world countries" and suggests that "[y]ou open the door to [non-White immigrants], and the next thing you know, they are defecating on your country and breeding out of control.").

188. *CNN Hire Beck: Illegal Immigrants Are Either "Terrorists," Outlaws, or People Who "Can't Make a Living in Their Own Dirtbag Country,"* Media Matters for America, Apr. 28, 2006, available at http://mediamatters.org/items/200604280003 (last visited Jan. 20, 2008).

189. Erin Texiera, Associated Press, Jun. 6, 2006, available at http://www.dailybulletin.com/orlet/article/html/fragments/print_article.jsp? (last visited Oct. 18th, 2007).

190. *Id.*

191. *Anti-immigrant Groups Borrow from Playbook of Hate Groups to Demonize Hispanics*, Anti-Defamation League Press Release, Oct. 23, 2007, available at http://www.adl.org/presrele/cvlrt_32/5154_32.htm (last visited Jan. 20, 2008) (noting that among other techniques, anti-immigrant groups describe "immigrants as 'third world invaders,' who come to America to destroy our heritage, 'colonize' the country and attack our 'way of life.'").

192. *Id.*

193. *Id.*

194. Andres Oppenheimer, "Time to Hit Back against Anti-Latino Bigotry," Miami Herald, Jul. 22, 2007, *available at* http://www.miamiherald.com/421/v-print/story/178206.html (last visited Jan. 20, 2008).

195. *See* Lani Guinier & Gerald Torres, *The Miner's Canary: Enlisting Race, Resisting Power, Transforming Democracy* (Harvard Univ. Press 2003).

196. *See* "The Invasion Continues," *supra* note 129 ("The beautiful countryside will be devastated, the cities polluted, and untold diseases will infect our population. We will cease to be a 'Western nation,' and become an unrecognizable amalgamation of third-world crime, disease, corruption, and human filth: a 21st-century cesspool.").

197. Heidi Beirich & Mark Potok, *Keeping America White*, Southern Poverty Law Center Intelligence Report, available at http://www.splcenter.org/intel/intelreport/article.jsp?aid=152&printable=1 (last visited Feb. 15, 2008) ("At a meeting of 'paleoconservatives,' former *Forbes* editor Peter Brimelow and others sound the alarm on non-white immigration.").

198. *See Broken Record, supra* note 170.

199. *Id.*

200. Ressam was captured near the Washington-Canada border en route to attempting to detonate explosives at Los Angeles International Airport on the last New Year's Eve of the millennium.

201. *See generally* Timothy J. Dunn, *The Militarization of the U.S.-Mexico Border, 1978-1992: Low-Intensity Conflict Doctrine Comes Home* (Univ. Texas Press 1996) (examining the efforts to militarize the border).

202. *Id.*

203. Ediberto Román, *The Alien Citizen Paradox and Other Consequences of U.S. Colonialism*, Fla. St. U. L. Rev. 1 (1998).

204. *See* Kevin R. Johnson, *The End of "Civil Rights" As We Know It? Immigration and Civil Rights in the New Millennium*, 49 UCLA L. Rev. 1481, 1486-89 (2002). As Johnson observes,

> Over the course of its history, U.S. society consistently has viewed new waves of immigrants as racially different outsiders. At different historical moments, German, Irish, Jewish, and Italian immigrants all were deemed to be of different and inferior racial stock. Benjamin Franklin, for example, decried the settling of German immigrants in Pennsylvania and considered them to be of a different race than the English. . . . Lawful exclusion of certain groups of immigrants reinforced their status as racially inferior, thereby contributing to the construction, and maintenance, of racial categories. At first glance, the racialization of European national origin groups is wholly incongruous with modern notions of race, particularly the almost reflexive treatment of all Europeans as white. Classifying European immigrants as nonwhite becomes understandable only with the realization that race is a social and legal creation. The social assimilation, or "whitening," of various immigrant groups, such as the Irish and Jews, which occurred slowly over time, reveals how concepts of races are figments of our collective imagination, albeit with real-life consequences. The racial classification of various immigrant groups reflects the fluidity of racial constructions. Immigrants from Asia, the focus of the initial federal immigration laws, long have been classified as racially different. Differences of physical appearance contribute to the resilience of the racial classification of persons of Asian ancestry, which contrasts with the erosion of such classifications for European immigrants. Immigrants from Mexico and Latin America continue to be racialized in the United States. . . . Physical appearance, class, cultural, linguistic, and religious differences contribute to this racialization. *Id.*

See also Kevin R. Johnson, *Symposium: Citizenship and Its Discontents: Centering the Immigrant in the International Imagination Racial Hierarchy, Asian Americans and Latinos as "Foreigners," and Social Change: Is Law the Way to Go?*, 76 Or. L. Rev. 347 (1997).

205. Neil Gotanda, Asian American Rights and the "Miss Saigon Syndrome," in *Asian Americans and the Supreme Court: A Documentary History* 1087, 1088 (Hyung-Can Kim ed., Greenwood 1992). In his work, Professor Gotanda discusses "the Miss Saigon Syndrome" and addresses the label of foreignness in what he calls the "other non-whites dualism." *Id.* at 1095.

206. *Id.*

207. *Id.*

208. *Id.*

209. *Chae Chan Ping v. United States*, 130 U.S. 581 (1889) (holding that entry into the United States could be denied to Chinese laborers because the legislature had authority under the sovereign powers delegated by the Constitution to exclude foreigners and that any existing treaty with China did not strip them of their power).

210. *Id.* at 600.

211. More recently, writers have even questioned the propriety of the disenfranchisement of felons. *See, e.g.,* Afi S. Johnson-Parris, *Felon Disenfranchisement: The Unconscionable Social Contract Breached*, 89 Va. L. Rev. 109 (2003).

CHAPTER 8

1. 128 S.Ct. 2229, 171 L.Ed.2d 41, 76 USLW 4406, 76 USLW 4391, 08 Cal. Daily Op. Serv. 7144, 2008 Daily Journal D.A.R. 8677, 21 Fla. L. Weekly Fed. S 329, U.S., June 12, 2008 (NO. 06-1195, 06-1196).

2. *Id.*

3. *Id.*

4. *Id.*

5. See Peter Spiro, *The Impossibility of Citizenship*, 10 Mich. L. Rev. 1492 (2001) (an emerging body of postnational scholarship is challenging citizenship and the nation-state).

6. Linda Bosniak, *The Citizen and the Alien* (Princeton Univ. Press 2006).

7. Immanuel Kant, *Fundamental Principles of the Metaphysic of Morals* (1865).

8. *Id.* at 52.

9. *Id.* at 53.

10. *Id.* at 59.

11. *Id.*

12. Inter-American Court of Human Rights, Advisory Opinion OC-18/03 of September 17, 2003 (Juridical Condition and Rights of the Undocumented Migrants).

13. *Id.*

14. *Id.*

15. *Id.*

16. *Id.*

17. *Id.* at 92.

18. *Id.* at 94.

19. *Id. at* 96.

20. W. E. B. Du Bois, *Black Reconstruction in America: An Essay toward a History of the Part Which Black Folk Played in the Attempt to Reconstruct Democracy in America, 1860-1880,* 289 (Free Press 1963).

Index

500-bushel class, 22. *See also* Citizenship, Greek concept of; Solon

Abraham, David, 62, 169n23ch. 5
Ackerman, Bruce A., 161n27
Adarand Constructors, Inc. v. Pena, 177n5
Advisory Opinion on the Rights of Undocumented Migrants before the Inter-American Court of Human Rights, 154-155
Afroyim v. Rusk, 161n20
Aleinikoff, Thomas Alexander, 189n186
Almeida, Joseph, 165n72
Alvarado, Lorenzo, 194nn85, 89, 195n126
Amar, Akhil Reed, 160n9
American Revolution, 59
Amour de soi, 73. *See also* Rousseau, Jean-Jacques
Amour propre, 73. *See also* Rousseau, Jean-Jacques
Anderson, Benedict, 163n54
Aquinas, Thomas, 42, 50. *See also* Christianity and Citizenship
Arendt, Hannah, 5, 161n22
Aristotle, 8, 15, 17-19, 20, 21-22, 28, 42, 45, 50, 57, 72, 123, 150, 160n14, 163n53, 165n65. *See also* Citizenship, Aristotelian construction of
Arneil, Barbara, 171n58
Augustine, 41. *See also* Christianity and Citizenship
Ayres, Ian, 193n44

Baca, Lawrence, 178n6
Baker, Thomas E., 161-162n29
Balderrama, Francisco, 86, 194nn78
Balibar, Etienne, 163n46
Balzak v. Porto Rico, 86, 104, 187n125. *See also* Citizenship, modern gradation; and Territorial Island inhabitants of the U.S.
Banaszak, Lee Ann, 190n234

Barron, Jerome A., 58, 163nn50
Bartley, Abel, 177n4
Bartolus of Sassofferrato, 45, 51
Bash, Dana, 190n249
Beirich, Heidi, 198n197
Bhala, Raj, 162n45
Bickel, Alexander M., 160nn11, 12
Bishop. *See* Clergy
Bishopry. *See* Clergy
Black Codes, 128. *See also* Modern de facto subordinates in the U.S., African Americans
Boortz, Neal, 139
Booth, William James, 164nn42, 50, 52
Bosniak, Linda, 8-9, 13, 133, 153
Boumediene v. Bush, 147-148, 149. *See also* Citizenship, future of
Bowe, John, 195n125
Bracero Program, 134, 135, 136. *See also* Modern de facto subordinates in the U.S., Mexican Americans
Bracey, Christopher, 127-128
Bradley, Joseph, 113
Bradwell v. Illinois, 112-113. *See also* Women, modern views on
Brandeis, Louis D., 5
Braverman, Dan, 180n51
Brown, Dee, 180n47
Brown, Henry Billings, 101, 102, 128
Brown v. Board of Education, 13, 120, 128. *See also* Modern de facto subordinates in the U.S., African Americans
Browne, Ray, 193n51
Bruni, Leonardo, 51-52, 56
Bunting, Glenn, 197n175
Burnett, Christina Duffy, 178n18, 191n13
Bush, George Walker, 118, 137, 142

Cabranes, Jose, 160n15, 161nn25, 28, 186n118
Calabresi, Massimo, 196n141

Calavita, Kitty, 194nn87, 96, 195n106
Calhoun, William, 196n129
Califano v. Torres, 189n187, 190n227
Campanalismo, 40
Campbell, Karen, 190n243
Caracalla, 23
Cavalry, 22. *See also* Citizenship, Greek concept of; Isin, Engin F.; Solon
Chae Chan Ping v. United States, 85, 86, 145. *See also* Citizenship, modern gradation
Charlemagne, 40
Chemerinsky, Erwin, 164n56
Cherokee Nation v. Hitchcock, 85-86. *See also* Citizenship, modern gradation
Cherokee Nation v. Georgia, 90-91. *See also* Indigenous peoples of the U.S.
Chinese Exclusion Act of 1882, 122n12
Chinese Exclusion Cases, 85, 96, 122, 145. *See also* Citizenship, modern gradation; Indigenous peoples of the U.S.; Modern de facto subordinates in the U.S., and other non-Whites
Chinkin, Christine, 163-164n59
Christianity and Citizenship, 29, 30, 39-43, 48, 50, 57. *See also* Citizenship, Dark Ages concept of
Chrysostom, John, 41. *See also* Christianity and Citizenship
Cicero, 42, 53
Citizenship: Aristotelian construction of, 17-19, 20, 21-22, 160n14, 165n65; components of, 7, 156; Dark Ages concept of, 29, 30-48, 150; defined, 5, 6; dialectic, 10; future of, 147-157; Greek concept of, 8, 15-22, 24, 25, 26-27, 35, 150; historical development, 4, 12; importance of, 4, 5; modern gradation, 1-4, 6, 7, 9, 11, 27-28, 55-56, 78-81, 83, 84-146, 163n48; nature of, 4, 12; Plato's concept of, 16; Roman concept of, 8, 15, 22-28, 32, 33, 35, 42, 45, 51, 125, 150; transition from ancient to modern notions of, 49-54; and women (*see* Women). *See also* Aquinas, Thomas; Bosniak, Linda; Bruni, Leonardo; Enlightenment; Indigenous peoples of the U.S.; Marshall, Thomas Humphrey; Pocock, John Greville Agard; Renaissance; Riesenberg, Peter; Women
Citizenship Clause of the Fourteenth Amendment, 84. *See also* Citizenship, modern gradation

City-state. *See* Citizenship, Dark Ages concept of
Civic humanism, 51. *See also* Citizenship, transition from ancient to modern notions of
Civil religion, 72. *See also* Rousseau, Jean-Jacques
Civil Rights Act of 1866, 125. *See also* Modern de facto subordinates in the U.S., African Americans
Civil Rights Act of 1875, 127. *See also* Modern de facto subordinates in the U.S., African Americans
Civil Rights Commission Report on the 2000 presidential election, 129, 151. *See also* Modern de facto subordinates in the U.S., African Americans
Cives, 15, 35. *See also* Citizenship, Roman concept of
Civitas, 25. *See also* Citizenship, Roman concept of; *Civitates foederata*; *Civitates liberae*
Civitas sine suffragio, 26. *See also* Citizenship, Roman concept of
Civitates foederata, 25. *See also* Citizenship, Roman concept of
Civitates liberae, 25. *See also* Citizenship, Roman concept of
Clark, Lorenne, 65
Clergy, 33, 40, 41, 46. *See also* Christianity and Citizenship; Citizenship, Dark Ages concept of
Clesthenes, 20
Cleveland, Sarah, 91, 182nn66, 75
Climate theory, 67-69. *See also* Montesquieu, Charles
Clinton, Hillary, 142
Close, Ellis, 129
Cohen, Ruth Schwartz, 115-116, 190n232. *See also* Women, modern view on
Cole, David, 159n4
Coloniae, 25. *See also* Citizenship, Roman concept of
Congressional Research Service Memorandum: Discretion of Congress Respecting Citizenship Status of Puerto Rico, 185n109
Constitution, 75. *See also* Rousseau, Jean-Jacques
Corporation of the Presiding Bishop v. Holdel, 110. *See also* Territorial Island inhabitants of the U.S.

Corpus Iuris Civilis, 38
Cose, Ellis, 193n44
Cottle, Amber, 193n48
Coulter, John Wesley, 189n215
Crossman v. United States, 187n125
Curial class, 23. *See also* Citizenship, Roman concept of
Curtius, Ernst, 168nn100, 104

Daniel, Peter Vivian, 124, 165n90
Daniel, Stephen, 169n17ch.5
Dark Ages, *See* Citizenship, Dark Ages concept of
Davis, Peggy, 193n44
Declaration of Independence, 59, 60, 63. *See also* Jefferson, Thomas
Delany, Samuel, 191n14
Delgado, Richard, 132
De Lima v. Bidwell, 85, 100, 188n166. *See also* Citizenship, modern gradation; Territorial Island inhabitants of the U.S.
Deloria, Vine, 179n42, 180nn47, 53
Demiorgoi, 20. *See also* Citizenship, Greek concept of
Dennis v. United States, 162n42
Despotism, 66, 69. *See also* Montesquieu, Charles
Dickenson, Donna, 64, 171nn53, 62
Dobbs, Andrew, 196n140
Dobbs, Lou, 138-139
Dobie, Madeleine, 171nn78, 105, 172n120
Dodd, Chris, 142
Dooley v. United States, 86, 187n125, 188n178. *See also* Citizenship, modern gradation
Dorr v. United States, 86, 104, 187n125. *See also* Citizenship, modern gradation; Incorporation; Territorial Island inhabitants of the U.S.
Douloi, 19. *See also* Citizenship, Greek concept of
Dowdell v. United States, 188n178
Downes v. Bidwell, 85, 100-101, 102, 104-105, 184n104, 187n163. *See also* Citizenship, modern gradation; Incorporation; Insular cases; Territorial Island inhabitants of the U.S.
Draco, 20
Dred Scott v. Sandford, 85, 93, 96, 102, 122, 123-125, 128, 148, 165n90, 170n44, 177nn1, 6. *See also* Citizenship, modern gradation; Indigenous peoples of the U.S.

Drimmer, Jonathan C., 160nn10, 16, 191n15, 192nn36, 38
Driscoll, Barbara, 194nn91, 93
Du Bois, W. E. B., 119, 126, 127, 156
Dunn, Timothy, 199n201

Elective Governor Act of 1968, 107. *See also* Territorial Island inhabitants of the U.S.
Elk v. Wilkins, 85, 92-93, 122. *See also* Citizenship, modern gradation; Indigenous peoples of the U.S.
England, 46, 47. *See also* Citizenship, Dark Ages concept of; Hobbes, Thomas
Enlightenment, 50, 51, 52, 53, 54. 55-81, 150. *See also* Hobbes, Thomas; Locke, John; Machiavelli, Niccolo; Montesquieu, Charles; Rousseau, Jean-Jacques
Epictetus, 41
Epstein, Lee, 163n49
Equestrian class, 23. *See also* Citizenship, Roman concept of
Eupatridae, 20. *See also* Citizenship, Greek concept of
Ex parte Milligan, 159n6, 162n42, 163n47
Ex parte Quirin, 159n6

Faulks, Keith, 166n15
Fears, J. Rufus, 166n93
Federalist No. 10, 62
Feudal system, 33. *See also* Citizenship, Dark Ages concept of
Fing, Gary, 163n49
Fisk, Catherine L., 163-164n59
Florence, 33, 44, 47, 52-53, 56. *See also* Citizenship, Dark Ages concept of; Machiavelli, Niccolo
Foner, Eric, 163n55, 191-192n24
Fong Yue Ting v. United States, 85. *See also* Citizenship, modern gradation
Fourteen Diamond Rings v. United States, 86, 187n125. *See also* Citizenship, modern gradation
Fourteenth Amendment, 84, 86, 92, 93, 98, 103, 104, 105, 114, 119, 120, 121, 125, 127, 128, 131, 150, 151. *See also* Citizenship Clause of the Fourteenth Amendment; Citizenship, modern gradation
Fox, James, 161n27, 165n72
Franklin, John Hope, 192n30
Fraser, Nancy, 162n34

"Free peregrine," 23. *See also* Citizenship, Roman concept of; Isin, Engin F.

Garcia, Juan Ramon, 195n108
Geomoroi, 20. *See also* Citizenship, Greek concept of
Getches, David, 180n55, 181n58
Gibbon, Edward, 164-165n90, 168n82
Gibson, John, 139
Gilbert, Lauren, 194n77
Gilchrist, Jim, 141-142
Gingrich, Newt, 63
Ginsburg, Ruth Bader, 177n5
Giuliani, Rudy, 140
Goetze v. United States, 86, 187n125, 188n178. *See also* Citizenship, modern gradation
Gonzalez, Jose Julian Alvarez, 185n113
Goodell v. Jackson, 177n6
Gordon, Linda, 162n34
Gotanda, Neil, 145
Granberg, Ellen, 190n243
Grant, Michael, 82, 164n40, 165nn79
Gross, Feliks, 166nn3, 18, 19, 167nn53, 56, 168n93
Gruber, Aya 163n49
Guam Organic Act, 106. *See also* Territorial Island inhabitants of the U.S.
Guest worker program, 137. *See also* Modern de facto subordinates in the U.S., Mexican Americans
Guiccardini, Francesco, 44, 53
Guiner, Lani, 198n195
Gurwitz, Johnathan, 197n178
Gutierrez, David, 133, 194nn94, 97

Habitator, 35, 37. *See also* Citizenship, Dark Ages concept of
Habitatores, 35. *See also* Citizenship, Dark Ages concept of
Halperin, David, 164n26
Hamdi v. Rumsfeld, 159n2
Hamdi, Yaser Esam, 3, 4, 6, 159n2
Haney-Lopez, Ian, 190-191n6
Harlan II, John Marshal, 5, 160n15
Harris, David, 193n43
Harzig, Christiana, 166n1
Hawaii v. Mankichi, 86. *See also* Citizenship, modern gradation
Healy, Thomas, 163n49
Heater, Derek, 5, 160n13, 162n33, 164nn10, 22, 165nn59, 88, 166nn102, 103, 166n2, 167nn35,

67, 68, 168nn108, 131, 169n149, 169nn3, 7 10, 14, 21ch. 4
Herrera, Deborah, 187n156
Hippies, 22. *See also* Citizenship, Greek concept of; Isin, Engin F.; Solon
Hirschman, Nancy, 171n56
Hobbes, Thomas, 55, 56, 58-59, 60, 62, 71, 72, 78, 79. *See also* Enlightenment
Ho, Daniel, 163n49
Hoerder, Dirk, 166n1
Holland, Nancy, 66
Hoplites, 22. *See also* Citizenship, Greek concept of; Isin, Engin F.; Solon
Housewifery. *See* Women, modern view on
Huckabee, Michael, 140
Huns v. Porto Rico S.S. Co., 86. *See also* Citizenship, modern gradation
Huus v. New York & Porto Rico S.S. Co., 187n125, 188n178

Imhoff, Gary, 197n169
Incolae, 35. *See also* Citizenship, Dark Ages concept of
Incolatus, 35, 36. *See also* Citizenship, Dark Ages concept of
Incorporation, 103, 104, 105. *See also* Territorial Island inhabitants of the U.S.; White, Edward Douglass
Indian Citizenship Act, 184n97. *See also* Indigenous peoples of the U.S.
Indigenous peoples of the U.S., 87-97, 151, 152. *See also* Citizenship, modern gradation
Insular Cases, 85, 97, 100, 101, 122, 148, 152, 188n178. *See also* Citizenship, modern gradation; *Downes v. Bidwell*; Territorial Island inhabitants of the U.S.
Isin, Engin F., 22, 23, 162n32, 164nn1, 37, 41, 53, 166n95

Jackson v. Goodell, 182n81
Jahoda, Gloria, 180n47
Jay, John, 160n16
Jefferson, Thomas, 59
Jim Crow. *See* Modern de facto subordinates in the U.S., African Americans
Johnson, Andrew, 128
Johnson, Kevin, 134n80, 145n204
Johnson v. M'Intosh, 89, 93, 95, 180n50, 182n93. *See also* Indigenous peoples of the U.S.
Johnson-Parris, Afi, 200n211

Jones v. United States, 86. *See also* Citizenship, modern gradation

Joo, Thomas, 159n4

Jus sanguinis, 146. *See also* Citizenship, components of

Jus soli, 146, 178n8. *See also* Citizenship, components of

Kaczorowski, Robert, 192n26

Kagan, Donald, 166n111

Kang, Jerry, 163n49

Kant, Immanuel, 153-154, 155, 156

Karst, Kenneth L., 160n15, 161n26, 167n57

Kennedy, Stetson, 192nn31, 35

Kepner v. United States, 86. *See also* Citizenship, modern gradation

Kettner, James H., 161n27

King v. Morton, 110. *See also* Territorial Island inhabitants of the U.S.

Kirshner, Julius, 166n110

Kitzinger, Rachel, 164n40, 165nn79, 82

Klein, Christine, 193n58, 194n63

Korematsu v. United States, 162n42

Kymlicka, Will, 163nn46, 51, 52

Laborers, 22. *See also* Citizenship, Greek concept of; Solon

Lailas, E. A., 170n41

Lamm, Richard, 197n169

Latin War, 26. *See also* Citizenship, Roman concept of

Leibowitz, Arnold, 187nn130, 140

Lialas, Elaine Andrews, 167n34, 168nn96, 103, 106, 117

Lindh, John Walker, 3, 6, 159n1

Lobreglio, Kiera, 194nn76, 90, 92

Lochner v. New York, 113. *See also* Women, modern view on

Locke, John, 55, 56, 59-66, 72, 74, 79. *See also* Enlightenment

Lone Wolf v. Hitchcock, 85, 94-95, 122, 182-184n93. *See also* Citizenship, modern gradation; Indigenous peoples of the U.S.

Lopez, Gerald, 197-198n179

Lopez, Ian Haney, 178n9

Lowell, Waverly, 178n17, 191n12

Lugay, Arvin, 162nn43, 44

Luna, Guadalupe, 194nn62, 65

Lycurgus, 15

Lytle, Clifford, 180n53

Macchiavelli, Nicolò, 45, 51, 55, 56-58

Madison, James, 160n16

Magna Carta, 47. *See also* England

Malcolm X, 121, 128. *See also* Modern de facto subordinates in the U.S., African Americans

Malkin, Michelle, 162n43, 196n127

Maltz, Earl M., 163n49

Manifest destiny, 131. *See also* Modern de facto subordinates in the U.S., Mexican Americans

Man's state of nature. *See* State of nature

Manumission, 24. *See also* Citizenship, Roman concept of; Slave

Manville, Philip Brook, 164n43

Marbury v. Madison, 79

Marshall, John, 88, 91-92, 101, 180n55

Marshall, Thomas Humphrey, 7, 9, 10, 13, 152, 156. *See also* Citizenship, components of

Marsilius of Padua, 42, 50-51

Marso, Lori, 78

Mayali, Laurent, 166n110

McCain, John, 140, 143, 159n4

McCammon, Holly, 190n243

McClure, Kristie, 171n56

McCutehen, Joe, 141

McKibben, Lizabeth, 189n190

Medicine Lodge Treaty of 1867, 95. *See also* Indigenous peoples of the U.S.

Merchant class, 32, 34, 43-45, 47, 49, 150. *See also* Citizenship, Dark Ages concept of; Citizenship, transition from ancient to modern notions of

Metics, 19. *See also* Citizenship, Greek concept of

Metoikois, 19, 20. *See also* Citizenship, Greek concept of

Minor v. Happersett, 160n15, 161n21

Mittelstadt, Michelle, 197n151

Modern de facto subordinates in the U.S.: African Americans, 118, 119-131, 149-150, 151; Mexican Americans, 119, 120, 131-44; and other non-Whites, 145-146. *See also* Citizenship, modern gradation

Modern *de jure* subordinates in the U.S., 83-118. *See also* Indigenous peoples of the U.S.; Territorial Island inhabitants of the U.S.; and Women, modern view on

Monarchy, 66, 71, 79. *See also* Hobbes, Thomas; Montesquieu, Charles.

Montesquieu, Charles, 55, 56, 59, 66-71, 72, 79, 80. *See also* Enlightenment
Mowery, Christine, 190n243
Muller v. Oregon, 112, 113. *See also* Women, modern view on
Municeps, 35, 36. *See also* Citizenship, Dark Ages concept of
Municipia, 25. *See also* Citizenship, Roman concept of

National Bank v. County of Yankton, 189n194
Nation-state, 50. *See also* Citizenship, transition from ancient to modern notions
Natural law, 24. *See also* Stoics
Navarette, Ruben, 197n165, 198n186
Nay, Annette, 170n29
Nederman, Gary J., 164nn24, 31, 33
Neuman, Gerald, 104, 187n155
Ng Fung Ho v. White, 161n17
Nicolet, Claude, 165n76, 166nn104, 109
Nineteenth Amendment, 114, 115, 117. *See also* Women, modern view on
Nishimura Ekiu v. United States, 85, 86. *See also* Citizenship, modern gradation
Norman, Wayne, 163nn51, 52
Norton, Eleanor Holmes, 193n49
Nouveaux riche, 43. *See also* Merchant class
Noy, David, 165n87
Nyland, Chris, 171nn79, 88, 106, 172nn114, 119
Nye, Andrea, 171n66

Obama, Barack, 119, 120, 151
Ocampo v. United States, 188n178
Okin, Susan, 65
Olinger, David, 197n158
Operation Wetback, 132, 136, 138. *See also* Modern de facto subordinates in the U.S., Mexican Americans
Oppenheimer, Andres, 198n194
O'Reilly, Bill, 138
O'Sullivan John, 131

Pachon, Harry, 193n57
Padilla ex re. Newman v. Bush, 159n3
Padilla ex re. Newman v. Rumsfeld, 159n3
Padilla, Jose, 3, 4, 159n3
Parekh, Bhikhu, 171nn81, 84
Parker, Johnny, 160n15, 161n23
Pateman, Carole, 63, 171nn60, 61
Peace of Constance, 31

Pelosi, Nancy, 142,
Pendleton, Florence, 193n50
Pentakosiomedimnoi, 22. *See also* Citizenship, Greek concept of; Isin, Engin F.; Solon
Perez v. Brownell, 161n19
Pericles, 51
Periokoi, 19. *See also* Citizenship, Greek concept of
Phillips, Noelle, 197n150
Pirenne, Henri, 167n44, 168nn74, 81, 129
Plato, 15, 16-17, 18, 41
Plenary powers doctrine, 84, 85, 87, 88, 99, 122, 145. See also *Chae Chan Ping v. United States*; Chinese Exclusion Cases; Citizenship, modern gradation; Insular Cases; *Johnson v. M'Intosh*; *Nishimura Ekiu v. United States*; *United States v. Curtiss-Wright Export Corp.*
Plessy v. Ferguson, 13, 85, 120, 122, 128. *See also* Modern de facto subordinates in the U.S., African Americans
Pocock, John Greville Agard, 7-8, 21, 164nn3, 23
Podgor, Ellen S., 159n1
Polis, polites, 15, 16, 18, 22, 23, 31, 41. *See also* Citizenship, Greek concept of; Isin, Engin F.; Solon
Polity, 16. *See also* Citizenship, Greek concept of; *Polis, polites*
Porter, Robert, 96, 182n80
Potock, Mark, 143, 198n197
Pratt, Julius, 186n120
Preuss, Ulrich K., 162n2
"Priors," 44. *See also* Merchant class

Ramos, Efren Rivera, 187nn138, 161, 190n231
Rankers, 22. *See also* Citizenship, Greek concept of; Solon
Raskin, Jasmin, 193nn46, 52
Rebarb, Theodore, 170n49
Rehnquist, Chief Justice William, 5, 161n18
Reid v. Covert, 105. *See also* Incorporation; Territorial Island inhabitants of the U.S.
Renaissance, 50, 52, 53, 54, 150. *See also* Enlightenment
Repatriation, 134, 136. *See also* Modern de facto subordinates in the U. S., Mexican Americans
Republic, 66, 69-70. *See also* Montesquieu, Charles

Ressam, Ahmed, 144
Riesenberg, Peter, 8, 9, 10, 53, 56, 164n8,
 165nn72, 73, 166n107, 166n13, 167nn26,
 46, 51, 54, 57, 58, 69, 168nn98, 114, 128,
 169nn135, 138, 145, 169nn1, 4, 9, 18ch.4.,
 169nn 2, 4, 8ch.5
Ritter, Gretchen, 163n59
Roberts, Dorothy, 190n248
Rogers v. Bellei, 105. *See also* Territorial Island
 inhabitants of the U.S.
Rollings, Willard Hughes, 184n100
Román, Ediberto, 162n31, 184n101, 185n106,
 186n121, 187nn127, 143, 189n197, 198n181,
 199n203
Romney, Mitt, 140
Rosenfeld, Michel, 162n45
Rousseau, Jean-Jacques, 55, 56, 59, 71-78, 79,
 80. *See also* Enlightenment
Rumsfeld v. Padilla, 159n3

Saito, Natsu Taylor, 96, 159n5, 163n49, 165n62,
 177n3, 178nn7, 11, 179n43, 184n105, 185n115,
 190n5
Salazar, Ken, 142
Salmon, Edward Togo, 166n94
Schenck v. United States, 162n42
Schochet, Gordon, 64
Schurz, Carl, 126
Secure Fence Act, 137. *See also* Modern de
 facto subordinates in the U.S., Mexican
 Americans
Sedition Act of 1798, 162n42
Segal, Jeffrey, 163n49
Senatorial class, 23. *See also* Citizenship,
 Roman concept of
Seneca Falls Convention, 114. *See also*
 Women, modern view on
Serf, 33, 34, 38. *See also* Citizenship, Dark
 Ages concept of
Serfdom. *See* Serf
Shanley, Mary Lyndon, 171n61
Sherwin-White, Adrian Nicholas, 165n81
Shklar, Judith, 172n110
Shubert, Adrian, 166n1
Skinner, Quentin, 168n113, 169nn142, 151
Slave, 18, 23, 44, 68, 69, 76, 123-124. *See
 also* Citizenship, Dark Ages concept of;
 Citizenship, Roman concept of; Modern
 de facto subordinates in the U.S., African
 Americans

Slavery. *See* Slave
Snow, Kate, 199n249
Social contract. *See* Locke, John; Rousseau,
 Jean-Jacques
Socrates, 164n52
Solomon, Neil, 189n195
Solon, 15, 20, 22, 166n111
Somers, Margaret R., 162n34
Spencer, Glenn, 141
Spirit of extreme equality, 67. *See also* Montes-
 quieu, Charles
Spirit of inequality, 67. *See also* Montesquieu,
 Charles
Spiro, Peter, 152, 184n101, 200n5
Stack, John F., 161-162n29
St. Ambrose, 41. *See also* Christianity and
 Citizenship
Standardbearer of Justice, 43
Star Trek, 162n41
State of nature, 71-72, 76. *See also* Rousseau,
 Jean-Jacques
Stephens v. Cherokee Nation, 85. *See also* Citi-
 zenship, modern gradation
Stephens, George, 169n22ch.5
St. Jerome, 41. *See also* Christianity and
 Citizenship
Stoics, 24. *See also* Natural law
Story, Joseph, 62
Strath, Bo, 168n113, 169nn142, 151
Strauss, Paul, 193n50
Stumpt Juliet, 160nn7, 8
Subditus, 35, 36. *See also* Citizenship, Dark
 Ages concept of
Sugarman v. Dougall, 161n18
Swarms, Rachel, 195n121

Takaki, Ronald, 195n112
Tancredo, Tom, 140-141
Taney, Chief Justice Roger Brooke, 93, 102,
 123-124, 186n123
Terborg-Penn, Rosalyn, 190n247
Territorial Clause of Article IV, 87, 98, 99, 101,
 104, 110, 112. *See also* Indigenous peoples
 of the U.S.; Territorial Island inhabitants
 of the U.S.
Territorial Island inhabitants of the United
 States, 97-112, 151. *See also* Citizenship,
 Modern gradation
Territory of Guam v. Olsen, 189n193
Texiera, Erin, 198n189

Theory of universalism, 24. *See also* Citizenship, Roman concept of

Thetes, 22. *See also* Citizenship, Greek concept of; Isin, Engin F.; Solon

Thomas, Paul, 77, 78

Thornbury, James, 110, 111

Thuraios, 20. *See also* Citizenship, Greek concept of

Torres, Gerald, 198n195

Torruella, Juan, 187n125

Trachtenberg, Zev, 172n130

Trask, Haunani-Kay, 189n211

Treaty of Guadalupe Hidalgo, 131, 132. *See also* Modern de facto subordinates in the U.S., Mexican Americans

Treaty of Paris, 98, 99, 100. *See also* Territorial Island inhabitants of the U.S.

Tumulty, Brian, 197n166

Twenty-Third Amendment, 129. *See also* Modern de facto subordinates in the U.S., African Americans

Unitarians in Poland, 36

United States Constitution, 55, 72, 78-81, 84, 121. *See also* Citizenship, modern gradation; Enlightenment; Fourteenth Amendment; Nineteenth Amendment; Twenty-Third Amendment

United States Supreme Court. *See* Citizenship, modern gradation

United States v. Celestine, 93-94. *See also* Indigenous peoples of the U.S.

United States v. Curtiss-Wright Export Corp., 86. *See also* Citizenship, modern gradation

United States v. Kagama, 85, 122, 178n10. *See also* Citizenship, modern gradation

United States v. Nice, 94. *See also* Indigenous peoples of the U.S.

United States v. Ritchie, 88. *See also* Indigenous peoples of the U.S.

United States v. Rogers, 90. *See also* Indigenous peoples of the U.S.

United States v. Sandoval, 94. *See also* Indigenous peoples of the U.S.

United States v. Stanley, 192n32

United States v. Verdugo-Urguidez, 189n179

Urban citizenship, 49. *See also* Citizenship, transition from ancient to modern notions

Urban professional class, 44. *See also* Citizenship, Dark Ages concept of.

Utter, Jack, 162n43, 163n50, 180n53

Van Devanter, Willis, 94

Van Dyke, Jon, 189n198

Volpp, Leti, 159n1, 163n49, 165n62

Vyverberg, Henry, 172nn121, 123

Wacher, John, 166n99

Waite, Morrison Remick, 5, 160n15

Walzer, Michael, 12

Wardle, David, 169n20ch. 5

Warren, Chief Justice Earl, 5, 161n19

Weber, Max, 30, 31, 33, 35, 44, 166n7

Weiss, Penny, 176n173

White, Edward Douglass, 103

Wilkins, David, 179n42, 180n46, 184n99

Wilkinson, Charles, 180n55, 181n58

Williams, Robert, 180n49

Wohletz, Ken, 168n83

Wollstonecraft, Mary, 77

Women: Dark Ages, 38, 41; Greek view of, 15, 17, 19; Hobbes' views on, 59; Locke's view on, 61, 64-66; Machiavelli's views on, 57; modern views on, 112-118, 152; Montesquieu's views on, 68-71; Roman views on, 24-25; Rousseau's views on, 56, 76-78; transition from ancient to modern notions of, 51. *See also* Citizenship; Hobbes, Thomas; Locke, John; Montesquieu, Charles; Rousseau, Jean-Jacques

Woolman, Joanna, 159n5

Worcester v. Georgia, 89, 90. *See also* Indigenous peoples of the U.S.

Working freemen, 23. *See also* Citizenship, Roman concept of

Xenoi, 19. *See also* Citizenship, Greek concept of

Yamamoto, Eric K., 159n5

Zeugitai, 22. *See also* Citizenship, Greek concept of; Isin, Engin F.; Solon

Zilbershats, Yaffa, 161n24

About the Author

EDIBERTO ROMÁN is Professor of Law at Florida International University School of Law and the author of numerous articles on international and constitutional law, social justice theories, and legal history. He is also the author of *The Other American Colonies: An International and Constitutional Law Examination of the United States' Nineteenth and Twentieth Century Island Conquests* and editor of NYU Press's series Citizenship and Immigration in the Americas. Last but not least, he is a proud father of four, and soon to be five, children, and a descendant of the beautiful and proud people of the U.S. colony known as Puerto Rico.